VOICES FROM THE VALLEYS

Stories and Poems about Life in BC's Interior

Compiled and Edited by
Jodie Renner

Library and Archives Canada Cataloguing in Publication:
Voices from the Valleys : Stories & Poems about Life in BC's Interior
Compiled and Edited by Jodie Renner
Library and Archives Canada Cataloguing in Publication
Includes index.
ISBN 978-0-9937004-3-9 (paperback)
Canadian literature (English)—British Columbia
Canadian literature (English)—21st century. I. Renner, Jodie, editor
PS8255.B7V65 2015 C810.8'09711 C2015-906822-3

Contributors, in alphabetical order:
John Arendt, Howard Baker, Michelle Barker, Della Barrett, Clayton Campbell, Fern G.Z. Carr, Virginia Carraway Stark, Danell Clay, Linda Crosfield, Debra Crow, Shirley Bigelow DeKelver, Keith Dixon, Elaine Durst, Bernie Fandrich, Beverly Fox, R.M. Greenaway, Sterling Haynes, Dianne Hildebrand, Norma J. Hill, Eileen Hopkins, Yasmin John-Thorpe, Chris Kempling, Denise King, Linda Kirbyson, Virginia Laveau, Loreena M. Lee, Denise Little, Alan Longworth, Ken Ludwig, Jeanine Manji, Katie Marti, Kate McDonough, Herb Moore, Janice Notland, Sylvia Olson, James Osborne, Vic Parsons, L.M. Patrick, William S. Peckham, Anita Perry, Seth Raymond, Jodie Renner, Seanah Roper, Ron B. Saunders, Paul Seesequasis, Wendy Squire, Kristina Stanley, Tony Stark, Cheryl Kaye Tardif, Mahada Thomas, Ross Urquhart

All proceeds from book sales, after production expenses, go to Médecins Sans Frontières / Doctors Without Borders Canada (MSF).

Cover photo of Emerald Lake and Wapta Mountain in Yoho National Park, near Field, B.C., Copyright © 2015 Murphy Shewchuk
www.murphyshewchuk.com

Cover design by Travis Miles of ProBookCovers.com

A big thanks to Kristina Stanley (x2), Norma Hill, and John Arendt for final proofreading, and to Michelle Barker for her advice on a few poems.

PRAISE FOR VOICES FROM THE VALLEYS

"When I sat down to review Voices from the Valleys, I was prepared to be entertained. Instead I was enthralled with a lively range of fiction and non-fiction stories and poems about towns and valleys and characters that rang so true to my own experiences, growing up in, and returning as an adult to my hometown of Lillooet and Southern British Columbia. This anthology belongs on the bookshelves of anyone fascinated by the history, colour, and texture of rural BC. Supplemented with amazing photographs and sketches, the authors have brought my favourite places to life."

– **Christ'l Roshard**, former mayor of Lillooet, former editor of Bridge River – Lillooet News

"*Voices from the Valleys* reflects the uniqueness, diversity and cultural richness that exists in BC's interior. This wonderful collection of stories and poems is a treat for anyone."

– **Gary Doi**, former school superintendent and creator of the Inspiring Hope book series

"What truly captures the unique beauty of a region are the people who live there. *Voices from the Valleys,* a creative and special collection from passionate and talented authors, is a delightful read."

– **Dan Albas**, MP for Central Okanagan-Similkameen-Nicola

"A visual artist might use canvas, oil, or watercolour to capture the tones and textures of our vivid interior valleys. My delight with *Voices from the Valleys* is the spirit and emotion of our regions' stories expressed in the words of poets and authors: art in a written form. A wonderful and moving read."

– **Craig Henderson**, Naramata author, historian and broadcaster

"Congratulations to Jodie Renner for bringing together such a stimulating collection of writing in *Voices from the Valleys*! This collective literary project showcases the diversity of BC experiences through a delightful variety of expressions."

– **Jane Shaak**, Executive Director, Shatford Centre, Penticton, BC

"Written by some of British Columbia's finest writers, *Voices from the Valleys* is a delightful collection of fiction, non-fiction and poetry. Well worth picking up and hard to put down, many of the stories slide the reader into the unique and beautiful geography of BC's Interior. Though many of the topics are familiar, the skillful writing makes them new and intriguing."

– **Coco Aders-Weremczuk**, President, Federation of BC Writers

"*Voices of the Valleys* is an absolute treasure, a tapestry of talent. I have always known the Shuswap Okanagan was a treasure trove of gifted writers. Jodie Renner has now provided the showcase proving this to be true. I found the variety of writing to be energizing and a delight to read."

– **Kay Johnston**, President of The Shuswap Association of Writers, Chair of Word on the Lake Writers' Festival, author of the best-seller Spirit of Powwow

"*Voices from the Valleys* is a thoroughly captivating collection of stories and poetry. I found myself travelling through time and places, experiencing the authors' amusement, surprise, wisdom, and delight along the way."

– **Connie Denesiuk**, former president of the B.C. School Trustees Association and director of the Canadian School Board Association

"The level of skill in these writers is par to bestselling authors. Well worth a cuddle-up in a comfy chair for an evening of reading. Thank you to all of the authors who took the time to entertain, teach, and engage their audience."

– **Janice Perrino**, Executive Director, South Okanagan Similkameen Medical Foundation

TABLE OF CONTENTS

UPPER FRASER RIVER VALLEY, BRIDGE RIVER VALLEY

CARIBOO – CHILCOTIN

NORTHERN BRITISH COLUMBIA

INTRODUCTION

As the organizer and editor of *Voices from the Valleys – Stories & Poems about Life in BC's Interior*, I'm absolutely delighted by the quality and diversity of voices brought to life in this collection of glimpses into typical, yet unique, experiences in the vast, rugged Interior of British Columbia, Canada.

As soon as we sent out a call for submissions to this anthology, writers throughout the province started spreading the word, and contributions came pouring in – entertaining short stories, fascinating memoirs, and touching, thought-provoking poetry, depicting life in every region of the interior of the province, from the '50s to today.

This anthology focuses on stories and poems about life in BC's Interior, mostly small-town, rural, and wilderness experiences in the southern half of BC. For this first of a series of stories and poems about life in British Columbia, Canada's most western province, we'll start at the Rocky Mountains and the Kootenays in Eastern BC on the Alberta border, then head west to the South Okanagan (Osoyoos, Oliver, Okanagan Falls, Penticton, Summerland, Naramata) and Similkameen (Keremeos, Cawston). From there, we'll work our way up through the Central Okanagan (Peachland, Kelowna) and the North Okanagan (Vernon area) to the Shuswap (Salmon Arm area). Then we'll head over to the Thompson and Nicola Valleys (Kamloops, Merritt), through Lytton, where the Thompson and Fraser Rivers meet, to the Fraser Canyon, Lillooet, and west of there, the Bridge River Valley. Back to Lillooet, we'll go northward to the vast Cariboo – Chilcotin region (Quesnel, Williams Lake, 100-Mile House, Anahim Lake, west to Bella Coola), then continue on to northern BC, to Prince George, Fraser Lake, Smithers, and area, then farther northeast to the Dawson Creek – Fort St. John region.

Peruse these pages and you'll find true stories about challenging experiences in remote areas, encounters with BC's deer, bears, moose, and other wildlife; the tragedy of forest fires; humorous people-watching stories; touching memoirs; tales of tragic incidents; and funny-only-in-hindsight true stories.

If you enjoy reading short memoirs and other creative nonfiction, you'll find stories about life as a boy in a remote coal-mining town, a community tragedy involving a young child, a near-tragedy of a family snowmobiling on an ice-covered lake, a frightening run-in with an angry moose, the resourcefulness and ingenuity of a settler and farmer, ranchers determined to build a road to civilization, experiences of a doctor in the '50s and '60s in the Chilcotin with rudimentary equipment, and various uplifting experiences with nature.

If you like immersing yourself in compelling fiction, you'll enjoy sassy and humorous stories, coming-of-age adventures, a family's harrowing escape from a forest fire, romance involving "snowbirds," a family intervention and rescue of a troubled brother, a '40s ranching story, a historical paranormal tale, a story about remote wives in the '70s, and more.

You'll find beautiful, thought-provoking poetry about early ranching life, rock climbing, a beloved motorcycle, the loss of orchards, prospecting, a raven, a tragic forest fire, encounters with wildlife, and special moments from various regions in BC.

A huge thank-you to our fifty-one contributors! This project turned out to be much more ambitious and way more work than I had imagined, but it's been a truly rewarding experience working with so many talented writers with personal stories to share. It's wonderful that together we were able to create this unique collage of fascinating stories and poems about life in our huge province.

A big thanks to our talented photographers and artists, as well! A special thank-you to professional photographers Murphy Shewchuk and Mike Biden for donating their photography to this very worthy project for charity.

Note to our American readers: this book uses Canadian spelling, apparent in words like *colour, flavour, centre, kilometre,* and *travelling*.

All proceeds from book sales, after production expenses, go to Médecins Sans Frontières / Doctors Without Borders Canada (MSF).

~ Jodie Renner, organizer and editor, November 2015

ABOUT BRITISH COLUMBIA, CANADA

British Columbia (BC) is Canada's westernmost province. It's bordered by the Pacific Ocean on the west, the Rocky Mountains and Alberta on the east, Alaska on the northwest, the Yukon and Northwest Territories on the North, and the U.S. states of Washington, Idaho, and Montana on the South.

BC is a very diverse region in its terrain and climate. The landscape ranges from some of the highest mountains in the world in both the Rocky Mountain Range and the Coastal Mountains, to lower mountains, interior plateaus, rolling hills, and flat agricultural lands. The variable climate has created temperate rainforest along the Pacific coast to semi-arid desert-like regions in the southern interior, from a subarctic climate in the north to mild winters and hot summers in the south.

BC has ten mountain ranges as well as numerous coastal inlets, thousand-year-old trees, and an abundance of lakes, rivers, and streams. The northern half of BC is rugged and remote, with its harsh winter climates, wildlife, forests, rivers, and lakes. There, nature rules, not man.

In BC, with snow on higher elevations much of the year, you can ski and golf on the same day–and go hiking, rock-climbing, fishing, boating, swimming and cycling on the same weekend, if you have the energy!

First Nations, the original inhabitants of the land, have a history of at least 10,000 years in the area. Ethnic groups along the coast, include the Haida, Coast Salish, Kwakwaka'wakw, Gitxsan, Tsimshian, and Nisga'a. Inland are various Interior Salish and Athapaskan peoples, and also the Ktunaxa.

Some of the largest First Nations groups in BC's Interior include Stl'atl'imx, Nlaka'pamux, Okanagan, Ktunaxa, Kinbasket, Secwepemc, Tsilhqot'in, Haisla, Gitxsan, Nisga'a, Nuxalk, Dakelhne, Wet'suwet'en, Sekani, and Dunne-za. [Source: UBC Museum of Anthropology map]

The region became a British colony in 1858, and in 1871, it became Canada's sixth province.

BC has everything from wilderness and remote outposts to towns and cities of various sizes nestled on mountainsides and in valleys, and on the ocean, bustling cities like Vancouver and Victoria (our capital). With a population of about 4.7 million (concentrated in Vancouver and Victoria), BC is Canada's third most populated province, after Ontario and Quebec.

With a total area of 944,735 square kilometres (364,764 square miles), BC is larger than the state of California, and larger than many countries, including the UK and Japan. Its highest point is Fairweather Mountain, whose summit is at an elevation of 4,663 metres (15,299 feet). Its longest river is the mighty Fraser, at 1,368 km (850 miles). Seventy-five percent of the province is mountainous (more than 1,000 metres [3,300 feet] above sea level); 60% is forested. Even though only about 5% of BC is arable, the province is agriculturally rich, (particularly in the Fraser and Okanagan valleys), because of milder weather near the coast and in certain sheltered southern valleys. Its climate encourages outdoor recreation and tourism, though its economy has long depended on logging, farming, and mining. British Columbia's rugged coastline stretches for more than 27,000 kilometres (17,000 miles), and includes deep, mountainous fjords and about 6,000 islands, most of which are uninhabited.

BC Wildlife: British Columbia is one of the richest, most diverse areas in Canada for its wildlife. Twice every year, many whales, dolphins, seals, sea lions, and sea otters migrate along the BC Coast, and several species of salmon swim upstream far into the province's interior. The Fraser River, with its many tributaries, boasts the largest salmon run in the world. Deer, mountain goats, moose, caribou, elk, bighorn sheep, foxes, lynx, cougars, wolves, wolverines, coyotes, wild horses, black bears, and grizzly bears roam the forests of BC's interior and north, and beavers build their homes in rivers and streams. BC is also a birder's haven, with diverse birds ranging from Canada geese, bald eagles, falcons, hawks, owls, loons, swallowtails and great blue herons to trumpeter swans, quails, and many more. And of course, we have all kinds of snakes, including rattlers!

– J. Renner

MAP OF BRITISH COLUMBIA

KOOTENAYS AND ROCKY MOUNTAINS

Kimberley and low mountains, photo © Gary Doi

ABOUT THE KOOTENAYS

The Kootenay – Rocky Mountain Region, east of the Southern Interior – Okanagan Region, offers us rugged, sharp-peaked, heavily forested mountains throughout. Four of BC's mountain ranges pass through this area: The Monashees, the Selkirks, the Purcells and, of course, the famous Rockies. The highest mountain peak in the area is Mt. Goodsir at 3,562 metres (11,690 feet). The isolation within the mountainous terrain contributed to the uniqueness of the early language spoken by the Ktunaxa people of the region.

From its southern reaches along the US border and on north, this region abounds with outstanding natural habitat, including many provincial parks as well as Kootenay and Yoho National Parks. The Kootenays offers magnificent scenery, including many impressive lakes, rivers and waterfalls. One of the most popular locations in the Rockies is Takakkaw Falls, in Yoho National Park. The mighty Columbia River and the Arrow and Kootenay lakes, among others, wind through the valleys that rise to the majestic Rocky Mountain Range in the east.

In the southern portion of the region is the historic Kettle Valley Railway, which is now part of the Trans Canada Trail for hikers, bikers, and cross-country skiers.

Cities and municipalities of the Kootenays include Golden, Revelstoke, Field, Radium Hot springs, Invermere, Slocan, Cranbrook, Kimberley, Fernie, Nakusp, Kaslo, Ainsworth Hot springs, Nelson, Grand Forks, Rossland, Trail, Salmo, Castlegar, and Creston. So much to explore and truly experience! This region is prized for its pristine wilderness and outdoor recreation. It also has a long mining history and a thriving logging/renewal industry.

– *D.F. Barrett*

DEIRDRE HUNTING SEASON

Fiction

Kristina Stanley

Due to the shortage of deer in the area, our community restricted deer hunting to bucks with four-point antlers. The doe in the area needed more males. Well, so did I. I was forty years old, and my buck had just married a doe half his age.

In our small town nestled between the Rockies and the Purcell Mountains of British Columbia, everyone knew everyone. I did the books for half a dozen businesses on Main Street and was known as the accountant with the cheating husband. That's me. Failure at marriage extraordinaire. What did I do to deserve this? I'm a rule follower. I do good deeds. I volunteer. I've never even received a parking ticket. So what happened in my life surprised me.

The day Mother Nature blew the leaves off my tree, I came home unexpectedly. We'd hired a local company to clean our air ducts, and the guy doing the work was supposed to come the following day. He called and asked if I could meet him a day early. I rushed home, even though I was busy, unlocked the front door, and headed toward the back of the house. I'd told him I'd leave the kitchen door open for him.

Fifteen years of marriage pinholed to one moment. A naked woman standing in my kitchen, leaning against my sink, drinking water from my glass.

"Hey, Babe. Get back here. I don't have much time," my then husband called from our bedroom.

The glass of water froze at the babe's lips as if she'd stuck her tongue on a metal swing set in winter. I recognized her from my husband's office. Deirdre something-or-other.

"Which babe do you mean?" I called back.

Deirdre shot toward the bedroom. I followed, just to make sure my husband was actually in the room. I was hoping against hope someone else was using our home for a romantic rendezvous. Perhaps a friend of my husband's who couldn't afford a hotel room. Most women would be hurt or angry. But not me. In my head I was already writing a story. I'm weird that way. Coming up with fiction to hide facts I don't like.

I have to admit, I found a snippet of pleasure comparing my husband's forty-five-year-old body to the twenty-year-old who frantically tried to pull the blanket from the bed to cover her perfectly toned body. The blanket stuck under the corner of the mattress, and she slipped backward, landing on her backside. I'm so polite, I removed my robe from the back of the closet door and handed it to her. I think I even smiled at her. That's me being weird again.

I get the giggles at the worst moments, and I didn't want my husband to see my smile, so I looked away from him and out the window. A doe stared back at me. A witness to my life falling apart.

When I understood reality, I refused to set foot in our house again. I know, stupid me. I moved into a one-bedroom apartment. What I hadn't considered was the location. Location is everything, right? If I'd noticed I had to walk by my old home twice a day to get to Main Street and back, or if I'd known Deirdre moved in the day after I left, I never would have picked the place I did. Too late now. I'd signed a two-year lease.

After a year of walking by the home where I used to be happy, the deer hunting restriction was in place for a second season, and I still didn't have a new buck in my life. I needed to let go of my past, but I didn't know how. Where was the manual on how to proceed?

Early one morning, I stood at the corner across from my old house, waiting for the light to turn green, wishing I could rush past the house and put the wretched place out of my mind. I couldn't even cross the street on a quiet morning when there wasn't a car in sight. I'm a rule follower, remember?

I saw a doe eating leaves from the maple tree in the front yard. I had to laugh because my ex, or should I say the jerk who married a woman half his age, insisted we put hay bales around the tree to protect it. The deer stood with her front hoofs on top of the bale of hay, stretching her soft lips, removing leaves at a leisurely pace. Smart girl. Avoiding being hunted by staying within the town limits. Getting a good meal courtesy of a cheating man.

The doe stopped eating and turned her brown eyes toward me. The way she stared, I imagined she had a message for me. She meandered to the front porch, stepped up the three steps, and dropped a load of pellets right in front of the door. Odd message but certainly one my ex deserved. I hoped he would come home from his honeymoon to a porch filled with deer poo. A fitting wedding present.

No. That's mean. And I wasn't a mean person. I couldn't even swear properly. Who said poo? I needed a serious attitude change.

For three days I walked by the deer, and every day, she dumped her pellet pie on the stoop. On the morning of the fourth day, I understood what she wanted.

For the next week, while my ex-buck and his Deirdre holidayed on some tropical island, I paused by their front door and carefully scooped the poop into a baggie. Anyone witnessing my actions would think, *How typical. She's taking care of his place while he's away.* My inside smile grew. The townspeople didn't know the new me.

Every evening, I carried a baggie of goodness home and stored it in my freezer. The day before the happy couple were to return, I knew what I had to do—but did I have the guts?

After dark, I trespassed. Yup. Me. The woman who couldn't break a rule. I snuck around to the back of their house, dressed in black. Cat Woman on a mission. I climbed the bale of hay between a tree and the back window, reached to the top of the windowsill, and snorted aloud when my fingers touched the spare key. Foolish man.

My heart pounded as I slipped the key into the lock. I rested my forehead against the door. Could I really do this? Taking a deep breath, I stepped into the dark kitchen. What used to be *my* kitchen. I took a moment to silently thank the duct-cleaning guy. If he hadn't changed the appointment day, I might never have known. I switched on my flashlight and found the register nearest the kitchen sink. I unsealed a baggie and dropped frozen deer pellets down the vent. I tucked the empty baggie in my pocket and opened the next one. Six more to go.

"Doe, a deer, a female Deirdre," I sang, hoping my replacement had a keen sense of smell.

Whoosh, a baggie's worth of pellets slid down vent number two.

Flop, baggie three's contents hit a curve in the air duct and stuck.

When all the frozen pellets I'd collected rested somewhere in the bowels of the air duct system, I surveyed the home. With the cooler temperatures of fall, the furnace would send hot air through the vents, warming my special blend of potpourri, sending lovely odours through the house.

Days, weeks maybe, would pass before they figured out where the smell was coming from. My laughter echoed off the walls, filling the house one last time with my breath.

I crept out the back door and found the doe waiting for me. I winked at her, and I swear, she nodded at me in approval. I carefully locked the door, put the key back on the windowsill, and skipped all the way home.

Photo by Donna Beckley Galanti

SWIRL OF FINCHES

Janice Notland

A swirl of finches
roller coaster
through thinning branches
atop a cedar,
blessing with a flourish
as deft as a wand.

Displacing handfuls of snow
they fall needles
like miniature loggers
laying bare new seeds.

Diving in tandem,
folding back in unison,
carving off snow
heavy in March,
fooled into thinking it was spring.

Listen now over there
another distant sound;
a continuous buzz of a chainsaw,
contrasting sharply
the silence of snow
sealing up the land.

But oh these finches survive,
know so much
require so little,
it renews my heart
with awe and joy.

DRAGONFLIES AND THE GREAT BLUE HERON

Creative Nonfiction

James Osborne

For more than a decade, great blue herons had a special meaning for Jim and Judi. During those years, Jim had no hint their affection for these graceful birds would one day have a much deeper significance.

The couple enjoyed watching them from the deck of their summer cottage on the shores of Kootenay Lake, nestled in the mountains of southeastern British Columbia. The tall birds would hunt for food less than two hundred feet away, drawn by schools of minnows to a small bay screened from their deck above by a row of willows on the shore.

Jim and Judi could also watch the long-legged birds fish patiently in the reedy shallows of a sheltered cove where they often anchored their boat overnight. The blue heron became their mascot. Thus, it was fitting to celebrate their thirtieth wedding anniversary by commissioning a watercolour of a nesting pair.

And then the years slipped by, as they will. Those thirty years edged toward thirty-five. Their prized painting hadn't been framed. One day, Jim snuck the rolled-up watercolour out of their house and got it framed. On the night of their thirty-fifth anniversary, as they prepared to turn in for the night, there was the framed painting above their bed, where Jim had just finished hanging it minutes earlier.

Three years later, Judi lost a thirteen-month battle with cancer. And Jim was, well … lost, too.

At Judi's memorial service, a dear friend and former colleague led the service. In her remarks, Eva was determined to help Judi's young grandchildren and other children among the large assembly of mourners comprehend what was occurring.

Eva told this brilliant story:

> Once upon a time, a happy group of tiny bugs was playing on the bottom of a lily pond. One by one, the bugs began climbing up a lily stem and disappearing. Those left behind wondered what had happened to their friends. Then they agreed the next bug to venture beyond the surface of the pond would return and tell the others what they'd experienced.
>
> One day, a bug left and found itself on a lily pad. It fell asleep. When it awoke, the warm sunshine had dried its body.

> Instinctively, it spread the wings that it had grown while asleep and began flying away. The bug had become a beautiful dragonfly with four iridescent wings. Then it remembered the promise. It swooped back toward the surface of the pond and headed downward. The dragonfly hit the surface and could go no farther. It was not able to return. After a while, it finally realized the others would just need to have faith that it was going to be all right.

Before she died, Judi had asked Jim to make two promises: to live a healthy lifestyle, and to find someone with whom to spend the rest of his life. The first was easy. He struggled with the second. It was shelved for almost three years. Then he met Sharolie.

Soon, it was obvious Sharolie was an extraordinary woman, just as Judi had been. Sharolie understood Jim's still-raw grief. She encouraged him to talk about the experiences of the thirty-eight years that he and Judi had shared together. Sharolie said it helped her to know and understand both of them better. Like Judi, Sharolie was blessed with a generous nature. Both had the capacity to recognize in others virtues that many others might overlook, ignore, miss, or fear.

One day, Sharolie's instincts and deep spirituality drew her to visit a yoga ashram near Jim's place on the lake. Jim went along, partly out of curiosity but mostly to be with her. After all, they were still immersed in the euphoria of new-found love.

It was early afternoon and sunny when Jim and Sharolie arrived at the picturesque ashram overlooking Kootenay Lake. They parked their car at the main building. The two walked along a narrow winding path through dense trees, over a footbridge, and across lawns toward their destination, a domed temple, the centrepiece of the ashram.

Suddenly, a large shadow crossed their path. They heard a rush of wings overhead. Both Jim and Sharolie looked up. A great blue heron had swept low over them, then folded its six-foot wingspan and landed seventy-five feet away in a vegetable garden, on the far side of a tall fence. A few steps beyond the blue heron, four people were busy tilling and harvesting in the garden. The big majestic bird took no notice of them. It was unusual behaviour for famously shy blue herons.

Sharolie and Jim were in awe as they savoured the experience. Each found themselves exchanging meaningful looks with the blue heron. It took several minutes to pull themselves away. Full of questions, they continued on to the temple. Half an hour passed while they enjoyed the temple's extraordinary acoustics and ambiance. Then it was time to go.

The couple emerged from the ground-level main entrance to another startling surprise. A blue heron was standing in the middle of a thirty-foot circular lily pond, centrepiece of the main entrance. Like the earlier blue heron, the five-foot bird was staring right at them, calmly and unblinking. Could it be the same one they'd seen earlier? Jim and Sharolie were sure it was. If the first encounter was unusual, this one had to be exceptional. More was to come.

Enthralled, the couple watched the stately blue-grey bird for several more minutes, unwilling to break the spell. As they stood, transfixed, numerous other visitors walked by, going to and from the temple, glancing over their shoulders at the rare sight. Again, the blue heron paid no attention to those passing by. It remained there. Patiently and unblinking, it returned Sharolie and Jim's amazed gazes.

"It has to be a message," Sharolie whispered quietly. "It has to be from Judi. It has to be! The heron is bringing a message from her. I just know it."

Eventually, the couple walked slowly a few feet along the main sidewalk away from the lily pond. They turned back. The blue heron was still there, watching them. Again, it returned their gazes. Then Jim and Sharolie finally turned and made their way along a secondary walk beside the temple, to a cliff overlooking the lake. While enjoying the spectacular view, they were unable to wrest their minds away from the lily pond, now hidden from view. They headed back.

"I wonder," Jim said. "Do you think it's still there?" He was skeptical of Sharolie's assessment of their experience. Sharolie's face displayed a matter-of-fact look of silent confidence that spoke wordlessly, *of course*.

Sure enough, the blue heron was still there. Once again, it quietly returned their gazes. This was uncanny, they both agreed. After several more disquieting minutes, Jim and Sharolie reluctantly pulled themselves away from the blue heron and the lily pond and returned back down the path though the grove of trees to their car. Both wondered how long the blue heron might have remained there, had they stayed. They marvelled at the rare behaviour of the blue heron.

"Yes...I'm sure," Sharolie kept repeating. "I'm sure. That was Judi sending you a message ... sending us a message ... telling you it's okay now. I think Judi's saying she knows you've finally kept your second promise. She's going to be okay now."

Jim and Sharolie didn't know at the time that the blue heron episodes would be just one part of their love story.

After Jim and Sharolie met, he wanted his three daughters to share his joy at having found someone he knew Judi would happily endorse. The first daughter to meet Sharolie was Kim. She invited her Dad and Sharolie to a semi-pro baseball game.

The three adults and Kim's children had settled in to watch the game from the open-air stands. Suddenly, two enormous dragonflies swept around Sharolie and settled calmly on her hat.

"Oh, my God!" Kim screamed, jumping to her feet. "Look at that! Look! Dragonflies! Two of them! Oh my God! Oh my God! You know what that means, don't you?"

In her mind, Eva's parable of the dragonflies had come true. From that day forward, no one was going to dissuade Kim from believing those dragonflies were on a mission of approval from her late mother.

Since then, Jim and Sharolie have experienced hovering dragonflies, often in the most unlikely locations. And they've encountered blue herons, time and time again. Like the dragonflies, these encounters were often in unusual and unexpected circumstances. Close friends also reported sightings of blue herons, unusually close up and where they'd never seen them before.

Jim and Sharolie were married twenty-three months after they met. Shortly thereafter, the visits from the blue heron and dragonflies began to diminish.

Now, the visits are less frequent, although always welcome.

On these occasions, Sharolie will say, "Checking up. She's just checking up."

(Author's Note: *Dragonflies and the Great Blue* Heron is based on a true story.)

Source Credit: Eva's dragonfly analogy is drawn from a public domain story, "The Water Bug Story," at:

www.healingheart.net/stories/waterbug.html

FENCES

Linda Crosfield

for Vi Plotnikoff

We follow the hearse up the hill to the English Cemetery.
Snow falls softly, feathers the ground.

Across the river in Ootischenia
the other cemetery, *Blagodatnoe*,
overlooks the Columbia River.
Slate or marble markers lie amid the dry grasses
abandoned by all but the dead now,
surrounded by a wire fence.

Vi's in a plain pine box, in a pale blue dress,
her hands folded, her eyes shut.
Fastened securely at her neck
as if the sharp November wind might tug it off,
a kerchief—a *platok*, she'd say—
covers her head with pink flowers.

Off to the north in New Denver,
another wire fence, a chain link fence
keeps children in and parents out.

There's always singing at Doukhobor funerals.
Today, at the graveside,
a cappella voices rise to the sky, clouds part,
the sun shines welcome to my friend.

In the fifties, the RCMP came before dawn
and rousted from their beds the children of Sons of Freedom,
children whose parents didn't hide them
in cupboards or root cellars, under floor boards
or out in the woods, wherever they could get to in time.

On her casket, pink roses from her family who loved her.
A deer, a young buck, emerges from the woods,
watches while she is lowered into the ground.

The government said parents were wrong
to keep the kids out of school,
so it punished the kids as well as the parents.

Vi told stories of Doukhobor life, of aunts and young soldiers,
of girls and their weddings,
and stories as distant from her life as mine,
one of dead villages, dead with no children,
gone with their youth, gone with their laughter
as if the Pied Piper had lured them away.

Two hours at a time, twenty-four times a year,
parents could visit their children.
In winter they touched fingers
through the chain-link fence,
afraid to kiss, for the fence was cold
and their lips might stick.

After she's in the ground
and the deer has returned to the forest
we drive back to Brilliant,
to long tables laden with tea and sturdy bread,
with bowls for the funeral borscht,
lapsha, served by the ladies.

In the fifties, children like me,

same age as the kids in New Denver,
didn't know how to say *platok*, or *Blagodatnoe*,
didn't know the Doukhobor kids could speak Russian.
They kept that secret.

Last time I saw her,
propped against pillows in her hospital bed,
Spasiba I said.
Thank you for the stories.
Spasiba for helping us English begin to understand.
Thank you for telling.
Spasiba.

KEENE HILL

Fiction

RM Greenaway

Clare recalled the whispers and wails of the nonstop wind that summer. The heavens would rumble days on end over the East Kootenays, but rarely unleash into a full-on storm. The rain came down in spatters, warm as tears, but evaporated on impact. From the back porch of her house on Keene Hill, the skies and fields spread out south to north. She could remember standing uneasy and depressed, watching purple clouds bunch up in the west, heavy and slow one day, the next day steamrolling fast toward the Purcells. Mostly she recalled the omens.

The animals that roamed Keene Hill delivered signs of their own that summer, and had she paid heed, she'd have picked up and left. But she would also have lost, in the end. That's the way of fate-twists.

The grasshoppers tried to warn her. They were thick in the grasses and loud like castanets, and they'd aim for the face like hard, leggy pea-shot. There was also the black horse that broke into the fenced five acres where Clare and Eric's rental house sat, and went charging about in the June dusk till it broke out again, a horse she'd never seen before or since.

And the deer. Before the omens began, she'd take her coffee outside in the morning to watch them graze their way past, till finally they'd leap with fantastic grace over the fence and wander off into the mist. In a normal year the deer would ignore her, but that summer of signs they'd stand poised on the western boundary, staring her way until she lost nerve and retreated indoors.

Indoors she would turn on the TV for company. She and Eric didn't have cablevision, so only received the two free channels, one decent but disheartening, mostly news, and the other more in the way of light entertainment but with a bad signal; the pale antics of ghosts set to laughter was about all one could get from the screen. Eric said he'd buy a satellite dish and install it himself, even though it was just a rental house and they'd be moving on soon as he gathered enough beans. But satellite signals cost money, and the trucking business for him had been a bust lately. Lots of reasons for that: the blockades and strikes and tariffs, the caroming economy, the cost of gas. And the truck breaking down, of course, at the worst possible times, like a thing cursed.

So Channel 3 with static was Clare's best link to the broader world that summer. And for narcotic escape, only the cheapest, hardest beer Eric could find to fill their fridge.

Their house sat at the turnaround of a dead-end road called Ermacora. Above their lot line, separated by a wonky metal fence, sat the trailer park. The trailer park was full of mostly pensioners, some bad-apple kids, and two certifiable crazies. One crazy was Miss Zino, small as a six-year-old child, with the withered body of a very old lady and a fairly smooth but misaligned face. And bulgy eyes and a weird grin. She never talked much, just gaped at everybody from her little porch. The residents shunned her. Clare tried to be nice, though, and would smile and wave if she was walking the acreage and got close enough. Ms. Zino never waved back, but one oppressively hot day, with hints of hurricane stirring the air, she and Clare became locked in a real conversation.

"How long you been living up here, Miss Zino?" asked Clare.

"Since long before you's born," said Miss Zino.

Over thirty years, then. Clare stood calculating, her hair whipping about like fanned flames, trying to keep it tamed with both hands. "Really? That long?"

"Hundreds of years," the old woman said. "I was born in the soil under your feet. I grew up with the pine cones. They built this trailer around me as I sat in this very chair."

"Is that right?" Clare said, and tried to go civilly on her way.

But Miss Zino had more to say, adding to Clare's stock of dread. "A dangerous place, your house."

Clare thought of the nails sticking out here and there, and had to agree. "It's not well-finished," she said. Which was a wild understatement. She knew her landlord, Mr. Boka, who lived at the far end of the property in a little bungalow, had built his tiny place and their huge place all by himself on an impossible budget. The big house was constructed of salvaged goods, a patchwork monument to his thrift. Green lino tacked down next to pink, a yellow fridge, black stove, and motley chandeliers dangling in the oddest places. The house stood two floors high, with an unfinished, dungeon-like basement, hollow walls, and brownish well-water you had to boil before use. But the rent was good, and Eric liked the place because it was rough—no landscaping bullshit to manoeuvre his gear around, and he could work on his rig without being harassed by any goddamn tulip-worshipping neighbours.

Dangerous it was. Not the kind of place to bring a child into the world. Clare very much wanted to bring a child into the world, but not into a place like that. It wasn't the nails so much as the raw mood of the place. She said to Miss Zino, "Well, it was sure nice talking—"

"What if there was to be a fire? Whatcha going to do then?"

The neighbour's wash rucked and buckled on its line. Crows shot past like kamikaze pilots. Clare's shadow was blurred in the weeds and stretched out long, telling her it was high time to move on. But she'd been raised to be polite, which meant answering when asked. She said, "Well, guess I'd call nine one one, wouldn't I?"

"Nine one one," Miss Zino echoed, and seemed tickled by the words. "Nine one one," she called mockingly into the air. "'Course you'll call nine one one, and the good firefighting fairies will come a-fluttering down to put out the blaze, eh?"

Big hideous grin, teeth you could count on one hand, bulgy eyes gleaming, and around them the rumble of distant thunder.

"But there won't be a fire," Clare said. "Why should there be a fire, Miss Zino?"

"Lightning," Miss Zino said, pointing inside to her kitchenette.

That night there was a lightning storm like nothing Clare had ever witnessed, and crashing rain, and thunder that made the house flinch on its foundations. The next morning the sunlight came blindingly through the steam rising from the earth, and there was no TV signal whatsoever. Eric liked to watch the news first thing, so without hesitation he went striding off through the prickly weeds and a blizzard of grasshoppers to fetch the landlord and complain.

Mr. Boka was a huge man of few words, probably because of his poor English, but really nice, if you got to chatting with him about the price of real estate or wine. Bit of a recluse, but if anything went wrong in the house, he'd be quick to come fix it. So he came trudging back with Eric, and outside they went to see if there was anything they could do—in the cheapest way possible—about the TV reception, and off Clare went as directed to buy a dozen beer, Gunpowder brand, eight per cent alcohol and only $7.99 for a six-pack.

It was about a fifteen-minute drive up the 95A to Marysville, so she killed two birds and picked up some groceries at the same time. By the time she got back, Boka was gone and the TV was working pretty much the same as it was before the storm, Eric sitting there watching bombs dropping on the Middle East.

"No better, huh?" Clare said, disappointed. She'd been counting on the picture being clearer once Boka fiddled with the bicycle wheel on the post he'd got rigged for an antenna out back. Eric said nothing. He never did like answering inane questions, especially when the answer was plain enough.

So in accompaniment to their silence, to the anchorman's drone of more bad news, the afternoon wind came sweeping in, and night fell, and that night Clare heard a ghost.

"God, Eric," she cried, sitting upright straight out of sleep. They used the downstairs bedroom and left the top floor pretty much to itself. Bunch of boxes up there and her sewing machine which she never used. "Did you hear that?"

Eric's uppermost eye shone through the darkness at her, a hazel glint that warned of short patience. "Hear?"

"That," she said. "A voice. Hear it?"

Eric perked an ear to the silence for a bit, then rolled over and answered her concerns with a snore. Just the tail end of a dream, she told herself. But how *real,* that low but urgent voice coming down through ceiling or walls, words that she could only discern as *Wa-walo. Wa-wa-walo.* And though she didn't hear it again, the sound was so awful, so bizarre, that she tossed for hours.

The next day Eric went on a two-day cargo haul up to Revelstoke, and Clare was alone in the dimming house. By noon the mysterious purple clouds had draped their early twilight all over Keene Hill, and the wind had started up its obsessive whining through the building's nooks and crannies. And then the ghost upstairs began to thud.

Thump. Thump-thump. Thump thump thump. Silence. Thump.

Of course it wasn't a ghost. A window stood ajar up there, and the wind was rocking some bit of furniture against the wall. With a beer in her for courage she walked upstairs, whistling cheerfully. But no windows stood ajar, and the next thud, louder than the others and much too close, sent her skittering in her socks back down the hall and out the front door, down the driveway and a stone's throw along the grit of Ermacora before she came to a full stop.

"My God," was all she could say. "My God." And she got in their pickup and drove into Cranbrook and spent the night in the cheapest motel she could find.

She was back in the house when Eric's rig pulled in the next evening, and as he climbed down she brought him a freshly popped beer and told him about the thumping.

"Well, yeah," he said. "It's the stuff."

"Stuff?" she said. "What stuff?"

"The ballast Boka winched up," he said. "Affixed the antenna up there to get it higher. Didn't do shit. I'll sort it."

Sitting by the TV, she could hear him propping the ladder, climbing up. His boots clomped about on the metal roof, dragging around the ballast

Boka had put up there, whatever it was. She looked out the back window and saw for the first time that the bicycle wheel was indeed gone from its tall post.

She laughed at her own skittishness. She'd blown fifty-seven bucks on a motel room for nothing. So the ghost was banished, she was a fool, and everything should have been fine after that. But it wasn't. Wasn't fine at all.

Eric, she could swear, was possessed. Some evil spirit had gotten into him. It wasn't too obvious, at first. He was the surly type, so his mood was hard to gauge, but something was definitely eating him. As summer waned to autumn he'd stay lodged in his armchair, beer in hand, hour on end. Nothing unusual there, except the TV was off. He'd sit and brood, eyes following Clare wherever she went. No longer did he spend the day outside souping up the pickup, a once-favourite pastime, and no longer did he drag Clare by the hand into the bedroom on a whim. And their conversation, such as it was, became a bone-dry creek bed.

Clare would say, "Why don't you go on out and flush the rad, Eric?"

"Rad don't need flushing."

He was not pleasant company. It was a relief when he went off on overnight hauls, and soon as he came home she'd feel another tension headache coming on.

He was jumpy and ill-kept. Gone were his vanity, his fear of being caught with food in his teeth. And he couldn't or wouldn't sleep. Clare would wake in the small hours to an empty bed, and she'd find him sitting in that old armchair in the living room, the house shifting and whispering around him, his face pale and vacant amidst shifting streaks of moonlight.

"Hear that?" he called out one night, from his armchair.

Clare scrambled out of bed and clung to the living room doorframe. "Hear what?"

"That," he rasped, eyes wide and throat working. "That tapping."

She heard no tapping, but fear is contagious, and she'd been born with weedy nerves. She suggested they go stay in a motel, maybe.

"No," he said. "Not gonna be scared off by a little blood."

"Blood?" she said. "What you mean, blood?"

"All down the side of the house," he said. And it wasn't a joke, because Eric didn't know how. "Blood and entrails, Clare."

Her voice rose three notches. "Where?"

"Forget it," he said. "Must have been a bird hit the house, is all. Go back to sleep."

She crawled into bed, but Eric stayed put, sunk in his armchair and staring at the dead TV. Next day Clare went and looked at the backside of the house. Saw blackish streaks coming down, like something had been dripping off the eaves, but could have been anything. Sure didn't look like blood. Not fresh blood, anyway.

Winter came, and so did the whipping snow, and so did the repo men. They took away the Kenmore washer one bitter cold day, saying Boka had defaulted on payments. Eric offered to square it up to keep the machine, but the repo men ignored him, wheeled the appliance away to their truck and scudded off without a backward glance.

And the next day a uniformed policeman came by. He was big and burly as Eric, with wary brown eyes and a bristling mustache. His breath billowed white as he introduced himself as Constable Shane and asked if Matthew Boka was around, by any chance. Eric pointed out Boka's house down at the northeast corner of the property, and he and Clare stood on the front stoop and watched the cop bumble his sedan across the clotted terrain and park in front of Boka's bungalow.

"I haven't seen Mr. Boka around lately," Clare remarked to Eric, now that she thought about it.

"Truck's there," Eric said.

But Mr. Boka's little blue Datsun was always there, except for once every couple of weeks when he'd go to Cranbrook for supplies.

"Frickin' cold," Eric said, and ushered her inside.

"Let's watch TV," she said.

"Let's not."

She lingered by the side windows, watching the police car till it came bumbling back toward the gate. But instead of heading out to Ermacora it stopped again in their drive, and the policeman climbed out and started to walk around behind the house. Clare moved to the back window and watched him stalk through the blanched and brittle weeds. The policeman glimpsed her at the window before she could dodge out of sight, and he smiled a bit and lifted a hand in greeting. She smiled a bit and lifted a hand too, but he was already moving on. He was looking this way and that. Looked up at the sky. Down at the foundations. Up at the siding. Fixed on something; she guessed it was that blackish stain, maybe. Huffed out a breath, and kept walking his circuit around the house. She moved to the side window, and then the front to follow his progress, and was flooded with hopelessness as he got back into his car and drove away.

That night in bed she told a sweaty, sleepless, twitching Eric that she wanted to move outta this horrible place. "Why?" he said. "We don't pay no rent, and you like him. Don't you?"

"I like who?" Clare said. "And what d'you mean we pay no rent? We pay six fifty a month."

"He won't accept no rent from me no more," Eric said. "He says we can stay for free, baby. I think he likes you."

"Who, Mr. Boka? Are you talking about Mr. *Boka*?"

"Always had his eye on you," he said, sweating and twitching. He'd laid down fully dressed, she saw now. Hadn't even taken off his boots. His once carefully groomed goatee had become just a plain scruffy beard since winter set in, like a horse gets hairier when the snow flies. His eyes were always red-rimmed, his hands forever clenching. "I think he likes you," he said again. "Hear him tapping away there in Morse code? Hear him, baby? Calling you?"

"I don't hear nothing," she said, and tried to ease out of bed. This was it. The Eric she knew was gone for good, and the man who'd taken his place was downright scary. "Gotta pee," she said, finding her slippers, wondering how she could gather her clothes and get dressed and out the door and into the truck and away down Ermacora without him noticing.

And damn but she should have seen it coming. Should have just made a naked dash for it. With rattlesnake speed Eric reached over and snatched her wrist before she could push off from the bed. He pulled her against him and seemed to cuddle her there, as they'd done in happier days, spooned together with his arms latched around her midriff, his breath hot in her ear. "Cold as a deep freeze out there, and he's been asking for you. Think we better do what the landlord says, angel-boobs."

"Eric," she whimpered. "What're you talking about?"

"He don't blame me," he said in her ear, in a pleading sort of way. "Don't worry that he's mad or nothin'. He knows it's just an accident. I was trying to help, is all, moving the ladder for him. It got tangled, eh, his foot in all that safety rigging he had knotted up. It weren't a proper harness. Wouldn't have happened if he had a proper harness, fuckin' cheapskate. Christ. Didn't know what to do, baby." Eric was whimpering now almost as bad as she was. "Didn't know what to do. I freaked. Thought he was dead. But he wasn't dead, was he? He never did die."

Clare started to shake in her husband's embrace, hardly hearing now his terrifying gush of words. "He's okay with it," Eric rasped. "He told me so. But he's lonely, out there, and cold. Wants to cut a deal, and it's only right, Clare, because I owe him a big one, living rent free and all that. Be nice if you'd go keep him company for a while, don't ya think? Warm him up with yer feminine charms."

"No," she cried, but she was already getting manhandled like a rag doll out of bed, and like a reverse rape forced into her dressing gown. "No!" she screamed, as he wrangled her arms through the sleeves and cinched the belt around her waist. He tried to hoist her up like a gunny sack, but she lashed out with fingers tensed into claws and got him across the face. He reeled a fist back and cracked her a stunning blow to the cheek. And again, and once more, and that was one too many, and she didn't know what happened after that.

Until the slapping cold breeze woke her, and she found herself slung over his shoulder as he grunted his way up a ladder. She focused first on his woolly blue jacket and the rear of his jeans, and then the rungs and the ground below, but didn't understand where she was till she looked sideways at the night's panorama of valley and clotted sky fuzzed with moonlight. She was so cold, so in pain, but playing dead seemed about all she could do. Play dead and wait for her chance to escape.

Eric got a handhold on something, probably whatever rigging Mr. Boka had used when he was up here in the summer propping his goddamn money-saving bicycle wheel against the chimney. Eric hauled himself up with difficulty, loaded with Clare's extra hundred and fifteen pounds. He was upright on the metal roof, counter-balancing his weight against its slope. He made his way along sideways, slithering and regaining his balance, then tight-roped precariously along the roof's peak. Clare was gasping now, not playing dead so much as paralyzed by fear. Only when he straddled the ridge line and unloaded her with a thud on her back and the incline tried to take her did she come alive, scrabbling for screw heads, corrugations, flashing, anything to stop her rolling toward a deadly fall. She caught hold and lay flat, staring up into Eric's face with her teeth bared. The screw heads hadn't saved her, but Eric's knee had, pressed now into her stomach and holding her in place. But he wasn't looking at her. He was squinting above her with a look of strained courtesy, saying, "Whoa, what a fricking cold night, eh, Matt? How's things, man?"

Matthew Boka, he was talking to. Clare whipped her head around and stared an arm's stretch up into a sagged and blackened face, two rotten berries for eyes, mouth a tattered cave and hair petrified into brittle chaos. The corpse was seated against the chimney stack, roped into place. Her thoughts flew back to the summer, the night of the horrific thumping when Eric had climbed up to sort Boka's "ballast." He wasn't sorting no ballast. He was hauling a heavy dangling body up onto the roof so it wouldn't hit against the siding with every gust of wind. Hauled it up, tied it in place, and left it there. Left Mr. Boka there to blister and boil in the hot summer sun, right over Clare's head, decomposing, his blood and body bits sloughing into the gutters and down the drain pipe and into the soil. And that's what the unholy stink had been, that one particularly gnat-infested day, that stink Eric blamed on a dead cat out in the rain barrel, and he'd gone outside and done some serious hosing until the stink disappeared. Except it never did disappear, and the air was forever tainted, and Clare never did enjoy the beautiful outdoors after that, and by the looks of it, never again would.

"Clare's come to join you," Eric wheedled in a small voice she'd never heard from him before. He had a virgin coil of rope looped around his shoulder and was drawing his favourite hunting knife from its sheath, and she knew for sure that she was betrothed to a carcass. She stared at the blade tip and thrashed under Eric's weight. "Fantastic view," he muttered, as he leaned to grab her again, not to gut her, she realized, but to pull her to the chimney, where she would be tied alive and kicking to Boka's mouldy flank, off at this weird angle probably invisible to road or trailer park and any hopes of rescue, and left to perish most horrifically.

Eric would have done it, too, he was that mad. Would have left her screaming herself dry and he would have climbed back down and gone on living there, maybe for years, till something gave. But it never came to that, because as he hauled her up against Boka and was whipping his rope straight to start binding the living woman to the dead man in unholy matrimony, there came a sudden holler from below, a man's shout, a hard and furious "YOU! HOLD IT!"

Eric looked sideways and teetered, losing his grip on Clare. Released, she slid like a dead weight, tearing her hands on screw heads until she hit the eaves and toppled over, just catching hold—to cheap tinny gutter that whined and gave under her weight as she dangled, cheap fasteners that popped and squealed. Her hands were numb-cold and bleeding and couldn't maintain their death grip, and down she went with a mile-long wail, crashing into the arms of Constable Shane, who sprawled to the ground beneath her.

But she wasn't a heavy woman, and Shane was massive, and they both survived the most violent and unexpected embrace of their lives.

Later that night, in the warmth of the police station, she was told who had saved her life. Aside from Constable Shane, that is. Seems the insomniacal Miss Zino had spied action on that distant rooftop from her trailer and had the wits to go outside on her deck and shout out "Nine one one" into the crisp midnight breeze. Seems this nocturnal hooting angered a neighbour, who phoned the police. Constable Shane paid his diligent visit, without lights or siren, because it was just a nuisance call, and as he tried to explain the niceties of community living to Miss Zino, she had pointed out what must have been vague silhouettes jiggling about up there, and complained that it just wasn't right for people to be fooling around on rooftops in the middle of the night. It just wasn't right.

Clare is doing well, now, except she hates wind, grasshoppers and televisions. In the year that followed her ordeal, Constable Shane persistently asked her out, and she persistently said no. He was a big man, like Eric, so she wouldn't let him nearer than across the table of the local diner, two coffee cups standing guard between them. Over one such coffee one late afternoon he said, "How can I prove it to you, Clare, that I won't hurt you?"

"You can't," she said. "I'm damaged goods. Sorry."

He laid his hand on the table between them, palm down, and said, "I won't be so bold as to touch your hand, then. How about *you* go ahead and touch *mine*?"

She didn't take him up on the strange offer, that day. But he went through the same routine the following week, and this time she pushed at his knuckle with her index finger. Just an experimental prod. Soon to be followed by a hand-in-hand walk through the windless lowlands where he lived, out behind the bird sanctuary.

One thing led to another. A dinner and dance, a canoe trip up the Kettle River. A quiet wedding ceremony in his home. Their home. And then the child she'd always dreamed of landed in her arms. So sometimes omens be damned, right? Sometimes.

THE LOOK OF COLD

Janice Notland

Winter howls,
searching to settle
somewhere familiar.

The cold remembers my house:
moans eerily,
rapping at my window panes,
slapping at my door.

Chased inside I light a fire,
warmth of wood
a comfort
against the strident wind.

Throwing off layers of clothes,
at the window warming icy cheeks,
I'm excited at being alive.

My weighted feet
make earth my home
but lift my mind to wonder.

As overhead a flock of birds,
outlines shattering a grey chill,
sail through – on particles of light.

SETH'S GOODBYES

Vignettes of an early childhood in the '50s in a coal-mining town in the Rockies

Seth Raymond

I turn off the ice-laden wipers and then the engine of the Ford pickup. I lay my head on the steering wheel. When I look up, wet snow has already plastered over the windshield. The hot engine ticks as it begins to cool.

The porch light comes on and Mom stands in the doorway in her slippers and housecoat. Jeez, she looks small and frail. With a sigh I open the truck's door, flip the seat forward, and drag out my suitcase.

"I thought you went off the road in this awful weather," she says, as she hugs me.

"I took it slow. The truck is good in these conditions."

Mom hugs me again. In the kitchen she makes me tea and gives me a piece of her apple pie she baked that afternoon. We don't mention Dad.

I lay in the guest room that night feeling the sway and swing of the long drive. In the morning, Mom, as always when I visit, prepares sourdough pancakes, fried eggs, and bacon for my breakfast. The sourdough is the real deal. Mom started the original starter dough decades ago.

She, of course, wants to come. She resists but finally agrees to let me go alone, at least for this morning. Even the nursing home's staff expresses worry about her when I phone them about Dad. She needs a break if only for this morning.

As I drive to the Nursing Home, the local radio station informs me it has stopped snowing in Castlegar but to expect snow later in the day. Plough trucks are out and people are busy shovelling driveways.

I park and walk up to the glass doors. The doors won't open until a code number is typed into a number pad by the doors. There's one outside to get in and one inside to get out. I punch in the number Mom gave me this morning. The door clicks and I push it open. I wipe my boots dry on the rugs.

Lost souls with empty eyes shuffle towards the doors to freedom, their arms waving languidly as if immersed in water. An assortment of wheelchairs sit parked to the left of the doorway. These are occupied by those who can't wander anymore but still beseech you as you pass to … do what? I do not know.

I keep my eyes on the floor until I reach the nursing station. The nurse recognizes me, "You're John's son, aren't you? You live up in Prince George. You were here in the fall, weren't you?"

I nod. "I'm Seth. I don't get down too often."

"I see Dorothy is not with you. That's good. She's here every day—twice a day—without fail. I don't know how she does it." She puts on a serious look. "Your mother must have told you it won't be long now."

I nod and notice her name tag. "Ruth, can I go see him?"

The nurse closes Dad's room door as she leaves. I stand and look at the figure laid out under the covers on the bed. There's a peak where his toes still stand and then a section of rumpled blankets where his body used to be, and it's topped off with a skeletal head propped onto a pillow. Who is this? My eyes keep wanting to look away.

They don't dress him now, just keep him clean. No food, no water—no extraordinary efforts. I pull up an upholstered chair and take the limp bag of bone and skin that used to be Dad's hand. I want to be anywhere but here. I want to be anytime but now. I let the years roll back to my early years in the now-extinct coal-mining town of Michel.

Old photo of town of Michel

Michel was sandwiched in a narrow valley in the Rocky Mountains, along with the mining and coke operations of the Crowsnest Pass Coal Company, the Crowsnest Highway, the Canadian Pacific train tracks, and a meandering Michel Creek. Two long rows of near identical, two-storied, side-by-side duplexes occupied a strip of land between the creek and a mountain side. The strip was scraped flat and was covered with gravel and crushed coal. A median strip composed of mismatched outhouses and coal sheds separated the strip into two roadways. The houses were long-ago red and each of their stoops ended on the black dust of the road. A small hospital, Michel Hospital, sat at the end of the row closest to the creek, and at the other end, a road led between the houses back to the Crowsnest Highway.

* * *

Three duplexes up from the hospital on the creek side, in the half farthest from the hospital, a small lad of four or so is having a bath in the kitchen sink. He's sitting, knees drawn up, in a white porcelain sink full of bubbles.

I stop splashing to push at Mom's hands as she rubs my face with a cloth. "My clean little lad. Yes you are." I squirm and try to pull the cloth away.

A long squeak and a bang as Norma and her grown daughter Eleanor, our neighbours on the other half of our duplex, enter through the screen door.

"Oh, getting a bath, are you?" Norma says.

"You can't put a saddle on me," sings Eleanor. Eleanor starts to slowly circle the kitchen, slapping her side and singing the same line over and over.

"Eleanor. Eleanor." I laugh as Eleanor dances.

"Shush, Seth," commands Mom as she lifts me out and places me standing on the linoleum-covered counter and towels me off. The towel is rough.

Norma pinches my leg. "You're getting big, you."

Eleanor keeps circling and slapping, "You can't put a saddle on me."

"The kettle's hot, Norma," says Mom, "Make us some tea. This young man is going to bed as soon as he gets his pajamas on."

"Eleanor. Eleanor." I hold out my arms.

Norma laughs. "Sit down, Eleanor, and be quiet." Eleanor sits at the kitchen table. "Sit still now, and Seth can sit in your lap. You can't move or you'll drop him."

Eleanor sits still. Mom pulls the soft flannel pajamas onto my legs and buttons up the top. She carries me over to Eleanor's lap.

"No galloping, Eleanor, or off Seth goes to bed," reminds Norma. Eleanor's thighs quiver as her legs secretly gallop. Her lips barely move as she silently sings. Norma helps Eleanor put her arms around me. "Not too tight, Eleanor. Not too tight. Be nice and gentle."

Eleanor's strong arms tremble; her big hands enclose me as if afraid.

"Don't move or he goes to bed," says Norma. "And no crying. Eleanor, you hear me? Don't you cry, or he has to go to bed. Don't you cry."

Eleanor bows her head and the curtain of her long, black hair falls about me. Through the shadow of her breath, I look up into her dark eyes as the tears slowly build and start to rain onto my face. My finger traces the big teeth peeking from behind the silently singing lips.

* * *

I run sniffling down our street towards the hospital and my house. The houses are on my right, and the row of outhouses and coal sheds are on my left. The houses on this side back onto the creek and our back fence is almost falling over into it. The houses on the other side of the outhouses and coal sheds back against the mountain. Their backyards press against the skirt of waste rock and coal towering above their rooftops—the spoil bank.

Grey snow is melting, and mud puddles are everywhere.

A few people come out onto their front steps. A man comes out of his outhouse tucking his shirt in and fastening his coat. He stands there looking. It's snowing lightly; the large wet flakes melt in the black puddles. Dad catches up to me and kicks me in the arse. I speed up, fall down with a splash, and quickly get up again and run on.

"Hey, John," calls out a woman. "What have you got there?"

I risk a look behind me at Dad advancing, his work pants supported by red suspenders going over his long-sleeve underwear top. The black gumboots on his feet advancing fast, splashing through the water. Smoke trails from the hand-rolled cigarette hanging on his lip.

He stops to answer the lady. "I get off shift and here's his Mom and my little girl at the company bus stop. His Mom's worried about where he is. So off I go and I find the little bugger up at the old coal tipple with Billy and Joey, and he knows better. I'm not finding him dead up there one day and me having to tell his mother."

His stopping allows me to make quite a bit of headway, but Dad closes it with a few big strides.

The woman laughs. "You've gotta learn them, John." Another kick hurries me on.

Far ahead, I see Mom out on our steps. My sister Margaret is standing in the road in her yellow rain suit. Eleanor is running circles about her. I faintly hear Eleanor singing her song. Norma is standing beside Mom.

I start to cry more loudly.

Mom moves down another step. She calls to Dad, "John?" Her voice struggles with the distance.

* * *

"You can't put a saddle on me," hollers Eleanor. She gallops around me, slapping her rump.

"Come on, Eleanor, let's go get Hawk."

Eleanor gallops up beside me as we proceed down the snowy street. “You can’t put a saddle on me.”

Hawk is waiting. Through the falling snow, I can see his shape outside his gate. The snow is wet and sticky, coming down hard at a slant. Gusts fling the wet stuff in our faces.

Hawk is excited. “Billy, Joey, and Pete are waiting. They’ve made a fort.”

“Yeah, but we’ve got Eleanor.”

“You can’t put a saddle on me.” Eleanor trots around Hawk and me.

“Eleanor, let’s make snowballs and go chase the bad kids.” Eleanor bends and starts squeezing the snow, making water pour out. Her large, powerful hands are covered with colourful mittens that Norma has knitted her. A string goes from the back of each mitten through her sleeve, across her back, and down the other sleeve to the other mitten. Her mittens are soaked in a moment.

She hands me the first snowball. It’s like grey crystal. You can see inside the specks of dirt and coal from the roadway.

I get Eleanor to make Hawk and me four each: one in the throwing hand, one in the other hand, and one each in our two coat pockets.

We’re ready. Billy, Joey, and Pete have made their fort up against Joey’s outhouse. They see us approaching and start shouting insults. Eleanor trots about, singing, “You can’t put a saddle on me.” They think they’re safe behind their chest high wall. They like to call Eleanor names. They’re afraid of her. She’s caught one or more of them before and had to be restrained from hurting them. But they think they’re safe now.

“There are the bad kids, Eleanor. They want to put a saddle on you.” Eleanor stops her galloping and slapping her thighs. Her dark eyes follow my pointing hand to the snow fort and the three heads poking out above its walls. Billy, Joey, and Pete start throwing snowballs.

“You can’t put a saddle on me!” Eleanor shouts at them. We three stop as the closest snowballs fall at our feet. Eleanor prances on the spot, her feet up and down, and both hands lightly flapping. Her mittens swing loose on their string.

I hand her a snowball. Eleanor is big and old. And she can throw a rock—or a snowball—very fast and very far. But they think they are safe in their fort.

The ice ball smashes into the outhouse wall behind Joey, Billy, and Pete with a thudding sound. Slush slides off the roof. Eleanor chants her ditty.

Hawk hands her another snowball. She takes it in her bare hand, her mitten swinging on its tether. Another loud blossom of ice appears above their heads. They duck down but Hawk and I know they'll have to bob up to throw their own missiles and check if we're advancing.

Eleanor starts to lose interest and begins the hand movements preparatory to galloping, so I hand her a snowball. She chucks it. No heads are visible but the ice ball disintegrates a portion of the fort's rim. Heads bob up. Hawk hands her another snowball. And this one connects, taking Pete right in the face and knocking him over backwards.

Hawk and I know it's over before the screaming begins. "Come on Eleanor. Let's go." The three of us race off, Eleanor slapping her thigh and singing.

* * *

Billy's folks have left Billy with us for the day. Someone died.

Billy and I sit in the back seat of our green car. It has little yellow arms that come out when Dad signals a turn. Mom and Dad are in the front. My sister, Marg, is sitting on Mom's lap. We're going to Fernie to shop, and Mom says we can eat in the Chinese restaurant that has the fish tank in the front window. There's big orange fish and black ones with bulgy eyes and funny tails that don't seem to work well. I can stand and look at the fish. I can see through the tails, which are filmy and wavy, not stiff and tough like a trout's tail. Their mouths are O's that expand and contract.

Billy brought a Batman comic with him, and he's reading it to me. It's like the Batman serial Hawk and I saw last year at the movie theatre.

"Why is Billy reading to you, Seth? Why don't you read to Billy?" Mom has turned her head to look at me behind Dad's seat.

"Seth can't read, Mrs. Raymond," says Billy. "The teacher has to help him a lot."

I see Dad's head make a little nod and shake. Mom looks at Dad. "Don't, John. Not a word."

Mom says, "Well, you keep reading then, Billy. Just don't get carsick now."

* * *

Mrs. Burns places the chair in the hallway. "You wait here, Seth. I'm just going to have a talk with your mother."

I sit down. She goes into the classroom and returns with a picture book of dinosaurs. "I know you like this book. We won't be long." She closes the door.

Some dinosaurs are really big, even bigger than our car. Some dinosaurs are small, even smaller than a cat. Mammoths are not dinosaurs.

Dinosaurs lay eggs. Dinosaurs don't have hair. Mammoths feed their babies milk. Mom feeds Marg milk. What do dinosaur babies eat?

Mom has wet eyes. She kneels down, takes the dinosaur book off me and puts it on the floor. She pulls me out of the chair into her arms. The chair clatters as it falls over. Mrs. Burns comes out of the room and picks it up, and then she turns and takes it into the classroom and closes the door after her.

The dinosaur book lies on the floor. Mrs. Burns forgot it in the hallway. After a while, Mom lets me go and gets up. She takes my hand. "We must go get your sister. I told Norma I'd only be an hour. I need to get supper for you and your sister."

* * *

It's nighttime. A loud thump has woken me up.

Norma and Ivan are downstairs in our kitchen. Ivan's voice rumbles like thunder far away. I like his sound. Ivan is Eleanor's daddy. Mom has stopped crying. She stopped as soon as Norma and Ivan came into the house.

"I'll go get him, Dot," says Ivan. "It's not the boy's fault if he's retarded, just like it's not Eleanor's. And it's definitely not your fault."

"Ivan! For Christ's sake, you're thick as stone." Norma sounds angry.

"It'll just be a fight, Ivan. You know how he is. Leave him be." Mom talks very softly. "He'll be home when the bar closes. Or he'll continue drinking over at Tommy's place. Let it be."

"Go back and have your supper, Ivan. It still should be hot. I'll stay with Dot."

I hear Ivan's heavy feet, and the screen door squeaks and bangs. A moment later another bang tells me Ivan is in his house.

I lay on the bedroom floor by the heat grate over the kitchen stove. Mom and Norma are over by the sink. The kitchen tap squeaks on and water runs. I hear Dad's metal lunch kit open and the crinkle of wax paper. I hear sounds of dishes clinking in water.

"I'm so sorry, Norma. I hope John's bellowing didn't wake Eleanor."

"For god's sake, Dot, why did you tell him as soon as he walked in the door? He and Ivan just got off a double shift, so they could hardly see straight. Why not let him eat his supper at least? Or even wait until morning?"

"He was at me right away. He didn't even take his boots or coat off. He wanted to know what the teacher said."

"So what did you tell him?"

"I told him the teacher said Seth was slow. That's all I said. It was all he heard."

"He didn't hit you?"

"No. John doesn't do that anymore. There was only that once. He just threw his lunch kit against the wall, tossed the chair across the room, and stormed out."

"Did he wake the kids? We need to check the kids are asleep."

Feet are coming up the stairs. I jump back in bed under the covers and pull the pillow over my head. There's whispering and rustling around Marg's crib.

Hands arrange my covers and Mom says, "He hates small noises. He always covers his head with the pillow."

The whispering and shuffling leave the room.

* * *

I'm big enough to go to Sunday school by myself, and I get ten cents to put in the box. Mom makes sure my hair is combed nicely, and I have to put on my good pants and shirt. It's warm and sunny, so I only have a sweater over my shirt and I wear my good shoes. I have to pick up my feet and not kick rocks with my good shoes.

Mom and Marg watch me as I walk down the street. I don't look back until I'm at the hospital. Eleanor comes out of her house and gallops in the road. Mom waves to me. Marg and Eleanor run in circles. A gust of wind blows black dust, and I can't see them anymore.

I walk past the hospital where Mom cooks and cleans sometimes for Dr. Glasgow, who came to our house to make Marg come out of Mom. Norma and Eleanor look after Marg and me when Mom works for Dr. Glasgow. I stay on the path through the field. The houses are behind me. The field narrows to a point with the black-sided mountain nearly coming to meet the creek. There is the swinging bridge. On each side concrete and wood pillars hold up cables, and the bridge hangs from them. I walk onto the bridge, then stomp side to side, far apart, first one foot then the other, to make it sway.

Billy and his sister are almost to the bridge. I run across and hide behind one of the big trees flanking the Anglican Church. Billy and his sister will soon go inside. Parents are walking their children to the church. Cars pull up and park. Parents and kids go into the church. The kids go to Sunday school and colour pictures of Jesus and angels, while the parents go listen to the minister. Dad calls the minister a sky pilot.

My hiding place is the fourth tree. The first is by the church entrance where everyone goes in and out, and the other three follow along the length of the church. Soon no one is walking or driving up.

I don't go to church and colour pictures of Jesus. Not anymore. Last week I kept my ten cents and went to Dicky's store. Dad says Dicky sells meat from cows that eat fence posts up the Elk Valley. Dicky didn't say anything, and he didn't get mad, so I bought a chocolate bar.

Today I buy a box of Cracker Jack. I return to the church and sit under my tree. The tall trees are skinny and not bushy, and they are old and have really big trunks. Their leaves fall off in the winter. I can't say the name of the trees, but I like them more than church and Jesus. They reach up to the blue sky.

I wait for Billy and his sister. When people come out and cars drive up again, I'll go meet them. We'll walk back over the bridge, to the path through the field, and then to our separate houses. I save each of them some Cracker Jack so they won't tell. The prize is a stupid ring—I'll give it to Marg.

* * *

Dad and I are studying at the kitchen table. Mom is making supper and helping Dad with his arithmetic for his engineer's ticket. Dad finished Grade 6. He hates the reading and the arithmetic for his engineer's ticket.

I hate studying too. Mom has me copying words today. Today is a ten words day and tomorrow will be a ten arithmetic problems day. I copy them three times and then she gives me a spelling test. Then I write my fixed mistakes three times, and I have another spelling test. When I can spell and say all the words correctly, then I have to use each word in a sentence. I say the sentence, and then I have to print it. If I make a mistake, I have to fix it and write the sentence again.

"I can't concentrate with that boy yammering away."

"He's not that boy, he's your son."

"Let him go play, for Christ's sake. I need to finish this assignment and send it in."

"Seth, go upstairs and finish writing your sentences. I'll be up in a minute."

Dad is on night shift. He goes to work after I'm in bed. We all are home for supper today.

* * *

We stand by the railway station. There are a lot of people. Hawk is here with his family. I see Billy and his family.

The highway is behind us, as is the hotel where Dad gets drunk and Freddie the Barber cuts hair. “There it is!” shouts Dad. “For Christ’s sake, kid, pay attention and pick up your feet. I’d swear he’s in a world of his own.”

Mom has Marg by the hand. She lifts Marg up into her arms. Dad suddenly grabs me and places me on his shoulders. I can see everything from Dad’s shoulders. “There it is,” says Dad, “the last of the steam trains.” The last steam train smokes and clangs past. Its horn blares. A man waves from the cabin in front. People wave back. The man in the train blows the whistle some more.

Dad talks to Eleanor’s dad, Ivan, “It’s the end of an era. It’s modern times from now on.” He puts me down and tells me to run to my mother.

Men walk across the highway to get drunk in the hotel. Moms and kids walk across the highway to the homes on this side of the creek. Mom, Billy’s mom, and lots of others walk across the highway, past Dicky’s store, past the church, to the swinging bridge. I like the swinging bridge even more when other people are on it.

“Mom? Mom?”

Mom stops chatting and looks down on me.

“What? What is it? You can see I’m talking.”

“Mom, Eleanor’s dad saw the last steam train. But Norma and Eleanor didn’t.”

“Eleanor would be too frightened with all the people and noise. She couldn’t come.” Mom’s eyes went up and she continued talking to the lady.

* * *

Bimbo’s truck is full of our furniture. The truck has BIMBO’S MOVING printed in large red letters on the big white box. It has four wheels, not just two, in the back. Bimbo stands and smokes by the open door of the truck. Dad smokes and talks to Bimbo, then Bimbo climbs in using a handhold on the side of the truck. The truck starts and slowly moves away.

Neighbours are talking to Mom and Dad, shaking hands and hugging. Marg is being kissed and ladies get down on one knee to hug her and stroke her hair. Norma is crying with a handkerchief crumpled in her hand. Ivan shakes Dad’s hand. Norma gives Mom a present and more hugs. Hawk and Billy are standing by their parents.

I can hear Eleanor faintly but I can’t see her. Norma turns and climbs up the steps to her side of the house. When she opens the door I can hear Eleanor’s song better. The screen door slams and Norma closes the door.

Mom tells Marg and me to get into the backseat of our green car with the yellow hands that stick out to signal. Dad and Mom get in and Dad drives away. People wave and shout.

I climb up on the seat to look out the back window. “I didn’t get to say goodbye to Eleanor, Mom. I want to say goodbye to Eleanor.”

“Shut that whining kid up or I will,” says Dad.

I start to cry. Mom turns around and makes me face forward. She wipes my face and blows my nose. Marg plays with the dolly someone gave her. “Be quiet now, my little lad,” she says. “We’ve got a long way to go today.”

* * *

“Mr. Raymond. Sir!” Someone has their hand on my shoulder. “Are you all right?”

It’s that nurse, Ruth. I realize I’m crying and my face is pressed onto Dad’s bed. I clumsily get up and turn towards the door. My shoulder hits the doorjamb as I push past the nurse.

I clutch the balancing rail along the corridor. I’m wading in thigh-deep water. My vision is blurred. I wipe at my eyes. Ancient siren voices murmur and flabby arms wave and beckon from the deep. The door won’t open. I push. I pull. I rattle the bar.

“Here, I’ll punch in the code,” says Nurse Ruth. And the door flies open.

A wet snow is falling. I breathe in the cold air.

WHEN TALKING ENDS

Linda Crosfield

My mother hits the wheelchair door release,
not that she's in one, but the doors are too heavy to push, she says,
talking steadily as she gets in the car, doesn't notice I'm listening to CBC,
an interview with Amanda, held captive in Somalia four hundred days
and lived to write a book about it, and if I want to know what happens
I'll have to read it because Mom's not going to stop talking.

Inch onto Gordon Road to see if anything's coming,
hear her sharp intake of breath. Haven't put her in an accident so far, ever,
but still that breath, which used to annoy me a lot more
than it does now, for her ninety-three years against my sixty-five
has tempered our relationship. If you live long enough
you can forgive anyone pretty much anything. Just ask Amanda.

We drive through town, slide around a cyclist on Gyro Park Road,
whiz past the display suite for the proposed new downtown housing
where I'd love to live but can't imagine downsizing enough to fit my life
into nine-hundred square feet, and besides, they wouldn't like it when
my husband peed off the balcony, and sooner or later he would.
You don't live thirty-five years on the same two-and-a-half acres
surrounded by trees and backyard mountains and not get in the habit
of peeing outside.

Stop-go-stop-go-stop, and we park across the street from the spa
where Lisa and Kimberley will wage war on our calloused feet,
but first the argument about who'll dig out change to plug the meter—
I have the required coinage but she wants to top it up. While talking.
Crossing the street, she takes my hand to foil the sun whose duel
with fencing shadows on the pavement beneath the trees
threatens to trip her, but she won't use a cane. They're for old people.

Inside the spa we're ushered into matching chairs.
Our feet plunge into stainless steel pools of almost-too-hot water,
we choose our colours and the pampering begins.

Old polish off, clipping and filing, scouring of callouses, pouring of tea.
On with the new, beige-pink-neutral for her, deep plum for me,
in honour of the ones still falling off the trees out back
and I could be/should be picking them up, but no—
I'm here having my feet tended to as if I were somebody.
My mother's somebody, and still she's talking.

We're all somebody. That there are places on the planet
where such self-centredness could be viewed as criminal shames me,
blames me, but I carry on, for this is something my mother likes to do
and at ninety-three how much longer will she be around to do it?
I've learned to grab these moments as we hold fast,
stand our ground, dig our toes into sands of memory,
raise a glass to the rightness of a late summer day
and I try not to think about when talking ends
and only the memory of this perfect slip of time remains
to cleave the sadness.

NIGHT NOISE – Janice Notland

A yard full of bears
bump and knock in a moonlit spree
round and round a fruit tree.

Sometimes, awake at night,
echo of valley dogs barking,
my ears prick up
hoping for bulky approaches.

Suddenly, a thud against the house
stops my breath.
My senses roam the darkness
as vague sounds float.

Bears are never there when I jump up
peering out to see them;
always disappointed, I continue my habit.

Later, sinking between worlds,
I watch lumbering forms
pad hazy terrain,
listen to crackling branches
recede into the night.

This morning on my daily walk
I count nine humongous patties,
fresh scat of undigested fruit
encircling the pear tree,
not a pear in sight.

I picture three or four bears
fattening up as winter
hails them across time,
plodding back to safe dens
to sleep and rest awhile.

There to dream of spring
bequeathed by nature's bounty in green.

THE OKANAGAN VALLEY

The Okanagan Region lies between the Cascade and Columbia Mountain Ranges in South-Central BC. It includes several lakes, all of which were once part of a large glacial lake. The largest is Okanagan Lake (home of the legendary lake monster, Ogopogo), which is 135 kilometres long and runs from Penticton in the south, through Kelowna in the Central Okanagan, and on to past Vernon, in the North Okanagan. From east to west are Swan, Kalamalka, Mabel, Mara, and Wood lakes and to the south lie Skaha, Vaseux and Osoyoos lakes. This valley spans from the Similkameen Valley along the US border east to Boundary River Country. In between is “Canada’s pocket desert” around Osoyoos, a dry shrub grassland that is the northernmost extension of the Great Basin Desert, where a large variety of sages, cacti, bull snakes, and the infamous rattle snake abound.

The Okanagan Syilx Peoples settled here thousands of years ago and still have a great impact on the cultural and economic life of the valley.

This region has one of the sunniest and warmest climates in Canada. And, due to its warm temperatures and well-drained soil, it is now recognized as one of Canada’s finest wine and fruit growing regions.

Heritage and culture in this area are strongly tied to the land, which is lush with orchards, vineyards and vegetable farms. There are also many historic and modern mines throughout.

Cities and municipalities: the four largest population centres are Kelowna, West Kelowna, Penticton, and Vernon. Enderby and Armstrong lie in the dairy and vegetable-growing region of the northern valley, and Okanagan Falls, Oliver and Osoyoos lie in the hot, dry, highly irrigated fruit-growing area south of Penticton. A vast variety of adventures and cultures can be found in the Okanagan.

The Okanagan region stretches north to Sicamous, which borders the Thompson and Shuswap regions.

SOUTH OKANAGAN & SIMILKAMEEN

THE SIMILKAMEEN

The Similkameen Valley in south central BC lies between E.C. Manning and Cathedral Provincial Parks to the west and Chopaka Mountain, near Cawston, to the east. The mountain range is a small sub range in the northeasternmost extremity of the Cascade Range. It straddles the border between BC and Washington south of the Similkameen River on the inland side of the range. The Similkameen River connects many southern communities.

Legends abound of the bravery and horsemanship of the Similkameen First Nations, many of whom speak the Syilx language and find innovative ways to bring life to our heritage through various cultural centres and events such as the rodeos at Princeton and Chopaka.

The southern end of the Similkameen, around the villages of Keremeos and Cawston, is part of a unique landscape known as "Canada's Pocket desert." With fertile soils and easily accessed irrigation, the valley abounds in thriving orchards, vegetable farms, and vineyards. In the north, Princeton and Hedley are best known for their history in mining and logging, and outdoor adventures are certainly enjoyed by all.

– *D.F. Barrett*

Keremeos, BC. Photo © Jodie Renner

A LIFE RECLAIMED

Fiction

Della Barrett

The lights of Vancouver's East End stretched up the dark street as if forever. Jack realized he hadn't seen stars and planets in weeks. With any luck, tonight would be the night—once this mess was over and done. Their strategy was risky, but Jack knew it was the only way, so he'd chosen darkness.

He leaned back against the rented black sedan, aiming for that look of nonchalance he'd seen so often in the can. He knew how to blend in. No bold black and white out here, just grey. Underneath, he was sharp, absolutely alert. Acutely aware. His eyes were peeled for two men—one his target. These people were never left to travel alone. Jack lowered his head and shrunk down as much as a big guy could. Subtle was his middle name. But he was tough. Ornery as a mule. Just ask his little sister, who two hours earlier had parked the vehicle outside the run-down apartment building.

Jack bent down and glanced at Sarah through the open windows. His leather jacket fell open and caught a cool breeze that whipped through the vehicle. It felt good to him, but he saw Sarah shiver. The sleeveless tank top she'd worn all day no longer did the trick. Wisps of blond hair swept across her grim face. "You okay?" he asked.

"Yeah. But it's almost midnight. I wish we could get this over with and go home." She rubbed her hands on her pants. "Are you sure he'll come this way? Maybe there's a back entrance."

"He'll come this way."

"I don't like this neighbourhood. There's a creepy homeless guy over there on the ground, leaning against the building."

"Yeah, I saw him. He's minding his own business. In fact, I think he's passed out. Harmless. Hang in there, kiddo. Just a bit longer, I'm sure."

He peered once again into the semi-darkness of the city. Two men were approaching. He lifted his solid weight from the car. "Sarah, be ready!" he hissed and heard her take in a sharp breath. He opened the back door slightly and hovered there, head down. Watching. Waiting. A number of scenarios passed through his mind. All meant trouble.

Luckily, the taller fellow was on the far side. He'd be able to get to the shorter one first. Perfect. They were walking fast, chatting, relaxed and unaware. Great. Now, if only...

"Howdy, boys," he said, when they were right beside him.

The two men paused for a split second. Jack ripped a right upper cut into the shorter man's jaw. His neck twisted. Head flung back. He was airborne. Hit the cement before he could moan. Jack whipped around and grabbed the tall one by the arm. As he yanked away, he lost his balance. "What the …?"

Jack shoved him to the open car door. The guy grabbed the doorframe and braced against it. That's when their eyes met. Jack saw the shock of recognition in his eyes—and the sudden bewilderment. He shoved him into the car, and scrambled in after him, shouting, "Go, Sarah. Go!"

She stepped on the gas before the back door shut. Thrown back and on top of his victim, Jack scrambled to sit upright. The tall one was reaching for the opposite door handle, clawing to get out. Jack pinned him down.

"Get off me! What the hell?" He writhed away. Jack stayed on top of him. He leaned to the side, reached in his pocket and yanked out a roll of duct tape.

Struggling, Jack managed to grab the guy's two wrists and wrap the tape around them.

"Oww. Dammit!" he hollered from underneath Jack's bulk. "Lemme go!"

Sarah glanced in the rearview mirror. "Shit!" she shouted. "You guys are scaring me."

"Just drive, Sarah. We're fine now." Jack sat upright, felt the sweat trickle down his temple.

"I see you've learned a thing or two in jail, bro," she said.

"Yeah, sis. Fast as lightnin', eh? And now I'm buff enough to sit on our poor, scrawny brother here."

Their captive jerked his elbow toward Jack. "Let me out," he shouted. "I'm not going anywhere with you."

"Too bad, Adam. We're goin'." Jack waved his hand. "It's time for you to break away from your pals."

"No! I don't want to break away." He kept struggling. "Stop the car, Sarah! Let me out. You can't do this. I'm your big brother!"

Jack saw Sarah clench her jaw. She wrung the steering wheel like it was an old washcloth.

"Yeah," Jack said, turning to Adam. "And you're my little brother. So you listen to me."

"No!" Adam twisted sideways, struggling to lift both hands to open the door. "Help. Help! Help!" he shouted out the open window.

Jack grabbed his arm, pulling him away from the door. He ripped off more duct tape and slapped it across his mouth. "Now," he said, leaning closer. "You have no choice but to listen to me.

"Mmpht!" Adam's eyes looked wild.

In next to no time, they were on the Trans-Canada Highway, heading east. Adam had calmed down, as if resigning himself for now. Jack stared out the window, searching for stars. He now had to focus on the next phase of this operation … getting out of Dodge. Once again, he glanced to the traffic behind them. No sign of a tail. He took a deep breath and told Adam they'd be home in a few hours. He told him they were doing this for his own good. That they were right and he was wrong about this whole mess in Vancouver.

Adam rolled his eyes and shook his head. "Mmuk yuu!"

"Oh! That's cute," Jack said. "I didn't think your leader let you curse!" He leaned his head back. *Time to try a new angle.* "We don't want to see you hurt, Adam. Don't you see it? Your cult is robbing you blind, and it's affecting all of us."

Adam responded by turning to face the window. His body was rigid and hard as the rocks that cut up the nearby mountainside.

On impulse, Jack turned on the overhead light. Swiftly, he leaned forward and yanked the duct tape from his brother's mouth, leaving the tape at his wrists fully secured. Adam jerked back and glared at him, his mouth set in a hard, grim line. His face had reddened. A little muscle on his jaw throbbed. He turned back to the window. Apparently, he had nothing to say.

Jack threw his hands in the air. Then he tapped Sarah on the shoulder. "You got any ideas, Sis?"

"Not 'til we get home safe," she said and kept driving.

"Pretty soon, kiddo," he said, turning off the interior light. "A couple more hours."

Adam turned to Jack. "You know they'll find me no matter where you take me."

"Now, that's what I want to talk to you about." Jack's voice dropped a note, but it sizzled with heat. "Your people phoned the house last week. Did you know that?" He pulled at his brother's shirt collar. "They wanted to talk to Sarah. If they come anywhere near our house or … or try to convert our li'l sister, I'll kill 'em. You got that?"

"No. You wouldn't dare."

"I didn't spend three years in prison for nothin', bro."

"That was for selling drugs after Dad died! That wasn't for … for murder!"

"A guy can learn from the pros!" He hoped he sounded convincing. "I learned a whole lot more there than you did spending that last three years with those…those mind benders."

Adam shook his head. "I gotta pee." Adam looked genuinely uncomfortable as he started rocking forward and back.

"We'll pull over somewhere."

Sarah began to squirm in her seat. "I gotta pee too, Jack."

"Well," he said, considering her point of view. "We're almost at Hope. There's a gas station at the edge of town. We'll stop there." He turned to Adam. "Just chill, Sarah's our personal chauffeur tonight."

"She's just a kid."

"I am not!"

"Just concentrate on the road, kiddo." Jack tapped her shoulder and pointed straight ahead. He liked the fact that she argued. Tough going losing your dad, but particularly tough on a teen girl. Clearly Sarah could hold her own.

At the gas station, there were a few people coming and going from their vehicles. "Hurry, guys," Sarah said. "I gotta go too."

Jack climbed out of the car, walked around, and helped his brother stand up. He pulled small, blunt-nosed school scissors from his pocket and cut the duct tape. Immediately, Adam swung away. "Help! Help!" he shouted. "Satan lover. Help!"

Shocked, Jack grabbed him and shoved him back into the car. His heart was pounding. "Shut up! Damn you. Shut up!"

"Help! Help!" Adam shouted.

"Radio. Sarah. Loud!"

Sarah restarted the engine. Instantly a rock tune blasted.

"Help! Help! Satan lover!"

"Drive. Drive, Sarah." They squealed away. Jack glanced over his shoulder at the onlookers. He prayed it was too dark for them to take down their license plate number.

Soon, they were at a roadside rest stop. There were no other vehicles. As Sarah hurried to one of the two outhouses, Jack took Adam to the other. Reluctantly, he undid the duct tape once more and waited outside the door. An owl hooted from a nearby tree branch, reminding him they were all alone.

Jack took a deep breath. It was the middle of night, in the middle of nowhere. Perfect. *No police or pedestrians for Adam to holler at. Nothin' here but stars and endless forest*. The wind whispered through tall pines as if to reassure him further. When Adam stepped from the outhouse, Jack blocked his way. He held up the roll of duct tape. “Do we need this on your mouth again?”

Adam glared at him and shook his head. Just then, Sarah came out of the women’s, wiping her hands on an alcohol cloth.

“Okay,” Jack said, “let’s get going.” They resumed their way in the black of night, heading northeast.

Less than two hours later, they rolled down the hill into Princeton. The sun was not yet up in the Similkameen Valley, but there were plenty of early-morning activities at the gas stations and breakfast nooks on the outskirts of town. When Sarah finally pulled the sedan into their home driveway, she said, “I’m dead tired. Driving these mountain roads at night sucks.”

Jack climbed out of the back seat. “There’s just one more job, Sarah,” he said, stepping up to her window. “You’ll drop this fancy sedan at Aunt Betty’s, remember? She’ll return it to the rental place in the morning. You’re supposed to leave the key under her flower pot at the back door.” Jack wagged a finger at her. “Then jog right back, okay?” He turned toward the house. “I gotta eat. And find coffee.”

“Yeah, me too, I’m starving!”

“I’ll make a few sandwiches.”

He hurried around to open the door for Adam, who glared as he struggled to stand up. “I can’t believe this! Don’t tell me Aunt Betty’s in on this kidnapping scam with you?”

“This ain’t no scam, bro. This is the real thing.” He leaned down to face Sarah at the wheel. “While you’re gone, I’ll get Adam to help me load up the groceries and a couple of extra propane tanks. Last time we forgot the propane for the fridge and stove.”

“And don’t forget extra batteries for the flashlights.”

Adam stopped in his tracks. “Oh, I know where you’re taking me.”

“Really?”

“We’re going to Grandpa’s cabin.”

“Maybe. Maybe not.”

They went inside. After a satisfying feast of grilled cheese sandwiches, Jack feeding his duct-tape-bound brother, they loaded up Jack’s jeep with sleeping bags and coolers full of frozen stew and vegetables and dairy.

Less than an hour east of Princeton they turned onto a gravel road leading deep into the mountains of southern British Columbia. Sheer rock cliffs rose up sharp and high along both sides of the Ashnola River road, blocking all service to their cell phones. Even when the valley widened slightly, the forest closed in. To Jack it was as comforting as a soft quilt on a cold night.

Photo of the Ashnola © Jodie Renner

"Now I really know we're going to the cabin!"

Jack said nothing. He loved the area. Long on timber, short on people. Perfect. The closer they got, the better Jack felt. The river had a mystical power. He could feel it wash away much of the stress he'd been under lately. Adam seemed to relax a bit, too. Halfway, they spotted a mountain goat and her kids. Jack pulled over to watch them trek sure-footedly across a hillside of jagged rock. Then he asked Sarah if she would drive once again.

In the back seat, Jack finally removed the duct tape from Adam's wrists. He held Adam's hand for the rest of the way. He told him he wasn't going to hurt him. He just wanted to understand. He explained that they'd been reading up on the ways of many cults. He said he'd learned that being book smart, as Adam was, didn't protect you from the likes of these leaders. You have to be street smart too. They find ways to use mind manipulation and deception to bring in and keep their people.

"It's not like that," Adam said flatly.

"Sure it is," Jack replied. "They get you to stop eating meat and other protein. Do you know why? Because they don't want you to think clearly! They want you foggy, so you'll do whatever they say, for Christ's sake."

"No," Adam replied, "you're wrong." He shook his head. "We're fine. We're just vegetarians."

"Healthy vegetarians eat beans and nuts for protein. They eat tofu." Jack pounded his knee with his fist. "When's the last time you ate tofu, Adam?

"Geez, Jack! Give it up. What the heck is tofu?"

Jack shook his head. He knew he had to get Adam away from it all. And the best place was Grandpa's cabin high in the wooded mountains of BC. Here the pristine wilderness had the power to cleanse the soul. *Here nature is the master. Here cult leaders have no power. Maybe here, we can move on together.*

As they neared the cabin, Adam started to groan, rocking forward and back. "I can't."

"It'll be okay," Sarah said.

"No!" He rocked faster. "Dad died here trying to save my dog. I can't stay here."

"Shhh," Sarah said quietly. "That's over now. We'll be okay. Give it a chance."

Good job, Sarah, Jack thought.

Around the next corner, the cabin came into sight through a stand of Ponderosa Pines. As they bailed out of the jeep, the first thing to hit them was the crash of river water over boulders. "Ahh," Jack said, as he paused to stretch his legs. A great sound. "As Mom would say, 'Don't go in empty-handed.'" He tapped Adam on the shoulder, his voice loud over the babbling river, "Remember, it's a hell of a long walk from here to anywhere." Grabbing a sleeping bag, he added, "Feel free to sleep as long as you want here. And eat as much as you want, especially meat."

Adam stiffened. "I don't know why you brought me here, Jack. This won't change a thing. Nothing will change how I feel about the Church of Unity Revelations. They were good to me. I want to go back! I don't know what your problem is."

"Sorry, bro. We're here to enjoy nature. Maybe go fishin'. That's all. Think of it as a holiday from your gang." He pointed to the sky. "Nature is the master here. We'll rough it here for a few days. You'll see, Adam—here you can be yourself. Get strong." He tossed the sleeping bag in through the cabin door.

By noon, after a late morning snack, Adam was sound asleep on the dusty, green sofa in the screened-in porch that overlooked the river. Jack and Sarah had decided it was now safe to sleep as well. Just to be sure, Jack curled up on a mattress in front of the porch door, while Sarah slept inside.

A few hours later, Sarah and Jack were in the kitchen. Sarah chopped cucumber and sweet onion for a salad while Jack stirred the large pot of beef stew they had brought from the freezer at home. Though they frequently glanced out the huge kitchen window, they were beginning to relax. Other than through the cabin, the only exit route for Adam was past this window.

Sarah put down her knife and picked up the small container of dried dill weed. She flipped open the lid. “I wonder how long we’ll have to watch him so closely. I wonder—”

“What’s up?” Adam walked in behind them, rubbing his eyes. His tone was solemn.

“Stew and salad for supper,” Sarah said, cheerily.

“We’ve got lots of protein,” Jack said. “And lookie here, we’ve got dad’s famous cheese biscuits fresh outta the oven.”

“Yeah,” Adam said, without a smile. His eyes swept across the counter top. “After supper you can give me the keys to the jeep.”

“No!” Jack and Sarah said at once.

Adam backed away, hands raised. “Okay. Okay. Just sayin’.” He sat down at the kitchen table and dropped his head in his hands. “I don’t understand why I’m so tired. I’ve napped all day. I should be used to this by now.”

“Used to what?” Sarah asked.

“At Unity, no one sleeps more than three or four hours a night. It’s a waste of time. Time that we could be praising the Lord.”

Sarah looked at Jack. They had discussed this at length. “Well, on that note,” she said, bringing the salad bowl to the table, “we can say a prayer for supper.”

Adam appeared to relax a little. Jack sat down beside him. “After we eat, we can go for a walk upstream. Maybe dig up some worms and take a couple of fishing rods with us.”

“Sure,” Adam said. He dropped his head and began to study his fingernails in his lap. Suddenly, he stood up. “I gotta go to the washroom. Can I go to the washroom?”

Jack glanced at Sarah and back at Adam. “Sure,” he said, wondering if this was a common question with the cult.

Adam paused at the kitchen sink. “Chickadees! And look, a hummingbird.” He pointed to the eves of the cabin with one hand and slid the other hand to his pocket.

Sarah came to the window. “Oh, yes. We’d better refill the feeder.”

Adam turned to the bathroom and closed the door behind him. Sarah shrugged and turned away. As she pulled plates from the shelf, they heard the click of the lock on the bathroom door. Sarah glanced questioningly at Jack. "We never use that lock."

Jack grabbed the door handle. "Adam!" he shouted. "Adam, open up. You weren't supposed to lock the door."

Not a sound. "What the hell?" Jack touched Sarah's shoulder. "Move back." With a swift kick near the handle, he smashed the door open.

Adam was sitting on the closed toilet, the kitchen knife in one hand, dark blood flowing from his other wrist.

"Oh my God!" Sarah cried. "Oh my God!"

Jack ran forward. "Get a rag, Sarah—a clean rag and ice, to slow the blood. Quick." Jack grabbed the bloody wrist. Blood surged through his fingers. Jack didn't pause. Unfortunately, he had seen this in prison too many times. "Christ, Adam. What've you done?"

Sarah returned with some tea towels and the first aid kit. She stood beside them frozen, eyes brimming over. Jack took the towels from her. "Set it on the floor," he said, pointing to the kit. "Take out a roll of gauze. Quick!" He wrapped it tightly around the bleeding wrist. Adam's eyes were glazing over. "Hold on, Adam," he shouted. "Hold on!"

Sarah ran from the room and came back with a bag of frozen peas. "This might work," she said, handing him the bag.

"Okay. Hold it on his wrist. We can't let him fall. He can't pass out."

Together they guided Adam through the cabin to the porch where he'd been sleeping earlier. Dazed, he dropped to the couch.

Jack kneeled next to him. Adam looked as if he might throw up. Sarah fell to the floor on the other side of Adam. Jack noticed she looked white as a ghost, her eyes were brimming with tears. She reached up and began to pound Adam's chest. "Don't ever do that again!" she cried. "Ever!"

Jack felt like pounding him too. "Why Adam? Tell us why. We want to understand."

Adam looked from one to the other. "I can't live without Unity R," he said, weakly. "I can't live without Dad, either. And this place bothers me. Dad died here trying to save Blue."

"I know," Jack said, gently holding his hand. "I know." He couldn't think of anything more to say. Sudden tears tumbled down his own cheeks. "But it was an accident," he said, shaking his head. He looked directly at his brother. "It wasn't your fault. You know that, don't you?"

Adam didn't respond. He seemed mesmerized by the tears on Jack's face. Jack tried again, "We … we all love you, Adam."

"That's not enough!" Adam's eyes flared and then glazed over. "That's not enough." He shook his head. "I can't go on this way. I—I'm not strong enough to..." He took a deep breath. "I need Unity to help me find purpose. Every time I look at you or Sarah or Mom, I see your lives wrecked because of me."

Kneeling on the floor, Sarah turned to Adam. Tears rolling down her face, she spoke quietly. "It's NOT because of you, Adam. We—we're all in this together," she said. "But we're okay now." She wiped her face with her shirt sleeve and heaved a deep breath. "We *do* understand what you're going through." Suddenly all the words came gushing out as if she'd been practicing them for years. "We've missed you, Adam. We don't blame you for anything. For three years we've been missing you, Mom and I. When we heard you were in Vancouver, we got excited. And, last night, when Jack and I found you, it was the happiest night of my life, even though I tried not to show it. And now … now you have to help me, Adam. You have to stay alive. Don't you see? I can't lose you again."

Wringing her hands in her lap, she started again. "When you disappeared so soon after Dad died, I thought I'd die. And then Jack went to jail. I'd lost all three of you! It was just me and Mom. We were total wrecks."

"But don't you see, it's all my fault?"

"No, Adam," she said. "I think you're overtired or something. Once you rest and…and get healthy again, you'll see it, I'm sure, Adam." She looked into his eyes. "You're alive! And it's wonderful. You're healthy and … and alive." She dropped her head into his lap and hugged his legs.

Adam reached out to her, tears brimming in his eyes. He patted her head softly. "I'll stay for a while."

As Adam and Sarah rested on the couch, Jack brought stew and cheese biscuits to the coffee table. Barely another word was spoken. Sarah broke a biscuit for herself and another for Adam. Jack ladled out the stew. They sat on either side of Adam, facing the cool, green forest and the river, picking at their food. Slowly the conversation started. Jack mentioned their dad making these same biscuits every time they came to this cabin. Sarah reminded them that it was always Adam's job to cook the morning bacon. Before they knew it, they had finished off most of the stew. As Adam set down his fork, a hummingbird flitted by the window. He heaved a huge sigh, but said nothing.

That night Adam slept almost twelve hours right there on the couch. At nine in the morning, when he woke, Jack was in the chair next to him.

"I needed that," Adam said, softly.

"He's awake," Jack called over his shoulder. Then he stood, walked to his brother and touched him on the foot. "We've got bacon and eggs ready to go for breakfast. And then we can go fishing." He pointed to some clothes on a chair beside the couch. "Get dressed and come and join us," he said, offering Adam a big smile.

Jack was standing at the stove when Adam stepped into the kitchen. One frying pan held six strips of sizzling bacon. The second held crispy hash brown potatoes. Jack cracked the first of the eggs into the middle. "Ready for breakfast, Antsy Adam?"

"Ahh, sure thing." He gently slapped Jack's shoulder. "No one's called me that in years."

Photo of the Ashnola © Jodie Renner

SIMILKAMEEN VALLEY MEMORIES

Memoirs

Debra Crow

My name is Debra Lynn Terbasket Crow. I'm a sixty-year-old Syilx Grandma. My mom was Virginia Leonard from the Kamloops Indian Band, and my dad was Ernest Terbasket of the Lower Similkameen. Band. I have lived in the Similkameen Valley all my life.

I was married for forty-one years to Doug Crow, until he passed away last year. We knew each other since Grade 1. I made the mistake of telling my father in Grade 2, "Guess what? It's a secret. I like Dougie Crow." My dad teased me all through elementary school. It was the last time I ever told him a secret. Then I married that Doug Crow.

I grew up with my cousins. I have one brother, Allan Lyle Terbasket, older by a couple of years. I also consider all my cousins my sister and brothers. We did all sorts of crazy things growing up.

As little people, we were left on our own a bit. We had no telephones, no TV, and no electricity in my home until I was in grade eight. Other homes I was at had electricity earlier. My mom and other moms would send us outside after breakfast to amuse ourselves. We were in a group a lot. I think different moms babysat all of us. Not really babysat, more like extended family hanging out. When we were smaller, around three or four, we stuck around the immediate home area. As we grew older we ventured farther, exploring our world that included the bottom land meadows, the cotton wood groves along the river, the haystacks, the mountains and deer trails.

If we managed to catch horses we could go even farther afield. The rule was if you can catch 'em and saddle 'em you can ride 'em. A saddle was a luxury and deluxe, a bridle a bonus. Picture me and my cousin Flash, saddling a horse, one person on the front of the saddle, the other person holding the back of the saddle. On the count of three, up went the saddle onto the big horse. We must have been five or so. It seemed like we were pretty short and the horse was pretty tall.

We had an unwritten code among us. The main thing was not to be a chicken shit, or the label would stick for a long time. When we were out trekking around, we would get bored and someone would come up with an idea of what to do. I don't recall how that happened. All of a sudden we would be off on an adventure. One of the things that got our brains working when we were bored was to check out what the adults meant when they told us not to do something. We had some interesting times checking out those rules. Stay away from rattlesnakes, don't swim in the river at high water time, don't cross the river, don't swim around the log jams, don't go to the clay banks, stay off of the haystacks. I could go on and on with those rules. The consequences of breaking those rules and getting caught involved going and finding a willow switch that would be used on your backside.

One day Allan talked me and Flash into eating dirt. That guy had the gift of the gab. We were playing cars in a fresh dug hole in the ground. It was a big hole, big enough for the cattle truck to back into, to load up the horses or cows. There had just been a fresh rain, you know how good fresh dug soil can smell after a rain.

I remember the conversation went something like, "Human beings need minerals to live, we get minerals and vitamins from what we eat, and plants grow in the ground. So the soil is packed with minerals and stuff good for us. See how good it smells."

Flash and I bought this line hook, line, and sinker, like two little fish on hooks. On the count of three, we each put a handful of beautiful smelling dirt in our mouths at the same time. Then spit, spit, spit, while my brother Allan and Flash's older sister Millie rolled on the ground, just a belly laughing.

Me and Flash raced to the creek on the other side of the house and put our heads in the water and rinsed and rinsed and spit some more. I felt kind of foolish for listening to my brother. That was a good lesson to not always listen to what Allan said and accept it as gospel truth, or you might end up eating dirt. It's good to laugh at yourself. I have such a clear memory of that afternoon.

Another not supposed to do was "Don't play with rattlesnakes." One summer day, the adults were gone and three of us were on our own—my brother Allan, Flash, and me. Flash and I were probably about seven. We were bored at home at Blind Creek. There is a creek that runs by that house. The rattlesnakes follow it down from Fairview Mountain. There was a snake den at the base of the hill too, so we would get snakes visiting from there. The adults believed that if you saw one snake, there was another one nearby. On this particular afternoon we never thought of that.

We saw a huge snake by the shed, where saddles and bridles and what-not were kept. Someone got the idea that it was so huge we should catch it, then we could show someone. My Aunt Betty used to can fruit and veggies in big two-quart jars. One of us went and got one of those jars. In the yard was a long pole with a hook on the end. It was used to catch snakes or pull them out of the tall weeds. Snakes in the yard were usually killed and buried by the adults. We got that snake pole and worked on that snake for a while that afternoon. I remember the sun shining; it wasn't hot, just warm out. I think we were concentrating as only a small group of kids could concentrate on a task on a warm afternoon.

We finally got that snake in that jar and then had a discussion as to who should put the lid on the jar. I think Flash did that. Then a discussion about how the snake needed to breathe or it would suffocate. So someone had to poke holes in the lid. That jar was absolutely full of snake. I had never been so close to one before. It was kinda creepy and scary.

Then we personified it and thought it would see us, recognize us, and be mad at us. I don't remember doing this, but my husband-to-be Doug lived down the road, where his parents had an orchard. He said we came down on our bikes to show him our prize in a bottle.

Doug used to think we were kinda wild. He remembers going with our crew on bikes and we were going to go find snakes or some adventure, and he asked us why we were doing that. We said because we are not supposed to. He said he just shook his head and didn't understand why we were doing it, but would go along with us anyways.

Next I recall we got bored with our snake in the bottle and needed to do something with it. Through childlike reasoning, we decided to put that snake in the freezer to make it go into hibernation until the adults got home.

When the adults got home, it didn't go as planned. We were in big trouble. Aunt Betty really didn't like rattlesnakes at the best of times, much less in her freezer. No one was impressed. We were directed to go and let the snake go.

I still feel bad, and now try to honour rattlesnakes. As a family we toss them off the road so they won't get run over. When we had the orchard, we would catch them and put them in a garbage can and take them up Fairview and let them go.

There is a lesson in everything we did, and some of our escapades are so clear in my mind. It feels good to share stories. We did keep ourselves entertained with what the valley had to offer us.

Again a brother story. My uncle Fergie, my mom's youngest brother, came down from Kamloops to stay with us for a while. He helped my mom out by doing yard work or painting or building something. I recall him as a quiet gentle person. He took us for a walk and showed my brother how to get rose bush to make arrows. He built a bow for Allan out of willow, I think.

As children, we watched western movies at the movie hall in Keremeos and saw John Wayne and other movies. We were always torn when we broke into groups—were we gonna be cowboys or wild Indians?

After that visit, it was winter, with snow on the ground. I wasn't in school yet, so probably about four years old. We were in living room, and there was a tall round heater in the corner, taller than me. Allan wanted to play cowboys and Indians. He set me up with a six shooter. I was pretty happy with that. He was the Indian and had the bow and arrow that Uncle Fergie made him. I peeked around the corner of the heater, and he shot me in the eye. My mom freaked out. The arrow didn't stay in, it just popped out. I think from my mom's reaction, there was probably blood coming out of my eye.

My dad wasn't home from the hill yet, he was logging. My mom dressed us up and we walked out to the road about a third of a mile in the snow. My eye started to hurt from the cold, so she walked us home. I think my dad came home then. Our emergency care, a nurse in Cawston, had a look at me and sent us all to Penticton Hospital. I had to stay there for about a week. A few years later, in Grade 2, I had to have glasses because my eyesight in that eye was no good. After that incident, the boys changed how they used the bow and arrow in their make-believe wars. They would wrap the end of the arrows with cloth so they wouldn't puncture anyone. So getting shot in the eye influenced future games of cowboys and Indians and made us practice more safety.

On other weekends we would try to corral some horses that were being pastured in Uncle Gabe's field. We would spend all afternoon doing this. We would put them in a corral that was attached to an old barn. Little kids on foot. This was a whole weekend entertainment. Corral the horses, sit on top of the fence, look closely at the herd, and decide which ones were tame and which ones were not. If they had cinch marks, that might mean they were tame. Then we would pick some horses to try.

My cousin Les, same age as me, would make an Indian bridle with hay twine. A loop was put over the lower lip of the horse, and two reins were fashioned. Then we'd have a discussion on who would get on.

There was a story and belief here too. The belief is that the horses wouldn't hurt a small person, so the smallest person had to get on and try it out. I think they took lessons from my brother Allan. I remember being shamed or peer-pressured into getting on whatever horse was caught and had the Indian bridle on. One time, when I got on a big horse, the whole herd started going in a big circle. I was on a huge white horse and the ground was a long ways down. He did have a gentle walk canter. One of the horses knocked over the poles holding them in the corral. The whole herd jumped out, with me in the middle on this huge horse, holding on for dear life. One of the thoughts going through my head was that without the fence how was I going to get off of him? My strategy was that when he got around to stopping and put his head down to eat I would slide down his neck. I have no memory of getting down, so that is what I must have done. No memory of being hurt, so it must have worked out okay.

On Sunday, the next step would be to either gather pennies or search for pop bottles to return to buy candy. We would ride on horses up to the confectionery store, on the Cawston straight stretch, about five miles away. Back then a quarter, dime, even a nickel would buy a lot of candy. Then we would ride home. That was our reward for two days work. We didn't know whose horses those were or if they were tame, we would just methodically work it. We loved horseback riding. I remember riding that huge white horse to Cawston, it was really mellow and had a big stride. When it jumped a ditch it was a nice jump.

We definitely entertained ourselves. I don't know if others got into what we did. I have some clear memories of some of the near misses. We did survive somehow, and here I am telling the story. Having no electricity and phones were a blessing. Even now, we go to the river a lot to swim. It's the only way to live with the heat in our beautiful Similkameen Valley. We are so blessed to live in God's country. I'm thankful to be born here and to still live here.

Similkameen River near Keremeos. Photo © Jodie Renner

WHISKEY JACK AND THE LONE MINER

Della Barrett

Dedicated to my dad, Murphy Shewchuk Sr., who was a miner and prospector for over forty years.

Warm afternoon breeze dries my grimy, wrinkled face
Just outside the mine tunnel entrance high above Princeton
I sit on a log in the shade of an ol' fir tree
Distant rush of a glacial creek adds to my day dreamin'
My ol' friend, Whiskey Jack
Is perched on a prickly branch not twenty feet away
He doesn't screech. He doesn't caw
He doesn't call me a 'cheep' old man
The gray jay is uncertain
Deciding: broken bits of cheese in my left hand?
Or freshly picked berries in my right?

Midday sun blinded me when I first stepped out
Of the dark mineshaft
Washed my hands in a pail of icy water and
Opened my tin lunch bucket
Now, with a few minutes to spare
Arms propped straight out across each muddied pant leg
I pass the time
My callused hands lay open, rigid
Displaying tidbit treasures in full view
It's been a rough morning mucking in the tunnels
Drilling and mucking

Leaning back against jagged bark of the fir, I rest my eyes
Cool forest scent is… Mother Earth
Warm summer sun is…
My thumb takes his weight and he is gone
So is the cheese.

SNOWBIRD MELTING

Fiction

Eileen Hopkins

Sitting in the lawyer's Calgary high rise office, Joy stared across at Merle in disbelief. "You want what?"

Merle squared his shoulders, but it was his lawyer who answered. "Half your pension, the SUV, and the cottage on Salt Spring Island."

Joy sputtered, lifted off her chair and hissed at her ex, "You sleazy bastard."

Her lawyer, Paul Schmidt, touched her arm and motioned that she should sit down.

"In that case," Paul said to Merle, "with all of the other concessions in place, my client will take half of *your* pension and the house in Calgary, Mr. Steward."

Joy squelched the red-hot surge of killing anger filling her heart as she and Paul filed out of the boardroom of Stock and Bule. *Should be Bull.* She waited until they were on the street before erupting. "What in hell was going on in there? Why didn't you nail his ass to the ceiling, the jerk. That cottage was the only thing I really wanted from that asset deposition." *The one thing he wanted more.*

"Joy, you weren't going to get it. You know that. He knew that. Not with all of the other concessions. You fight this and you will be paying Merle alimony for the rest of his life. Your retirement will look a lot different if you end up in court fighting for a seashore cottage that—be honest—is more a harbour of pain than pleasure. Of course, a fight might finance a private jet for Stock and Bule."

"Damn it, Paul."

Joy knew he was right. Her retirement savings were untouchable and she had to admit, that was a miracle that only Paul could explain. *I know—one of those concessions*. Still, it was a bitter pill. She had wanted to hurt him badly. Just as badly as he had hurt her. She had wanted to take that cottage and burn it to the ground.

Merle hunched over in his chair, staring at Stan Bule who stood just outside the door, reviewing the papers with a legal assistant. *Thirty years and this?*

"We are done here, buddy. Just the paperwork left. Always feels good being on the winning side, right? And hey, stop by for a brew this weekend. I have another project that needs your touch—at least, Laura keeps reminding me I do." Stan leaned over to shake Merle's hand.

Strolling along 8th Avenue in the shadow of the Calgary Tower, Merle's smile felt wooden—screwed in place. Victory and the cottage were his. It was his baby after all—every nail, board, and pane of glass were placed there by his hands. He knew Joy had loved the place just as much as he had. He had been inspired by her vision of what it would look like—from how the sun would bounce off the maple and white interior right down to the glass-fronted cabinets storing the collection of white dishes of every shape imaginable, gleaned from a multitude of flea markets and antique stores. He had loved all that, too. *Not anymore.*

Merle also remembered the angry times over recent years when nothing could convince Joy to take some time away from Calgary and Zed Architecture Inc. That damn city had kept her frozen in place, harried, distracted, filled with figures and data that fuelled Zed's movement from a junior to a senior player in the Calgary cityscape. Lately, Merle had preferred floating in fog and silence at their west coast refuge, Salt Spring Island, rather than fighting rush hour on Deerfoot Trail.

On the island, he had immersed himself in a seaside oasis with a log fire burning and, eventually, with Mona heating up the bedroom. Bored Mona. A renter, a temporary intruder on the gulf island, an author forcing herself into a quiet retreat to meet her publisher's demands. He had welcomed her easy attitude to her work. He had also welcomed her fiery, sometimes crazy sexy vision of what "between the sheets" really meant for a man and a woman. In the firelight, he lost himself in her softness, her eagerness, her no-prisoner independent way of loving and leaving. He never knew when she might show up again. He never pursued her or invited her, but oh, she was on his mind.

And then, Joy made a spur-of-the-moment decision to take a break and caught a late flight out so she could catch the early morning ferry.

Mona had slipped through the door at seven AM, wrapped in a sheet, sandals in her hand. Merle had thrown back the quilts and welcomed her into his bed. Afterwards, he had floated away into early morning drowsiness, holding Mona against his chest, the curve of her back fitting like a puzzle piece against his stomach. Glaring lights and a gasp woke him. Joy had stood there, in the doorway, backpack dangling from her fingers, her rosy cheeks glowing from the three-kilometre hike from the ferry terminal.

There was no going back. He had tried to apologize. He had promised. He had cried. And then he had stopped. It would never be enough.

A woman caught his heel with a stroller, and Merle shook himself out of his reverie. *No point in rehashing on 8th Avenue.* He hailed a taxi to the airport.

Joy sat on a box, tapping her foot. The house in Calgary still smelled like home but resembled a warehouse more than the beautiful townhouse they had bought ten years ago. She heaved a sigh, then stood up to look out the window again. She squinted in the bright sun. Her eyes hurt from too much wine at her retirement party last night. She quickly shifted her gaze from the sunny window to the bare walls and found herself focused on the empty spots that had been her life rather than on the actual walls that had somehow held it all together. Photographs and art from around the world no longer held her gaze. Joy could feel her heart start to tear, a corner at a time. *This ... this has to change. He can't destroy me.* The grinding gears of the moving truck interrupted her tumble down the well of nostalgia. *Go ask Alice, when she's ten feet tall. Saved by the big white truck. Maybe Alice is driving.*

Two hours later, the closing front door echoed through the empty house, the windows rattled and it was done.

Ensconced in a dim corner of the Eau Claire Starbucks, Joy inhaled the aroma of her chai latte. Her friend Carol was beaming at her as she shifted her chair a little closer to Joy's.

"It's serendipitous, Joy. Really. Don't you see it? You, homeless—well, okay, temporarily renting—driving down the highway to the sunny Okanagan. Come on. It works. It all works. And Jane's place is gorgeous—and vacant. You would … well, you could have designed it yourself, it's that beautiful. And it has a lake view and this amazing deck, and you can golf in February, and..."

Joy was not sold on the idea of driving twelve hours west to a little resort town called Osoyoos for a winter escape, even if it was warmer than Calgary. *Me with five hundred other prairie snowbirds.*

Joy grimaced. "And what does it even mean, Carol—Osoyoos? Sounds more like Japanese than English—OH-SOO-YUS. Or maybe someone sneezing, like, Ah-soyoos! And I'm a city girl, for God's sake. What do people do in Osoyoos in the wintertime? And it's a desert. Why would I leave a vibrant city like Calgary to live in a desert, even in the winter?"

"Just for the winter, Joy. And, it's not like a desert with sand dunes and camels. It's like … a dry, warm, sunny place, a Canadian kind of place, and—"

"...and with lots of old people wandering the streets with their walkers and canes, arm in arm, greeting everyone with a smile and nod." Joy finished Carol's nattering comment and looked away. "I am not sure I would, you know, uh, fit in … with snowbirds. I'm not even a senior citizen yet. Look at me. Do I look like a snowbird?" *As in old.*

Carol's eyes softened. "But, Joy, you just might love it. And you can leave your other life boxed up in your apartment in Calgary for the winter. Just think about it. Please."

Joy was embarrassed that it was so obvious to Carol that she still hurt like crazy inside when she smelled sawdust or walked over a new wooden floor. It had been months since she had seen Merle. The divorce would be final in four more.

"Well, show me the pictures again."

Two weeks later, Joy headed out of the city and followed Highway 3 through mountain passes, all the way to Main Street, Osoyoos. *Main Street—how quaint.* She pulled into a parking stall in front of the town hall and looked for the parking meter. Not one meter anywhere. *Free parking. Awesome. Give me a big cup of coffee, God, and I just might stay.* Gazing out the driver's side window, Joy marvelled at the very different landscape stretching across the lake and up into the mountains. The October sun bounced off golden patches of sandy soil as rust-coloured grape vines snaked up the mountainside. A layer of clouds circled the mountain tops like a halo. *Enough of the heavenly reminders.*

Grateful she had heeded her Aunt Liza's admonition many years ago that once you hit sixty, you don't have to meet a man nose to nose anymore—*just kick off those stilettos and let your toes breathe, girl*—Joy stepped out of the car on to the hilly street ready to hike, if need be, to the nearest cafe. She looked up the street—literally up as it climbed the mountain to the west—and then down towards the lake where she could just make out the word "Cafe" about three doors from where she had parked. *Down it is.* Five minutes later, she was enjoying the warmth of a quiet little coffee shop.

"Want room for milk, Ma'am?"

Joy had been so busy taking in all of the local art hung on the walls, she had forgotten about the coffee. The young woman's question brought her back to her reason for being in this quaint little place. "Oh, no, black is great." Grabbing her cup from the counter service, Joy turned to find a chair near the window and bumped into an elderly gentleman, leaning on his cane. Joy's coffee sloshed over the rim, spilling all over his black oxfords.

"Oh God, I am so sorry. I..."

"Harvey's my name, young lady. God is off taking care of the rest of the world right now."

Joy looked into Harvey's twinkling eyes. Managing to return his smile before moving away, Joy slipped into a comfy chair near the fireplace. There were only three other customers besides her and Harvey in the cafe: a young couple holding hands in the back corner and a forty-something guy reading a paper near the window. *Not Starbucks, but mmmm, good coffee.*

Joy pushed the door of the rented villa on Lakeshore Drive open with her shoulder, trying not to let go of any of the five miscellaneous bags she was juggling. As she turned she could see straight through the living room and all the way across the lake—a lake circled by brilliant yellows and greens and reds. *Okay, so Carol was right. It is beautiful.* Too tired to do more than dump the bags and defrost dinner, Joy sat at the dining room table and watched the lights across the lake twinkle in the distance. *Here's to retirement—and bed.*

The sound of pigeons cooing and tapping their claws on the metal cladding outside her bedroom window woke her the next morning. *My first morning as a snowbird—time to check out the lay of the land.* Joy caught her breath. She was having a hard time breaking the habit of using Merle's expressions as if they were her own. She ventured downstairs, thinking a run in the cool October air might inspire her, motivate her, do something, anything to get her into a happy retirement frame of mind. Walking with purpose, Joy rounded the corner of the parkade and rammed into the rather solid shoulder of a man bending over an overflowing garbage can. She took a quick step backwards, grabbing for the wall to steady herself while he pulled himself up from his crouching position. Joy was staring into the weathered and rugged face of a very tall and handsome man.

"Might want to watch where you're going on this fine sunny morning. We move a little slower out here in the sticks."

"Sorry. I was..." Joy fumbled for words like a junior high egghead who had just run into the high school football quarterback.

"Good morning, just the same."

She smiled and held out her hand. "Joy Steward from Unit 2."

"Joe. Caretaker and anything else you might need."

Joe's grey hair was pulled back into a ponytail. His black T-shirt looked like a faded rocker souvenir from the 1970s, and his cargo shorts were nondescript Walmart.

"Well, Joe the Caretaker, I am going for a run. Got any advice?"

Joe leaned against the cement pillar, thumbs hooked in his pockets. "Might want to watch out for rattlesnakes."

Joy waved goodbye. *Did he say rattlesnakes*? Her eyes swept the cement floor of the empty parkade. Heading down Lakeshore Drive, she found her gaze constantly watching what might lay ahead on the path. *Rattlesnakes*. She shook her head in dismay. She needed to get out more, find a friend, find something to get her through this winter in the desert, something that didn't involve rattlesnakes or men.

Breathing hard from her first run after weeks of packing and unpacking, Joy stopped beside a bench in Gyro Park to stretch and catch her breath. She watched a pair of ducks fighting over some delicious morsel and carefully kept her distance from two geese grazing on the grassy boulevard. It was the many snowbirds strolling in pairs along the path that really caught her eye. One grey-haired couple after another jogged, walked, or rolled past her bench and greeted her with a cheery good morning. *Friendly creatures, these snowbirds—and they don't poop all over the walkway.* Joy rolled her eyes at her own sick humour and headed back along the lake.

Who would've thought you could get groceries in fifteen minutes? Joy was still shaking her head in amazement as she backed out of her parking spot and headed down towards the lake. She parked in front of what was becoming her favourite coffee shop. Harvey waved to her from across the street. He stood in front of a little art gallery situated on the corner by the town hall. Running across the street to say hi to the elderly gentleman, Joy glanced at the gallery over his shoulder and asked, "You an art aficionado, Harvey?"

"Bonafide lover of the arts and the artists—my wife usually has a few paintings on the walls."

Joy laughed as Harvey winked.

"See you tomorrow, Harvey. Coffee's on me."

Joy was curious. What kind of art does this little town offer? Hmm … maybe painting classes? Mrs. Wilson always said I had an eye for design, even in fifth grade. An image of Mrs. Wilson and her eyeglasses hanging lopsided on her chest made Joy grin as she walked up the short set of stairs to the gallery door to investigate. She'd been an architect for years, so why not a painter now?

Joy was confronted with a small Closed for Renovations sign hanging on the door. She peeked through the glass door and could make out a tiny gallery. The place was stripped to the walls with a beat-up desk shoved into one corner. *Nice space. Great light.* In fact, the little space touched her architect's heart and sent bolts of excitement to her brain. *Some new flooring...oiled pine? And move that desk to the other corner, and...*Her interest was piqued. Joy scribbled down the contact number from the bottom of the sign. She needed to connect with someone besides good old Harvey. Maybe not a class, but how about a project?

After another solo dinner, Joy dialled the number, and was soon engaged in conversation with the very enthusiastic gallery manager, Nancy Connor.

"I am so excited you called about our mini project, Joy. You're a retired architect, and you specialized in commercial spaces? Really? This is amazing. We can usually find the brawn in our little town but rarely the visionary to drive it forward. Lunch...no, let's make that coffee first thing in the morning, if that works? I don't want to give you any time to change your mind."

Joy smiled as she hung up, already seeing images of the renovated gallery. Taking her wine with her, she walked out on to the large deck and marvelled at the stars reflecting in the calm water of the lake. Sitting down in a soft, wicker chair, she pulled her shawl a little tighter. *This could work.*

After their coffee together, Nancy called a group meeting for the next day. *She wasn't kidding about not wasting time.*

"It's how we do it in this little town, Joy," Nancy laughed into the phone. "It's pretty close-knit—sometimes you just have to call across the back lane, and you have a committee of six."

"That's amazing, Nancy—instant meetings." Joy smiled. "It's a date."

Joy ran upstairs to the gallery boardroom and greeted the committee members. She was surprised to see Joe sitting near the door and smiled as he invited her to take the chair near him.

"Nancy told me you two had connected. She was so excited she talked my ear off all night."

Nancy stood up. "If Joe is willing to share the floor, I think we can get started."

Joy could tell by the twinkle in Nancy's eyes and the wink from Joe that these two were more than committee colleagues. *Joe the Caretaker is into the arts—and Nancy.* She also noticed the six pairs of eyes eagerly glance in her direction as Nancy introduced her.

Joy rose from her chair and walked to the front of the room. "I'd have to draw up the plans, of course, and get a sense of what the budget would be, but here, let me draw a picture of how I see this space working for you. With a new hanging system, some lighting above, and a new floor—I think some kind of soft, scraped wood—and a little paint on the walls, you would have the most amazing space to highlight your art." Joy's passion flashed from her eyes as Nancy and the others grinned, and Joe pumped his arm in the air. *I think they liked it.*

Two weeks later, the budget was approved, and Joy was the new volunteer architect from the big city. Sitting on the floor in the empty gallery that afternoon, water bottles at their sides and backs against the bare walls, Nancy and Joy beamed at each other.

"It is such a relief to have you take this on, Joy. Carpentry was within my realm of resources, but designing was way beyond." Nancy gave Joy's hand a squeeze. "Oh, yes, you should know—we have already hired the carpenter for the job. He's the one who gutted the place last month—with Joe's help, of course. I emailed him the general plans and a rough draft. He gets back to Osoyoos late tonight—had to take a couple of weeks to sort out some personal business out-of-province. How about we get together tomorrow and launch Phase 2?"

Joy smiled back, feeling like a giddy girl on her first day of school.

Joy pulled into the parking space in front of the gallery at nine the following morning, gulped the last remnants of her coffee, and grabbed her purse. Hopping out of her car, she stood staring at a very solid male chest. Looking up, Joy dropped her coffee cup. "You."

Joy took a step back, gazing momentarily at Merle's bristly chin.

"What the hell are you doing here? A little bit on the hick side for your tastes, isn't it?" Merle tugged on his Canuck's tuque and glared at Joy.

"Please don't tell me you're the carpenter working on this job." Joy could tell from Merle's eyes as they rolled skyward that the answer to that was a resounding yes. "I don't believe this. Of all the places you could pick...why aren't you off on your island paradise? What, does Mona live here or something?" Joy snorted as she turned to leave.

"Hey, wait a minute. Can we just talk?" Merle stepped forward to catch Joy's arm.

Shaking him off, Joy tossed her head and stared into his stormy eyes. "Well, Merle, I am the new architect for the gallery renovation. From now on, you can call me Boss." She turned on her heel and stomped into the gallery. Six pairs of eyes dropped to the floor as her committee members all stepped sheepishly back from their various perches near the window overlooking the street.

"So, here's where I think we need to start." Joy ignored the sound of the door opening and closing and focused on Nancy and the committee. "I've drawn up the final plans and I think you're going to love them." *He can leave. I'm staying.*

Merle was waiting beside her car when the meeting broke up.

"Come on, Joy. This isn't going to work. You know that. Can't you find some other little project to keep yourself busy? Learn bridge? Take up line dancing? Buy a dog?"

Joy blew a big cloud of moist air into the crisp fall morning, watching it rise up and disappear right about the level of Merle's chin. She put her hands on her hips like a gunslinger waiting to draw. "I'm not quitting. If you aren't up to the job, then leave. There are lots of other carpenters who would love to work with me. But I'm not seeing too many architects lining up. Nope, not one." Joy stepped into her car and slammed the door.

Joy stood in amazement, staring at the pile of wood sitting in the back room of the gallery—old barn boards from Canto's ranch up on Anarchist Mountain.

"This...this is the jewel in the crown, the sun in the sky, the...well, this is going to be so perfect, Joe."

Joe's skepticism seeped up to his raised eyebrows and spilled out in one word. "Really?"

This was the exciting part of design—the part that Joy loved and refused to waste on a broken, angry heart. The old wood would shine with the touch of the right craftsman. This pile of scrap would produce the one feature that could make the gallery shine—an aged floor with the priceless glow of a century's worth of memories. But it would take some special skill to piece it all together. *Damn.* She had to admit, Merle was the perfect man for the job, even if it meant bumping heads now and again. *Suck it up, buttercup—you can do it. Can he?*

The pre-Christmas opening loomed closer. So far, Joy had timed her visits carefully, making sure Nancy or Joe or one of the others in the group would be there along with Merle. *See, I can be reasonable.* Merle was often heading out the door for coffee as soon as Joy had set her car's parking brake, which worked just fine. Joy was more than satisfied with his work, and that, after all, was what counted.

With just the final touches left, Joy waved her paint brush in big broad strokes in the air as she joked with Nancy and Joe and the rest of her six-person team about her expertise as a painter. "This will be the only painting of mine you will ever see on these walls." Inside, she felt like a conductor wringing out the final notes of crescendo from the orchestra before the crowd granted them a standing ovation.

"Can you believe it? Only one week to go. But first, we paint. I'll get up there and do the edging if someone will roll."

Joy loaded the brush with paint and climbed the ladder, reaching for the furthest corner. *Just a little farther*...the ladder shifted under her right foot and she lost her balance. Joy's head hit the corner of the old reception desk as her arms flailed wildly, trying to grab something besides thin air. Blackness enveloped her as she landed, but not before she heard her arm go crack.

Three hours later, Joy hobbled into her villa as Joe held the door. She clumsily searched for the light switch with her left hand. *I had to land on my right arm.* Nancy and Joe helped her get comfortable in the big arm chair. Wringing her hands, Nancy walked to the fridge.

"Let's see...maybe we should make a list of things you might need. Joe and I can go shopping and then I can keep you company—make sure there's no concussion."

Joy started to object. "No, Nancy. You have done so much already. It isn't necessary. I—"

"She's right. It won't be necessary. I've got it handled." Joy looked up to see Merle in the doorway, three bags of groceries weighing down his arms. Nancy looked at Joy and arched her eyebrows.

"It's okay, Nancy. You go. I have your number on speed dial." Joy waved with a smile pasted on her face. She didn't think the smile had fooled Nancy, but it made her feel better just trying.

"I know, I'm not your first choice for a nursemaid," Merle said as he set the grocery bags on the kitchen counter. "But I figured, with one of your arms out of commission, I might have a fighting chance to get a few words in before you could throw me out."

Joy grimaced silently at this intruder. She opened her mouth to speak.

Merle held up his hand. "But, first things first: my over-the-top, amazing, make-your-mouth-drool, broccoli, mushroom and cheese omelette—with a glass of milk, because wine and concussions don't mix."

Joy didn't have the strength to fight him. And his omelette really was delicious. *Damn, I missed this*. Joy rested her head on the back of the chair, meekly letting Merle take her plate. When she opened her eyes, he was sitting across from her, staring at her like he wanted to see inside of her heart instead of the thick skin he had been bouncing off of for six weeks.

"I screwed up big time, Joy. I don't know why."

Joy motioned for him to stop.

Merle took a breath and kept talking. "I have spent too many hours trying to figure that out. Weak? Stupid? All of the above?"

Joy raised her eyebrows as he continued.

"But I wanted you to hear this at least once. I am so very sorry I hurt you like that. No matter what, I am sorry. You don't need to forgive me, although...well, I just wanted you to know."

Joy sighed and shifted a little in her chair as she leaned forward just a few inches.

"Merle. Words are easy. Crazy as it sounds, what I really want to know is, what did you do with the cottage on the island? Obviously, you aren't there."

"Joy, there was nothing left in that cottage I wanted. I sold it, packed up, and came here. Stan and Laura Bule—"

Joy raised her eyebrows and tilted her head.

"Yes, that Stan. Well, they were building a summer home here on Osoyoos Lake and wanted me to do the finishing. Hell, what else did I have to do? I spent the summer hammering nails and well, I know, a lake isn't an ocean but somehow, the serenity captured me. That, and the most amazing woodworking shop sitting there, waiting for a buyer. You should see it, Joy. It has this loft and..."

As he continued, Merle's eyes lit up, the shadows disappeared, and magically, the man she had fallen in love with thirty years ago materialized right before her eyes. Joy felt the ice surrounding her heart start to melt. *Yes, Merle. I would love to see it.*

STANDING ROCK, SIMILKAMEEN

Della Barrett

On the cliffs
Above Standing Rock
Three ants scurry on the ledge
Past my wide, dried eyeballs
Black dust bites my throat
Sun sears my shoulders
Fingertips tremble
Ten meters up
Sweat trickles, cool
To steel-toed boots
My last salvation
A crow caws his disgust
Mocking my arduous ascent
Above Standing Rock
I turn, I twist
Return the scoff
Shale crumbles. Boot slides
I drop, scrape, scream
The rope at my waist
Jerks tight
Steals my breath
Stunned, I swing
Like a rag doll
At the mercy of
A wayward child
A quick breath
A prayer
I dig deep
To my sorry soul
Heave up
One last stellar effort
Ahh…top of the world
Horizontal earth
Fantastic!

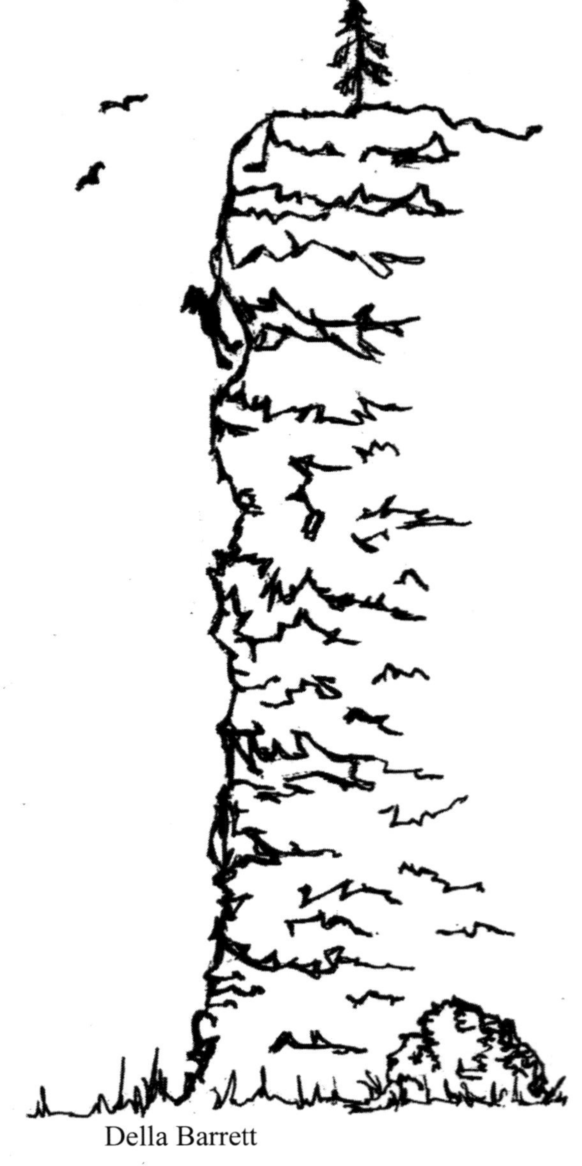

Della Barrett

CORNERED IN THE ORCHARD

Fiction

L.M. Patrick

"Who's ready for burgers?" Scott asked as he nudged the thick, juicy brown patties around the grill.

"I am," Billy said. "Amazing spread, Scott. All this to celebrate our last day of Grade 11? Wow."

Paul poured four glasses of his dad's homemade Merlot wine, then raised his glass. "A toast to the summer of '76. May it be the best summer yet."

Scott raised his glass and took a sip. His barbeque was off to a late start, but having the house to himself for the entire weekend more than made up for it.

"So, are we going to the bush party to get some beer?" Billy asked as he tackled his burger. "Wine's a good warm-up, but we definitely need beer."

"I'm with Billy. Gotta have beer," Tim said, as he squirted ketchup all over his fries.

Paul turned to Tim. "Are you sure you wanna go? You remember what happened yesterday when Danny Lopez almost thumped you out? He'll be partying tonight at the lake for sure."

"Yeah, Tim," Scott added. "If it weren't for Vice-Principal Greenway stepping in, Danny would have scrunched you into a paper ball and stuffed you in a locker." He had no desire to run into Danny tonight. "Besides, we don't need beer. We got tons of food and Mr. Schultze's wine. There's a scary movie on at midnight. We can't miss that."

"Forget about Danny. I can handle him," Tim said.

"Let's check it out. If we can't get any beer, we'll come straight back," Billy said.

Paul fidgeted. "You heard the news on CBC? Two guys broke out of Kamloops Regional Correctional Centre. Reports said they're armed and dangerous and heading this way. One guy's ex-wife and kids live here in Oliver."

Oliver never got in the news but now the little town was suddenly famous.

"What? Are you afraid to leave the house because of some news report?" Tim smirked as he grabbed his glass of wine. "Quit wimping out."

"We're heading to a bush party. Do you think the prisoners are going to be there waiting for us? Get real," Billy said.

Don't go. It's not safe out there.

Scott heard his Voice loud and clear. It never steered him wrong, so he trusted it. "Paul's right. I've got a bad feeling about tonight."

"Ooohh, a bad feeling," Tim said, making a face at Scott.

"Don't be such a wuss. We'll be there and back before you know it," Billy said.

Scott knew that once Billy and Tim had their minds set on something it was next to impossible to talk them out of it.

After they finished their barbeque, Scott and his friends climbed into Tim's ruby red 1965 Invader. Rust blotched the bottom of the car, and it seemed to be held together with nothing more than chicken wire, duct tape, and lots of hope and prayer.

Bombing down Fairview Road toward Main Street, the Invader was magically transformed into the Starship Enterprise. Scott shared his friends' passion for Star Trek, and whenever they rode together the legendary television show came to life. Tim jumped into the lead and declared immediate war against the Klingon Empire. Captain Kirk and Mr. Spock ordered torpedo launches to blast to smithereens the Klingon warships disguised as innocent-looking houses, trees and buildings.

Despite their inevitable victory, Scott's Voice was in no mood to celebrate.

This is a mistake. You should have stayed home. Be careful tonight.

Leaving Oliver behind and heading south toward Osoyoos Lake, Scott tried to push the Voice out of his mind. He cranked down the window and rested his left arm on the outside of the car door. Warm summer winds danced and swirled about his face, blew through his hair, and delivered the sweet smells of sagebrush and Ponderosa pine. The sprinklers in the orchards went tick-tick-tick as the car picked up speed, passing one orchard after another. Cherry season was here, and Scott could almost taste the thick, heavy clumps of ripe fruit hanging from the rows of cherry trees lining Highway 97.

For some reason, Scott forgot about the stick propping up Tim's driver's seat. By the time his foot knocked the stick, it was too late.

"Whoa," Tim yelled as his driver's seat collapsed to the right. "What the…?"

The Invader swerved off the pavement, sending the right tires to chew up rocks and gravel.

"The stick. The stick," Billy shouted from the front passenger seat. "Put it back."

Scott fumbled and dug through piles of garbage on the car floor to retrieve the lost stick.

With Billy pulling and Paul pushing the driver's seat forward, Scott jammed the stick back in place.

"How many times have I told you? You could have gotten us killed," Tim shouted as he veered the car back on to the pavement.

Scott huddled close against the door and tried to shove the incident from his mind. Tonight was off to a bad start.

Time to go home. Turn around. It's not too late.

The Invader turned a sharp left off Highway 97 and wound its way along Road 22. They crossed a white wooden bridge over the Okanagan River, and approached vehicles parked alongside the river road leading to Osoyoos Lake. As they turned off the pavement on to the river road, laughter and loud conversation cut through the sound of the Eagles floating lazily out of someone's car stereo.

"Let's turn around and point the car in the other direction. We don't want to back up all the way to the bridge when we leave," Billy directed as they came to a widening in the road.

They parked on the far side of the road, near the riverbank. Still stinging from the stick incident, Scott got slowly out of the car while Tim, Billy, and Paul wandered ahead.

"Looks like lots of people from Osoyoos. Let's see who has beer to sell," Tim said.

Scott didn't know too many people from Osoyoos. Keeping his head down he weaved between clusters of people, trying to avoid eye contact. In the distance a large group hovered around a fire. Safety in numbers, he thought. When he got to the fire, a space opened up in the circle and someone thrust a can of Kokanee into his hand. He mumbled a "thank you" and took a fast sip. The can was ice cold and foamy liquid cut through his dry throat. Led Zeppelin IV came to life through an open Ford Pinto hatchback, and he began nodding his head in time to the music.

"Hey, Scott, come here. I think I found someone."

Scott looked to his right and saw Paul beckoning him over.

"His name's Keith…something. He worked for my dad last year. He's got a few extra beer. Hey, where did you get your beer?"

As Scott was about to answer, cold shivers rippled across his shoulders and shot up his neck. His stomach clenched into a knot. *Watch out. Trouble's coming.* Turning back, Scott scanned the glowing faces around the fire, looking for a sign of something gone bad. Everyone milled around the fire, drinking and talking, some mesmerized by the flames. An evil presence was in the air, but Scott didn't know where it came from.

Time to go. Leave now.

"Come on, let's get outta here," Scott said, placing his can of beer on the dirt.

"Are you kidding? We can get beer."

"Forget the beer. Let's go. Where's Billy and Tim?"

Headlights shone through the dust, accompanied by the sound of low, rumbling car engines. As the headlights drew near, everyone's attention turned to the red Mustang, the black Camaro, and the dark green Charger.

Doors and trunks opened and slammed shut, followed by the sound of clinking beer bottles. Several older kids emerged from the cars. Leading the pack was Danny Lopez. Too late. Scott stared at the ground not knowing whether to inch away slowly or run.

"Uh oh," Paul said. "Danny just spotted Tim."

Tim staggered out into the middle of the dirt road with his arms wrapped around his stomach guffawing in laughter. "That's hilarious. I gotta remember that one."

"Hey, Danno. Isn't that the guy that plowed into you?"

Tim stopped laughing and squinted through his thick lenses at Danny, who caught sight of his victim.

The next series of incidents was a blur.

Billy raced up to Tim, spun him around, and yelled "Run!" while Paul broke out into a hundred yard dash through the silent gauntlet of onlookers.

Scott's chest felt as if it would explode as he tore up the dirt, pumping his arms and legs as fast as he could. Behind him, he heard shouts and curses and then the sound of a muscle car roaring to life. Up ahead, Scott's friends flung open the car doors and disappeared inside the Invader. Wheels spun and gravel and dust kicked up everywhere. Scott grabbed on to the open back door and threw himself head first inside the moving vehicle.

"Shut the door, shut the door," Billy yelled from the front.

Paul grabbed Scott's shoulders and managed to haul him inside. Scott gripped the driver's seat and after three failed attempts finally closed the back door and sat up. It was a miracle the stick stayed in place.

Scott stared at the approaching white bridge, wishing the Invader was truly the Starship Enterprise, launching into warp speed, away from the approaching Klingon warship.

"Turn right when we get to the road," Billy shouted. "I know a place we can hide."

Once the tires hit the pavement, Tim peeled a hard right onto a hairpin road winding between the sloughs. In the moonlight, Scott made out two abandoned barns, one on either side of the road.

"Hang left. We'll hide here." Billy gestured toward one of the large, collapsed wooden barns.

Tim tore off the road and ditched the car neatly behind the barn. He turned off the engine and cut the lights. Scott ducked low, held his breath, heart slamming against his chest. Seconds later, a car engine thundered past, then faded into the night.

"Let's give it a few minutes. We can double back and head to the highway … and back to Scott's place," Billy said in a low voice.

This was the first good news Scott heard all night.

Tim started the car, and the Invader crept around the barn and onto the pavement. Scott kept his window down, listening for the first sound of a muscle car. As the Invader pulled out on to Highway 97 and headed north to Oliver, he started to breathe easy again.

Rounding a corner, they saw police lights flashing up ahead.

"Maybe there's an accident," Tim said.

"No, looks more like a roadblock," Billy said.

Two RCMP police cruisers blocked the highway, stopping cars going in both directions.

Stay calm. Relax.

Through the front window, Scott saw flashlight beams waving the car forward.

"I've never seen a roadblock on '97," Paul said. "Why would they…?"

Scott knew the answer before Paul finished. The escaped prisoners.

A police officer approached the car and started talking to Tim.

A second police officer stuck his flashlight into Scott's open window and asked, "What is that? A stick?"

A harsh beam of light illuminated the clutter of garbage on the floor, including the dark brown piece of wood propping up the driver's seat.

"Oh yeah, the stick. Right. A bit of jerry-rigging to keep the driver's seat from falling backward," Tim said.

Awkward silence filled the car.

"Everyone out of the vehicle. Now," the police officer ordered.

They scrambled out and the officer pulled on the stick. The driver's seat fell backward, smacking him on the head and knocking his cap off.

Scott turned away, fearing what would follow.

"You can't drive a motor vehicle with a stick supporting the driver's seat. It's unsafe. And is that a hole in the floor?"

Scott had forgotten about the layers of garbage acting as a cover for the gaping hole in the floorboards.

After rummaging through more garbage in the trunk, the first officer pulled out a beaten up, red plastic jerry can. "What is this?"

"It's gas. For emergencies. My fuel gauge is kind of haywire, and the jerry can gives me enough to get back home. Most of the time anyway," Tim said.

"You can't store gasoline in the trunk. That's it. I'm impounding this vehicle."

Tim started to argue, but Billy grabbed his shoulder and yanked him back.

Scott, Paul, and Billy showed IDs while Tim's license and registration information was radioed in. The officer handed Tim some papers, telling him to report to the Osoyoos detachment for a car inspection. A tow truck would come by in half an hour to tow the Invader to Osoyoos.

As soon as Tim drove the Invader off the road, Scott noticed a buzz of activity around the two police cruisers. Before Scott knew it, the road block was down and the cruisers had spun around and disappeared toward Oliver.

"What are we gonna do now?" Paul said. "We're stuck. The killers will see us. They'll think we're here to ambush them. They'll start firing at us. We're gonna die."

"Yeah, and don't forget about Danny and his buddies," Tim said, staring down the road. "If the prisoners don't get us, they will."

"We have to wait here until the tow truck comes. Maybe he'll give one of us a ride back to Oliver," Scott said.

The boys hid behind the Invader in an orchard, waiting for the tow truck and avoiding any passing cars. An hour went by before the tow truck finally pulled up.

When Billy tried to climb in the truck, the driver yelled, "Whoa, wait a minute. You can't ride with me. It's against insurance rules. Come collect your vehicle tomorrow, and we'll see about repairs."

Scott stood with his hands stuffed in his pockets and watched the beloved Starship Enterprise being towed south to Osoyoos.

"We're doomed," Paul said.

"We'll have to walk. Hopefully we'll get to town sometime before morning," Billy said as he turned and began walking.

Tim sighed and added, "Yeah, if we don't get beaten up or shot."

Stay out of sight. Hide in the orchards.

"Is there another way to get back to my place? Does anybody know a shortcut?" Scott asked.

Billy turned to Scott. "No. We walk until we get to Road 7, which leads back to Fairview Road."

They trudged along the side of the highway for what seemed like forever. The sound of an approaching car engine made the boys scurry off into the nearest orchard.

Around the corner. Two of them. They're coming toward you. Take charge and protect your friends.

"Let's get off the highway for a bit. Let's take a break," Scott said, grabbing Paul by his arm.

Paul slowed but Tim and Billy kept walking ahead.

"I'm with Scott. Let's rest. We're in no rush to get back, right?" Paul said.

Scott ran ahead, turned around, and took a stance. "This is as far as we go. Two men are coming up ahead. Don't ask me how I know. I just know."

The two boys stopped and stared.

"You're kidding right? How do you know that?" Billy asked.

"It's a voice I hear in my head. It warns me about stuff, and it's always right. I never told you guys about it before. I was afraid you would think I was nuts or something. You gotta trust me on this. They'll be here any minute."

A warm, gentle breeze floated through the trees, waving the branches and rustling the leaves. A great grey owl hooted off in the distance.

"Step right up, right this way," Tim said in his travelling carny voice. "Psychic Scott's Paranormal Predictions. Tickets are going fast. No time to lose."

Billy chuckled and punched Tim on his right shoulder. "Hey, maybe we can get Scott to tell us when the world will end? Or when the Russians will invade?"

Scott's face felt flushed but he stood his ground.

"Psychic predictions or not," Paul said, "let's just take a break. My feet hurt. Twenty minutes, okay guys?"

After the laughing stopped, Billy said, "Let's make it fifteen minutes. Then we keep walking 'til we hit Scott's place."

Scott took the lead, hurting from the ridicule but grateful his friends listened to his Voice. The orchard was dark, and thick branches blocked out any light from the summer night sky. Tall damp grass swished against Scott's pant legs as he navigated between the rows of trees, ducking to avoid the low-lying branches.

"This is far enough," Tim said.

The boys dropped down on the orchard floor and leaned against a couple of cherry trees. Scott and Paul shared one tree, Tim and Billy the next.

Scott's feet were hot and sore, so he untied his shoelaces and loosened his shoes. The surrounding damp grass cooled his feet, and he felt a little better. The soft ground and the support from the tree made a comfortable chair. He started to drift off when he heard branches snap to his right.

Scott's mouth turned dry. Paul jerked and bumped Scott's shoulder. Scott leaned forward and turned his head. It was dark, but his eyes had adjusted, so he could make out Tim and Billy sitting up straight and alert under the next tree. He tapped Paul's shoulder, waved his hand at his other two friends, and then placed his index finger on his mouth and gestured "Shhh." The boys caught Scott's signals and nodded their heads.

"Where are we? How much longer?" a voice said.

"Can't be too far now. Cutting through these orchards slowed us down some," came a second voice.

"I need to stop. I got a cramp."

"Deal with it. We're wasting time."

A flicker of light lit up the orchard like a tiny beacon. From the glow Scott made out the shadows of two men a couple of rows over. Scott's stomach churned, and his arms began to quiver. He caught the smell of cigarette smoke and something else. Body odour? He wasn't sure. Billy held his right arm across Tim's chest, motioning for him not to move. Paul shifted and squirmed. Scott touched Paul's shoulder.

Stay put. Don't move. They can't see you.

One of the men hacked up and spat.

Scott looked at his three buddies. Tim was pressed against the cherry tree with Billy's arm holding him back. Paul was shaking now and the vibrations shot through Scott's left arm. What if his friends started to run? What would he do? He didn't want to be left alone in the orchard with two armed and dangerous men.

Billy and Tim will not run. Paul is thinking about running. You must stop him.

Scott grabbed Paul's baggy corduroy pants and held them in a tight grip. Scott leaned in and whispered, "Don't run. Don't move."

Paul turned his shaking head ever so slowly and faced his friend, a look of terror on his face. Scott inhaled Paul's stale breath and sweat. He gripped the pant leg tighter. A few seconds later, Paul responded with a trembling yet determined nod.

"You done? Let's get going," came a voice.

Paul's body jerked upright, and Scott thought it was all over. Paul was going to run for sure.

Another hack and spit and then the sound of grass whisking toward them. Scott held on to Paul's corduroys for dear life.

They cannot see you. Keep Paul still. It's going to be fine. Wait until they are out of sight.

Two tall, dark shadows passed by the cherry trees in front of the boys. The shadows moved at a steady, deliberate pace and disappeared into the next rows of cherry trees. Scott held his breath, half expecting the men to turn around and leap on top of them, guns blazing, knives drawn. The orchard turned to dead silence, punctured only by the great grey owl hooting once again.

Scott wasn't sure how long he sat under the tree. His left hand was now sopping wet. Paul must've peed himself. Scott didn't let go of the corduroys until he heard Billy say, "Psst. Hey. They're gone."

Scott kept close to his friends as they snuck out of the orchard and down to the highway. They stood at the bottom of the orchard and peered both ways, making sure the coast was clear. Heading north, Scott followed his friends in silence, everyone keeping tight against the orchards. The boys arrived safely at Scott's house just before dawn broke.

After that harrowing night, whenever Scott's Voice spoke, he no longer hesitated to tell his best friends. They accepted it as part of who he was and never joked about it again. Scott's Voice saved them a few more times and brought them even closer together. For the first time in his life, Scott began to appreciate and understand his Voice, realizing he was not so crazy after all.

OKANAGAN RAVEN

Paul Seesequasis

for S

Skipping on the ridge, raven's darkened silhouette dances in the sky,
as the white moon rises.
Every star emits a light-tale, of ages past, soft whispers singing
Her song.

Desert sage burns on the black hills,
She lights fearlessly there.
Her wings fan the flames higher,
as ten thousand orange embers lift.
Tiny flames flicker around the moon,
staining it a blood, blood red.

Across the Mesa, the ponderosas burn,
sparks in the night sky. A silvery
shadow-smoke haze, she dons a veil
that's black. The fire, fuelled by warm winds,
sing from the south. The scent of burnt
sage intoxicating.

Rat root on my tongue. In her eyes, four
directions. She lives with these flames. Intimately.
Like a lover she caresses the burn. She and this
fire have history. The smoke burns my throat.
She hops her raven dance,
and emerges on black wings.

The red moon in the east. Distant, prone hills
hold her secrets. Sleeping ancients
who last walked when time was young.
She moves parallel now to the fire,
spellbound in the burning desert.
The smell of sage and antelope brush
upon her. This is the end.
This is the beginning.
She is the fire.

The burning shines on her cheekbones,
her dark eyes, her raven wings.

Black wings outstretched, she dances
single or double beat, lighter than air.
None can match her, her dark feathery fineness.
She is the night, circling the moon
Her song, only hers.

By the side of the road, beckoning
teasing, preening, shuffling side to side.
She brings the flames down the mountains,
a glint in her eye, she dares you to get close.
The orange embers rise over the valley,
The fire is hers. And hers alone.

ONE HUNDRED AND SIXTY ACRES

Creative Nonfiction

Virginia Laveau

My dad loved to sing an old cowboy tune "One Hundred and Sixty Acres" after he bought rural property that size on White Lake Road in the South Okanagan, off Highway 97, about halfway between the Keremeos turnoff and Okanagan Falls.

Our closest neighbours were two miles down the road in either direction, and we were five miles from Dad's father's homestead where the White Lake astrophysical observatory sits.

Dad built our house in a valley surrounded by coniferous forests interspersed with birch and poplar trees. In summer, the air was sweet and heady with the aromas of Mountain Laurel, drying pine and fir needles, dusty dried bunch grass, and the moist musty scent of moss and loamy soil. We had two sections for gardening. One sat between our house and White Lake Road and the other was on the flat top of the hill behind us near a small spring-fed lake, which Dad named Lily Lake.

Lily Lake was encircled by reeds, with a fallen tree across one end. My siblings and I were fascinated by the buttercup-coloured, teacup-sized flowers that looked like they'd been moulded from wax. A pair of Mallard ducks nested there. At our approach, they would take wing, flying away with great urgency. But once we backed off, they would return to care for their young. Box turtles, a family of large and small, would line up in a row across a fallen log sunning. One by one they'd plop into the water disappearing beneath the surface. Before long before they returned to sunning, ignoring our non-threatening presence.

The vegetable garden on the flats in front of our home was easy to irrigate. Dad had attached a long garden hose to the outside tap mounted on the front of the house, and an oscillating sprinkler swayed back and forth. The problem came with the upper garden. Mom and we older kids had to lug heavy buckets of water up the hill to fill trenches dug alongside veggie rows.

"Jack, my back can't take much more of this. And the kids are tuckered out. What are we to do?" Mom asked.

"I'll think about it and let you know," Dad said.

A few days later, he came home from work with our station wagon rear stacked to the top with six-foot-long wooden sluices. He helped a farmer update his irrigation system. Wooden flues had been replaced by galvanized pipes with "big boomers," sprinklers with huge revolving heads perched atop wheeled metal frames. They roamed the fields, gushing gallons of water with each spurt.

"Since I did such a good job helping him install his new system, he gave me all this for nothing!" Dad exclaimed proudly. "Now all I have to do is adapt them."

And adapt them he did. From one of the local farming supply houses, he purchased a galvanized pipe fitting that was adjusted to fit like a sleeve over one of the flue's ends. He made a rubber washer from a split inner tube tire before bolting the sleeve into place. On the other end of the galvanized piece, he attached a reducer that would fit into the female end of a garden hose. For Dad this was cutting-edge technology. He had never worked with such new-age equipment on our farm, other than a small diesel tractor with which he harvested grass for hay to feed our animals.

The next morning he was up with the rooster ready to assemble his watering system. We made a family picnic day out of the whole affair and everyone was overjoyed to think of not having to haul buckets of water for the huge garden, which included one acre of potatoes and one acre of a variety of vegetables.

When the flues were installed, Dad stood for a moment with his hands on his hips smiling.

"Now for the most important part." Like a magician, he produced a cardboard box from the back of the station wagon. With glee he brought forth a small gas-powered water pump. Humming, he bolted it to the framework supporting the flues. Next he fed a long pipe into the lake and attached it to the motor.

"Here goes nothing!" He wrapped the pull cord around the motor's head and pulled. The motor burped and faded. He rewrapped the cord and pulled. This time it roared to life. Ducks took flight, turtles dived, and water poured from the spout into the waiting sluice.

"Hooray!" the family cheered in unison. The cheering died when the pump groaned and the water stopped flowing. Dad frowned and scratched his head.

"Perhaps it's clogged." He opened the panel. "What the—?"

At this juncture it must be remembered that Dad was a farmer and a hunter. The act of butchering and preparing animals both wild and tame exposed him to the most noxious odours and messes. Over time he had developed a cast-iron stomach that even the worst jobs couldn't upset. This time his cast-iron stomach let him down.

When he opened the panel pent up pressure was released and the pump chugged to life, spewing weeds and stinky mud all over Dad's face and down the front of his shirt and trousers. He bent double, gagging. Goo smeared onto his hair when he mopped his face.

My siblings and I had never before seen him behave in such a bizarre manner. We roared with laughter.

Time and again he dipped his hands into the water running through the sluice, scrubbing his face. Our laughter turned to clapping delight as the water flowed into the garden hose and spurted from the end of the large-headed rotary sprinkler rhythmically spraying in a large circle. Our delight became amazement when baby frogs, still wearing tadpole tails sprang from the sprinklers' large exit hole and rained down upon the garden. They bounced off the vegetation before hopping away. Moving the intake hose into deeper water ensured that clean water sprinkled. Our upper garden was a success, providing vegetables for canning and freezing, plus some for friends.

Dad loved the land and often sang his favourite song, "One Hundred and Sixty Acres." Sometimes he'd change the colour of the "hoss" to brown or grey, instead of paint. When he got to the part about "pocket money jingling in my jeans," he'd rattle his keys. He never kept money loose in his pockets. Bills went into the brown leather wallet in his hip pocket and the change into a round, black leather, zippered pouch. When he did take money from his wallet to pay for something he almost made it squeak. His grip was so tight the cashier had to pry it from his hand.

Don't get me wrong. My dad was not stingy. He would give you the shirt off his back and his last crust of bread if you needed them. Surviving the dirty thirties had forced him to make every dollar stretch, and even though it was the sixties, he continued handling money with restraint.

Dad loved to play guitar and mandolin and sing songs by Hank Snow, Marty Robins, Wilf Carter and Johnny Cash, to name a few, even yodelling when a tune required it and improvising with spoons and a washboard when instruments were not available. He passed on his love of music to his children. Some of us learned to play musical instruments, some pursued artistic endeavours instead.

Throughout the years my father worked at many types of employment, in fact he was fondly called "Jack-of-all-trades." He was a farmer, received on-the-job training in carpentry, plumbing, electrical installation, took a correspondence course to be a T.V. repairman (in the days when black and white monstrosities were filled with glass tubes instead of computer chips), and was a family car repairman. His being a self-taught mechanic stood us in good stead because we drove second-hand, older model vehicles that needed frequent repairs.

I was once responsible for one of those vehicle repairs. Mom asked me to take her Austin Mini to the hill garden to pick vegetables for supper. The winding dirt road was steep and full of pot-holes. I bounced my way steadily uphill, and after picking the necessary produce, crept downhill. It was late afternoon and the roadside trees created deep shadows, hiding the sawed-off tree stump in the centre of the road. The vehicle slipped into grooved ruts. It high-centred on the stump, breaking the rear axle of the car. In dismay I stared at the splayed wheels and the sagging back end of the Austin Mini. Oh, no! How was I going to explain this to Mom? It was her only transportation.

I hiked the rest of the way home, lugging containers filled with the good things of the earth, mentally kicking myself for ruining Mom's car. I dreaded what Dad would say.

He was really very good about it. That evening he went to the auto wreckers and purchased an axle from a larger car for next to nothing. After towing the Mini to the front yard with his tractor, he and his brother worked into the wee hours of the morning, taking turns sawing at it with a hacksaw, dulling several blades, until it was shortened to fit the Austin Mini's frame.

Dad never berated me for causing so much trouble. In fact, once the car was fixed, the episode was never mentioned again. But I thought about it a lot and vowed I would be much more careful while driving on rutted dirt roads.

Dad was self-taught about many things. Some ventures were carried out after reading an article, some by guess and by golly. He was fearless when faced with a challenge. Whichever problem-solving method he chose, the experience contained a lesson for me, like the time he built a smokehouse to cure meat.

That year we raised pigs on our farm. Dad decided to salt and smoke the pork himself rather than sending it to the local butcher, who charged an arm and a leg. After all, he had eaten enough ham and bacon; he should be able to figure out how to prepare them, shouldn't he?

One fine Saturday morning he and his brother constructed a smokehouse. As the oldest child, I was Dad's right-hand gal and gofer. I fetched and handed tools and supported boards as they nailed. It stood over six feet tall, like an upright deep-freeze, with a smoke hole in the top. Upon completion of the task they butchered the hog.

Everything about the curing process was trial and error. Dad put water in a sanitized, galvanized washing tub and poured in a generous amount of salt, then he added more, emptying the five-pound sack. Well, if a little is good, more is better, right?

How long was the meat to soak in the brine? His brother suggested overnight. Mom's sister suggested four days. Mom guessed at a week. But Dad figured the longer it pickled the better, so it sat in the cooling cellar, marinating for two weeks. He hung the hams and bacon slabs on heavy wire hooks and secured them to layered wooden laths stretching across the width of the smokehouse. Then he and I built a fire beneath it.

"Why birch wood?" I asked, staring at the large teepee of wood below the meats.

"It will give a sweet flavour to the meat. Remember the year we collected birch sap and made our own syrup? It should have that kind of sweetness. It was almost like maple syrup."

Remember? Maple syrup? How could I forget trudging through the melting snow in early spring, tapping birch trees and collecting plastic ice cream pails of sap? Mom spent all day boiling the juice, hoping it would thicken. It never achieved anything more than a watery consistency. When Dad tasted it he smacked his lips, remarking on its mild flavour. I didn't find it sweet at all. It didn't taste anything like maple syrup, which I enjoyed. It tasted similar to what the green inner layer of birch bark smells like. I hoped Dad was on a better track with the smoked meats than he had been with the birch syrup fiasco.

He waited until smoke belched from the hole in the roof, then he closed the door and rubbed his hands together and grinned. "That oughta do 'er."

Early the next morning we went together to check the meats. When Dad opened the door his jaw dropped. I poked my head around the doorframe to see what he was gaping at.

Oh, the pork was smoked, all right. Stalactites of solidified lard hung down from each piece of meat. The lowest wooden laths supporting them were scorched, barely holding their weight. Not only were the hams and bacon smoked, they were pre-cooked.

"Oh, well." He shrugged. "Next time I do this I'll make the fire smaller."

We toted the meat back to the house. His treasure, a slab of bacon, would be for breakfast, a family taste test. Mom carved thick slices and laid them into the waiting frying pan.

"This is the leanest bacon I've ever seen," she remarked.

Dad beamed. "Just wait till you taste it!"

A mouthwatering smoky aroma rose from the skillet. Soon crispy bacon rashers lay on our plates alongside farm-fresh fried eggs. Sweet home-churned butter glistened on slices of golden brown, homemade, whole-wheat bread toast. What a treat!

In our family no one nibbled. Large chunks of bacon, egg and toast were shovelled into gaping mouths. With equal rapidity, semi-chewed mouthfuls returned to each person's plate.

"This bacon is awful!"

"It's like eating pure salt!"

"And downing a charcoal briquette!"

Dad made no comment at all. His eyes glistened. He stoically munched his breakfast and swallowed it down, drinking more strong tea than usual.

"I know what I can do," Mom said, pushing the bacon to one side of her plate. "I'll boil the slab. That will cut the salt and smoke." And boil it she did. In fact she boiled all the meats from that smoking episode. That was the only way we could eat any of it. To this day I don't like highly salted, extra-smoky foods, especially bacon.

The next time Dad smoked meats he reduced the amount of salt, the length of time it cured, and the size of the fire. What came out of the smokehouse was delicious. His confidence was restored when his family ate the smoked meats with gusto and asked for seconds. That was when I learned that less is more.

Another instance of his unique problem solving skills was when we wanted to have a mid-winter turkey dinner. The Bronze turkeys we raised on the farm had attained a great weight. At the time we didn't own a deepfreeze, so the massive birds resided in a frozen food locker in Penticton.

"It's a monster," said Dad, wrestling the thirty-pound bird onto the kitchen table.

"I'm not even sure it will fit inside my roaster," said Mom, unwrapping it from the brown freezer paper. The bird dwarfed the largest roasting pan.

"Jack, it won't fit. What are we going to do?"

Rather than waste time and gas on an hour-long drive from our country home to Penticton to purchase a larger roaster, Dad came up with a solution to the problem. You could almost see the wheels turning and a little light bulb going off over his head.

"We'll cut it in half. It shouldn't be too hard. You can refreeze the other half. That way it will become two feasts." Dad always referred to Mom's meals as feasts. And no wonder. His mother had been a terrible cook. She had come from a wealthy English family, and as a girl her first cooking lessons were camp cooking while travelling by covered wagon via the Oregon Trail. Everything she cooked became a watery soup, even the choicest meats. Her biscuits were like hockey pucks. Two black and white Border Collies roamed the house, and their hairs were everywhere, in the air, in the butter, in the food. There is little doubt as to why his spending money, from his first job as labourer on a neighbouring farm, went to buy cheese, bread, bologna, and tinned meats to supplement the meagre fare at Granny Burns' table.

He cleaned one of his sharpest handsaws with soap and water and tried to cut the frozen bird. It was like attempting to saw cement. The blade bent into a u-shape and wobbled, merely scratching the turkey's skin. Never one to give up in defeat, he looked about his toolbox. He picked up an axe, examined it, and put it back. When he spotted his chainsaw sitting in the corner, his eyes lit up.

"This ought to work!" He cleaned the saw teeth and chain with dish soap and water.

"It's too cold to do this outside, so you'll have to plug your ears, kids," he advised his wide-eyed brood of four. "And stand back!"

Dutifully, we stepped back into the living room, hands cupped over our ears, gazing at the show with bated breath.

"Helen, slide that cutting board under the bird," Dad said. Mom strained to place a three-inch thick rectangle of laminated wood beneath the turkey.

"Brrp. Brrp. Brrp. Roar!" Blue smoke belched from the chainsaw. The windows rattled. Hot machine oil exhaust fumes filled the air. I toyed with the idea of uncovering one ear and enduring the noise in order to plug my nostrils.

Dad held the saw in a two-handed grip poised over the bird, then slowly lowered it. The roaring deepened as it worked. Frozen meat and bone sawdust spewed into the air and onto the table. Soon the turkey lay cleaved in two from breastbone to backbone.

With a triumphant smile he turned off the chainsaw.

Mom thoroughly washed both halves. Wrapping one in plastic wrap, she placed it into the empty fridge-top freezer, which it filled to capacity. By next morning the bird had thawed enough to be stuffed. She wrapped the stuffed area with tinfoil prior to baking. We enjoyed our turkey dinner, and even though our family of six were good eaters, there were plenty of leftovers.

Throughout the years we lived on the farm, I shadowed my dad, observing his style and techniques for problem solving. There were many lessons that I learned about coping with troublesome situations. The greatest one was to not solve problems by gosh and golly, but to do research before attempting a project I had never tried before.

Many years later, in hospital in Vernon, Dad sang his favourite songs, including “One Hundred and Sixty Acres.” The nurses got a kick out of his renditions. He had a song for every occasion and then some. The entertainer in him took over once he had a captive audience of nurses and patients.

The hospital staff encouraged Mom to bring Dad’s guitar, so he could really entertain. Fingering was impossible because strokes had impaired his left hand, leaving it like a claw. The guitar sat by his bed until Mom took it away. He died shortly thereafter.

As I write this memoir, the song “One Hundred and Sixty Acres” is rolling around in my head. Dad’s favourite country and western songs stick with me because I learned them while so young.

My husband and I now live in Barriere, B.C. When I am standing on a hillside with my eyes closed, breathing in the warm summer air, I get whiffs of sweet Mountain Laurel, pungent pine and fir needles, dusty dried bunch grass, and musty moss and loamy soil. I am transported back to my childhood and life on the farm, and I am at peace.

ELEGY FOR THE ORCHARD

Michelle Barker

Now it is the fashion in these parts
to plant vineyards,
trees having gone out of style.

And so whole orchards are razed
to make room for grapes.

Even the word – vineyard –
has the power to conjure
cobbled Italian roads,
old men with purple
grape-stained feet,
a slender flute glass,
and a violin,

which in an orchard
would be a fiddle.

Where is the charm
in the lowly apple?
Eve's bane doesn't tempt us.

That sensation
of passing an orchard
on a mid-summer's eve
and feeling the sudden chill
of shaded air, smelling
the sweet green of ripening fruit,
imagining paths
beneath the arms of trees –

it's only real estate.

[A version of this poem first appeared in *The Centrifugal Eye*, Volume 6, Issue 1]

NARAMATA CYCLE OF LIFE

Fiction

Ron B. Saunders

“Dad, wait for me,” Rebecca said. “I’ll come and help you out.” She opened the driver’s side door and went around to assist her father. *Why is he so ornery today?*

Joe fumbled with the door handle and struggled to stretch a foot to the ground. “Damn little cars. In my day a car was built to fit a man.”

Rebecca hurried to the door and held his elbow. “Let me help you, Dad. I don’t want you falling today. Ninety-five is not a good age to be injured. Why won’t you use your walker? You know how much steadier it makes you.”

Her father shook his head. “I’ll be fine. You make a better walker. Give me your arm, and I’ll hang on tight. Besides, how often do I get a chance to stroll arm-in-arm with a pretty girl?”

“Oh, Daddy, I’m seventy,” she said, a little flattered.

“Still gorgeous, sweetheart. Just like your mother.”

“And why did you insist we park so far away?” Rebecca pointed west. “The packinghouse site is three blocks away. Dad, this is silly—you won’t make it that far.”

“Don’t badger me, Becky. I want to walk down Robinson, the way I always used to walk to work. It’s a nice day. Look at the blue sky. The leaves are finally out. I can smell the lake air from here. The walk will do me good.”

“Let me get your jacket, in case you get cold.”

Joe narrowed his eyes. “No. I’m fine. It’s May and the temperature is just right. I can feel the sun on my face. I love the warmth of the sun. Reminds me of the old days in the apple orchards. We would start picking at five in the morning. It would still be bloody cold, but the sun would come up over the mountain and warm you through to your bones. Of course, by mid-morning it was roasting your arse off.”

“Okay, okay,” Rebecca said, shaking her head. She knew there was no point arguing with him.

The two shuffled down Robinson Avenue and approached Third Street. The Naramata Community Church came into view on the northeast corner. The small, whitewashed building was bordered by a rose garden, now in bloom. Two small crosses extended skyward from the roof peaks, like thin hands reaching for heaven.

Joe pulled Rebecca's sleeve and stopped. "Do you remember Sunday School here?"

"Yes, you always insisted I attend, even though you seldom showed your face in this church."

"I know, I know. I didn't care for sermons. Your mother and I just wanted you to get the basics of Bible learning and Christ's way. This village and the surrounding countryside were my church. A man could not dwell in a more magnificent cathedral."

"I remember you used to go for long hikes," Rebecca said.

Joe nodded and lifted a thin finger towards the low pine-covered mountains to the east. "Oh, yes. I would walk through the orchards and up the rise to the railway tracks, look down the lake—all shimmering with sunlight, and see the valley disappear past Penticton and Skaha Lake as far as you can see. Then I knew I was in God's presence. Indeed, the only time I was ever really aware of Him was up in those hills. And, when I looked into your eyes, and your mother's. I could see Him looking back at me, blessing me. I never found Him in this little white building. Although, I must admit, the most sacred event of my life happened here."

"You married Mom," Rebecca said, squeezing his arm.

Joe nodded. "On that day I was truly blessed. He gave me an angel. When she wrapped her arms around me, I could imagine the tenderness of heavenly wings caressing me, keeping me safe … warm … needed. She knew how to hold a man. When she came to me …"

"Okay, Dad, I get the picture," Rebecca said, her tolerance waning. She tugged at his arm. "Let's keep moving. I don't want you standing too long."

Tall, mature trees lined the street, bursting with an abundance of new pale-green leaves. Their mid-height branches extended over the road, affording pleasant shade as they approached the Naramata Store, then continued down Robinson another fifty feet. As they passed the store, Joe came to a dead stop.

Panic jolted Rebecca as she thrust her arm against his chest to prevent him from keeling over.

Joe's jaw dropped. He gasped and turned to her. "There isn't a goddamned thing left!"

Before them stretched a large open area surrounded by chain-link fencing. Spanning a couple of acres, the open compound lay barren. Nothing but flat, machine-groomed dirt and crushed concrete remained. No vehicles, machinery, or scraps endured. The Naramata Co-operative Packinghouse had vanished. Evidence of its existence now prevailed only in faded old photos and fragments of memory.

Rebecca's heart sank. "Dad, I know this must be shocking for you, but you knew this had happened. Why did you insist on coming if it was going to upset you?"

"I'm okay, sweetheart. I guess until you actually see it, the change doesn't sink in. This building was huge. It swallowed you up when you entered."

Joe released his arm from Rebecca's and hobbled to the fence. He wrapped his gnarled fingers around the wire mesh and reminisced. "The packinghouse was the heart of the operation. It was a beehive of activity, full of busy people receiving fruit, washing, sorting, packing, boxing, labeling, and shipping. Trucks were coming and going constantly. It was noisy. Machines clickety-clacked, conveyors hummed, people yelled and joked."

Rebecca stood beside him. "I remember visiting you here when I was little. The sorting girls would give me candies."

"Oh, yes." Joe smiled. "They were amazing—working so fast and carefully. The whole place smelled of fresh fruit, fir timber frame, and machine lubricant. We were happy—a family. We all lived, worked, laughed, and cried here. Naramata was a wonderful place to live, to grow up, fall in love, get married, make babies, grow old, and die. And the packinghouse crews were special. We knew it. We were the kings of the fruit industry—known around the world. At least, until those damn Yankee vampires sucked us dry with the big Washington orchards."

Joe sighed and fell quiet. She wrapped her arm around his shoulder and hugged him. He bowed his head and closed his eyes.

"Dad," Rebecca said, sensing her father needed some solitude, "I'm going to walk down to see the old hotel. Want to come?"

Joe raised his head and gazed at her through red-rimmed eyes. "No thanks, honey." He waved his hand along the fence. "I'd just like to stand here by the loading dock for a while."

"All right. You holler if you need me. I'll keep my eye on you."

Rebecca strolled to the end of the block. She stood before the Naramata Heritage Inn, the original hotel built in 1908 by the founder of the village, John M. Robinson. Her thoughts wandered to a past era.

Thank goodness they preserved it. It's such a beautiful reminder of wonderful times. Mom loved to come to the hotel to dine. Daddy made such a fuss over making a date with us. "I'm taking my princesses to the castle," he'd tell me.

Rebecca turned to look at her father. She muttered, "Oh dear, how's he doing?"

Look at him. He used to be so much taller than me—now our eyes are level. His hair, once full and black as coal, is so wispy and white. His shallow cheeks, sunken eye sockets, and almost transparent skin are all that's left of the rugged, ruddy, and chiseled features of my manly father's face. He was always such a good father—faithful, protective, and caring. My, my ... I've loved him for seventy years. Mother adored him, as he loved her. She was the centre of his universe since they were teenagers. She left us much too soon. He's never been the same, after all these years.

How strange. I prayed for a child of my own and was denied. And now, I have him—my helpless little boy.

Rebecca returned to Joe and took his arm in hers.

"My old man worked in the original packinghouses along the lakeshore," he said. "They were much smaller and privately operated. But the Naramata Co-operative Packinghouse replaced them in 1920, the year I was born. Dad got me a position there when I was fourteen."

"Fourteen was so young to be working full time."

"Yeah, I was just a gofer, but it was a job and I made money. I stayed on and worked my way up until 1943, when the whole damn building burned to the ground. It was a hell of a fire—started in the middle of the night. Something went wrong with the heater in the packer's lunchroom."

"Yes, Daddy," said Rebecca. "I think I've heard this story a few times."

Joe continued unabated. "Geezus, the weather was ungodly cold—twenty below and a brutal north wind. We tried to fight the fire, but the water lines kept freezing and cracking. We used gunnysacks to wrap around the hoses when they cracked. The temperature was so cold the sacks would freeze and keep the hoses working. We knew the building was a goner, so we sprayed the equipment to try to salvage it."

Joe paused and bowed his head. "That was in January, and you were born the following October. I guess after the fire your mother and I had time on our hands." He cupped his hand over his mouth. "Oh, Marian … you were so precious. I still miss you."

Joe swallowed hard and straightened up. "They built the new packinghouse right here in short order. It was operational by 1945. Such a grand building. We were so proud of it. I went back to work, and the rest is history."

Joe looked at Rebecca through teary eyes. She hugged him again, thinking how hard this visit was for him.

"Come on, Dad," she said. "I need to get you back to the Home. Your nurse will be anxious to get your meds into you."

Joe chuckled. "Yeah, Shirley the Pusher—never misses a dose." He spoke under his breath as they returned to the car. "Mission accomplished. Bring it on."

Joe wished Shirley a good night as she left his apartment to continue her rounds. He settled into his cherished old armchair. It was the only possession he had retained from their first house on Ritchie Street, a short walk from the packinghouse. *I love this chair*. There was no talking him out of it. Like an old friend, it was something familiar in an unfamiliar place.

I'm done. He laid his head back and descended into deep sleep. His respiration slowed, and then ceased. Joe let go and drifted away—departing his mortal existence.

He stood tall at the entrance to the Robinson Avenue packinghouse. The massive building towered before him. He ran his hand through a shock of black hair. Wearing a wide grin, Joe entered the doorway, and strode confidently toward his office. Passing the sorting conveyor, he nodded to the girls sitting in straight back chairs along its length, busily separating apples. A petite brunette wearing a floral bandana looked up at him. She smiled, and said with a wink, "Hey Joe, late for your shift again? Marian must have kept you busy this morning."

Joe accelerated backwards. The brunette and the packinghouse vanished into a distant point. Soft white light surrounded and suspended him. A quiet voice spoke, and he thought it sounded familiar.

"Joey, my love, come back to me. I want you," whispered Marian.

LOG CABIN ABOVE PENTICTON

Norma Hill

Deserted, lonely
In a field of waving sage and prickly dried grass.
Roof concave, sagging
Scraggly bushes pushing out empty windows
Door hanging lopsided against cracked, dry doorframe
Hinges long rusted away.
Lonely, deserted – and yet…
Can't you hear?
Echoing laughter of small children,
Far off voices of parents,
Proud, strong,
Connected to this place, this land.
Their land.

Splashing murmurs of water
Being drawn from the crumbling well.
Glancing sideways,
Can't you see them still?
Shimmery, translucent in the hot summer sun,
The children run out the door,
Laughing still,
A frisky puppy dancing at their heels.
In the shallow dip of the ground behind the cabin
Scattered posts lay helter-skelter,
New fresh green treelings
Springing up from their nursery mothers.
The neigh of a horse echoes
Against the mountainside,
And the steed's shadow flickers in the old corral's
Hard, cactus scattered basin.
From the branch of a great dry pine,
An old wood and rope swing
Stirs slowly in the breeze.
Alone.
Or perhaps not.

RAMBLINGS OF AN OLD, OLD SOUL

Mahada Thomas

I was on Syilx land picking poplar buds the other day,
when a curious woman walked by and asked what I was doing.
I told her I would soak the buds in olive oil
and create a pain-relieving balm for myself.
She wanted to know how I'd learned about that.
"From my medicine people," I said,
thinking of my witchy women friends and siStars,
who have shared earthly knowledge with me.
"You have such a neat culture," she said.
I stared blankly, thinking, *Which culture is that?*
She continued on her way, and I began to ponder...
I've lived too many lives to be this or that,
A woman, a man, red, yellow, white, or black.
I've lived in all four corners of the world and I remember.
I have lived as a slave, a queen, a healer, a hunter, a peasant.
I know myself beyond this lifetime; beyond my experience,
beyond my culture, my race, my profession, and status in society.
I am not this or that. I am both this *and* that.
I am That I am.
People are often curious about me and ask, "Where are you from?"
Seeking an explanation for the colour of my skin and the kinks in my hair.
The answer, London, Ontario, never satisfies.
They dig until my Jamaican heritage is revealed.
Wherever I go, people see a different culture in me.
In Greece, I'm Greek; in Spain, I'm Spanish.
In the Caribbean, they see my Ancestors in me. The truth is,
I am as the Jamaican motto states – *Out of Many One People.*
I see myself in the face of an Indian, an Irish woman, an African.
We are one. Spirit having a human experience.
Ego sees falsely, the separation of colour and gender.
Soul and Spirit are colour blind, gender-neutral.
I found myself picking poplar buds, dreaming of a world
where ego becomes transparent, and Spirit shines through,
to create a Soul-filled world, where
Humanity is Our Culture.

QUAILS IN THE GARDEN

Nonfiction

Yasmin John-Thorpe

When we built our retirement home above Skaha Lake in Penticton, we found we had disrupted a large number of quails living in the wild sage covering the landscape. I knew very little about quails, as they did not exist in the Caribbean where I grew up. I just knew a number of them live in a covey.

The gardener suggested we leave them an area of their own, or else they would dig up all our plants and flowering bushes and shrubs. Outside our office window, we left an oval area surrounded by large river rocks and filled with dirt, where the quails could scratch away.

Over the years, the families brought their chicks to feed on the chicken scratch seeds we scattered for them. We noticed they had some form of hierarchy for entering the "bath" area to eat. Older males would chase the younger, more eager chicks out of the oval if it were not their turn. But they were also very protective should the neighbour's cat approach or when the magpies hovered, searching for nests with eggs or babies.

A male and female duck found the quail bath and returned each year. However, after fifteen years, I finally lost the quail bath. It had attracted a flock of pigeons, who sat on our roof, taking turns filling their gullets. If startled, many flew into our glass enclosed deck, breaking their neck. Most destructive was the mess they left in our eaves, causing problems whenever it rained. The roofer said they were a health hazard. Everything was cleaned up at our expense. Two large plastic owls now adorn our roof, to deter pigeons and woodpeckers, while large river rocks have filled in the quail bath. Looking out the office window, there are no quails feeding in the dirt. They have moved on, and I do miss their crazy antics.

Drawing of quails by Della Barrett

PROVIDENCE CREMATORIUM

Michelle Barker

Penticton, B.C.

A small building
with a tall slim smokestack
sits beside the lake,

bike path behind it,
cemetery behind that.

Prime real estate
given over to the business
of dying.

But for the sign
you'd think they were smoking fish.

When I ride past on my bike
and see the haze above the smokestack,
I cringe at the idea

that I will smell death –
inhale it with the fresh autumn air

in which everything today
feels so alive.
But death doesn't smell.

It gives no sign of its presence
except for the wisp of warm air

I ride through
for but an instant –
like a hand on my arm.

[A version of this poem first appeared in *Autumn Sky Poetry*, Issue 17]

RISKING IT ALL

Fiction

Linda Kirbyson

Charlie placed a flashlight into his school knapsack and quietly shut the back door. He crept across the lawn, past several apricot trees, and down a gravel pathway to the garage. The door on the garage squeaked as it opened. "Damn it." He glanced back at the house for any lights turning on.

He stroked his dad's new blue 1957 Ford pickup truck on the way past, looking for the stashed keys. His dad always buried the keys next to the metal toolbox. He had told Charlie it was wrong to keep the keys in the ignition and tempt someone to take the truck for a joy ride.

As Charlie shone the flashlight along the sandy floor searching for the metal toolbox, a large black spider scurried over a stack of lumber, sending shivers up and down his spine. Although he was almost sixteen and tried to be manly, he hated spiders, snakes, and creepy bugs. He wondered what else lurked in the dark garage. But there was no time to think—Billy was waiting for him. Charlie fell on his knees and sifted through the sand until he found the keys.

He jumped into the driver's seat, ran his hands over the steering wheel, and peered over the hood. Even though he had to move the seat forward to reach the pedals, he felt invincible. His hands trembled with excitement as he turned the key, but nothing happened. He scratched his head and tried again, but the engine just sputtered. "Third time lucky," he said under his breath. This time as he turned the key, the engine purred. He let the truck idle for a minute and then slowly released the clutch. With a forward jerk, the truck lunged out of the garage, just missing a large wooden pole, and then chugged onto the dirt road that looped around the cherry orchard down to Okanagan Lake.

In the dark, he raced through lower Summerland, past Mr. Daniel's grocery store, the post office, and the fruit packing plant. If he wasn't in such a hurry, he would have gone all the way down to Crescent Beach. But Billy was waiting for him.

Earlier that day at school, Billy had asked, "Do you want to hang with us tonight?" Charlie thought he had died and gone to heaven. *At last a chance to hang with the cool guys!*

At the top of Switchback Hill, he shut off the headlights and coasted down a side road into the cherry orchard next to Billy's house. The scent of cherry blossoms hung in the evening air, and a chorus of frogs sang in the background as he circled into the orchard. He parked next to a pile of cherry bins and waited for Billy.

In the distance a dog barked. Billy came strutting down the dirt road, eyeing the truck. When he got close, he rubbed his hand along the hood and whistled. "Nice set of wheels. Can't believe you stole it."

"I didn't steal it—I just borrowed it."

Billy got in. "You're not such a Momma's boy after all." He adjusted the mirror to inspect his greasy black duck tail, then took a comb out of his back pocket and pulled it through his hair. He lit a cigarette, blew several smoke rings into the air, and watched them float out the window into the orchard, disappearing into the night sky. "You ready for some fun?"

"What kind of fun?" Charlie asked.

Billy smiled and flicked some ashes onto the rubber floor mats, then smeared them with his foot. Charlie hoped his dad wouldn't notice the white streaks on the mats or the stale cigarette odour.

Charlie started the truck and turned up the volume on the radio. Big Bopper was belting out Chantilly Lace, and they both began to sing along, "Oh baby, you know what I like. Chantilly Lace and a pretty face, ponytail hanging down..."

"Let's go find some action!" Billy yelled.

A full moon shone on Okanagan Lake as Charlie released the clutch and the truck bounced through the cherry orchard back to the road. Once on Peach Orchard Road, he revved the engine and quickly let out the clutch, laying a long patch of rubber. A musky oil smell filled the cabin while smoke drifted from the wheels. He smiled at Billy, hoping he had impressed him.

"Everyone's at Gartrell Road," Billy said while he rolled another cigarette. "Bet this could be a mean machine." He watched Charlie shift into third gear. "But racing's getting to be a bore."

"What're you talking about?"

"I've got another idea."

As they approached Gartrell Road, they saw Lizzie standing in the middle of the road, her long red hair pulled into a ponytail and her perfectly curved body moving in slow motion. Charlie's legs went weak, and he had trouble climbing out of the truck. He wanted to talk to her, but didn't know what to say, so he just stood there with his mouth open, watching her. She clutched a blue checkered towel in her hands and started to count backwards from ten. When she got to one, she waved the towel across the road. A jacked-up red Buick and a fancy yellow Chevy spun down the road, sending waves of smoke into the crowd.

Charlie couldn't wait to show Lizzie what his dad's truck could do.

Lizzie waved at Billy. Her brother drove the yellow Chevy that just blew past the red Buick.

"Glad you came," said Lizzie, smiling at Billy as she twisted her ponytail around her fingers. She rolled up the checkered towel. "Are you racing?"

"No, racing's a bore," Billy said. He pointed at Charlie. "We need some real excitement. This guy's a daredevil. He's driving across Trout Creek Trestle."

"What?" Charlie said, his heart thumping.

"Wow, that would be really cool," said Lizzie. "Aren't you afraid, Charlie?"

"I—"

"No," Billy said, "Charlie's just like me; nerves of steel. Nothing scares him. Right, Charlie?"

Charlie shook his head, but Billy was too busy with Lizzie to notice. He just kept on talking about Charlie driving his truck across the trestle, and with each rendition of the story, more people gathered around them.

It was like a thousand eyes were staring at him, but all he could do was smile nervously. His mind raced. Billy has flipped out. No one has ever driven across that trestle—it's for trains, not cars. And it's a 240-foot drop to the frickin' bottom of the canyon. There's no way I'm driving across it.

Charlie pulled Billy by the arm to the edge of the road. Never before had Charlie felt panic churn in his gut like he did right then. He felt like steam was coming out his nostrils, and all he wanted to do was punch Billy in the head to knock some sense into him.

"What the hell are you talking about?" Charlie said as he tightened his grip around Billy's arm. "I'm not driving across any damn trestle."

"What, you chicken now?"

"I'm going home."

"Don't screw this up." Billy grabbed Charlie by his T-shirt and kicked some gravel over his shoes. "If you go home now, then you better never come back to school. Everyone will know you're a chicken, and you'll never be able to hang with us again."

As the moon crept up the clay cliffs, it shone a bright beam over Charlie like an interrogation light. He could hear his mother saying, "Charlie, don't drive over the trestle. Never you mind what Billy says." But all Charlie wanted was to hang with the cool guys, and if it meant driving across the trestle, maybe he could do it. The trestle wasn't that long, and the next train wasn't until morning. Besides, he'd been driving the truck through the bumpy orchards for two years and nothing had ever happened. He could do this and hang with Billy forever.

"Why are you doing this?" asked Irene. She was Lizzie's cousin. Charlie wondered how they could be related, they were so different. At school she had told him that she hated hanging out with the cool crowd because someone always got in trouble. "You could drive off the tracks and die."

The reality that he could die hit him head on. Feelings of fear flooded his brain. What if the truck fell off the trestle into Trout Creek? He would die. What if an unscheduled train came? He would die. What if the trestle collapsed? He would die.

Several of the cool guys were leaning against the truck smoking cigarettes, waiting for the action to begin. "Irene, shut up and go home," said Ralph. "If you're such a chicken shit, just go home and cuddle your teddy bear and let the big boys play. Charlie is now one of us, and he doesn't want to hear you whining."

Charlie paced back and forth, trying to reassure himself. It's just a quick ride over the trestle and then you're one of them. You can do this.

The cry of a screech owl sent shivers up Charlie's back as he walked over to his truck. When he opened the door, he made a pledge with the Almighty: *Get me across safely, and I'll never take the truck again.*

Billy stood at the railway crossing acting like a bigshot director giving a play by play of what was going to happen. Charlie started the engine and inched up to the track. The crowd became silent. Lizzie brought out the checkered cloth, counted down, and dropped it in front of the truck.

Charlie steered the truck off the crossing onto the wooden ties, carefully balancing the wheels on either side of the metal rails. He saw Billy put his arm around Lizzie and heard the crowd cheer as the truck crept along the track to the start of the trestle. The trestle couldn't be more than 250 feet long. He could do this. He crept forward. As the pickup inched across the trestle, the steering wheel jerked repeatedly. He gave the engine a little more gas, but that was a mistake. He heard a whoosh of air coming from one of the left tires and the truck leaned to the left. *Oh no!* He'd punctured a hole in the tread—probably from a railway spike. Charlie's heart sank. *What do I do now?*

He wished he could go back, but it would be easier to keep going ahead. As he crawled forward along the trestle, the truck wobbled. One wrong jerk of the steering wheel and he could be over the edge. Clutching the steering wheel, he stole a glance out the window into the dark abscess of Trout Creek. He slowed down and the truck stalled. *Crap!* He tried to start the engine again and again, but it only sputtered. He could smell the gas in the cab. "Bloody Hell," he said. "It's flooded."

He slowly opened the door, but there was only a skinny ledge that offered no room to step out on. He was trapped in the truck. Trout Creek was more than 200 feet straight down, and there were no railings that would buffer a fall. If he or the truck slipped over the edge, he knew there would be no tomorrow. *I'm too young to die.* "Let's try one more time." But the engine just kept cranking over. Sweat flooded down his face and soaked his whole body. His trembling fingers slipped on the key with each turn. Finally the engine coughed, sputtered and started. He let out the breath he'd been holding.

As he clutched the steering wheel and coaxed the truck to move forward in a straight line, the left wheel rubbed along the metal track. The trestle stretched for another 25 feet before the landing platform connected with the roadway to the Experimental Station. "Just keep moving," he said softly under his breath.

Photo of KVR train trestle bridge © Keith Dixon

The truck's headlights showed his friends cheering at the far end of the trestle. Charlie smiled as he realized they were cheering him. "Charlie! Charlie! Charlie!" Suddenly he felt ecstatic knowing that he was now one of them. It didn't matter what his parents thought, it was all about his friends. He was now one of the cool guys. *I can do this.* The last ten feet of track went on forever. The wheels on the truck seemed to move in slow motion, and even the cheering seemed to move further away. Finally when he got to the end of the trestle for the victory, his friends had disappeared into the darkness. Just two burly cops stood on the track.

They were not cheering. Instead, they stood silently, shone their flashlights into his face, and yelled, "Stop your vehicle."

His head throbbing, Charlie pulled to a stop.

A cop approached the driver's side and shone his flashlight at him. "So you think you're a train engineer?"

"Me?" asked Charlie, sweating profusely.

"Do you have a license to drive a train?"

"No," Charlie squeaked.

"Then get out off the track."

Charlie carefully maneuvered the truck off the track onto the road and got out. He was glad he was soaked with sweat, so they couldn't see the tears running down his cheeks and dripping onto his soiled T-shirt.

"Hands on the hood, feet apart."

Charlie slowly moved like a robot, spreading himself across the hood. The cop patted him down.

"Where's your licence?"

"I don't have a license. I'm turning sixteen next month," Charlie said, sobbing.

"Did you hear that, Sarge? He hasn't got a driver's license, either."

The cops huddled beside the tracks, talking on a walkie-talkie. Sarge strolled over to Charlie and read him his rights just like they did on TV when someone was in big trouble. He snapped on the handcuffs and led Charlie to the cruiser.

"What's going to happen to my dad's truck?" Charlie asked.

"That's the least of your worries."

The lights on top of the cruiser flashed red streaks across the trestle. Charlie sat in the back seat feeling like he was falling into a deep dark nightmare. A tow truck pulled up and started hooking up his dad's pickup. He was suffocating. He banged on the windows, but the cops just ignored him. He folded into a fetal ball and rocked back and forth on the rear seat until he fell onto the floor. In the deep abscess of the backseat, his brain scrambled his thoughts as he tried to think about what to tell his parents.

The officer opened the back door. "Sit on the seat. We're taking you home, and I bet your parents won't be happy to see you."

"Where are my friends?" Charlie asked.

"What friends?"

As the cruiser sped down the highway to lower Summerland, Charlie's stomach tightened. He knew that his parents would be furious and that no matter what he said, it wouldn't make a difference.

As he stood between the two cops on his front porch, Charlie's heart pounded against his ribs. Sarge pounded on the door several times. The lights switched on in his parent's bedroom, and footsteps came down the steps and towards the front door.

The door opened. His dad, dressed in striped pyjamas, looked bewildered when he saw Charlie standing between two uniformed police officers. "What the hell is going on?"

"Your son thinks he's a train engineer. He'll explain," Sarge said as he pushed Charlie in front of his dad.

Charlie sniffled as he stood looking at his dad and saw his mom coming down the stairs in her housecoat and fuzzy slippers. Only broken syllables and sobs funnelled out of his mouth.

"Charlie! Tell us what's happened," his mom said. The colour in her face went from peach to pearly white.

Three small heads with huge sleepy eyes gazed through the wooden railings at the top of the stairs, listening to every word.

"Tell us!" yelled his dad. His nostrils flared while he took a deep breath and slammed his fists on the bookcase next to the door.

Charlie froze in the doorway, trying to come up with an explanation that would work. He had a pounding headache that made it hard to think, and each word he said vibrated through his brain like a jackhammer.

"I did something stupid," Charlie said. "I took your truck for a joy ride."

"What? What a stupid-ass thing to do," his dad said through clenched teeth. "You don't even have a license. What were you thinking?"

"I just wanted to hang with Billy and be cool."

"But that's not all," Sarge said.

"After I picked up Billy, we went to the drag races."

"You didn't!" screamed his mom.

The cops stood solidly on either side of Charlie and smirked as his parents tore him apart. The future of Charlie becoming one of the "cool guys," or what they liked to call them, juvenile delinquents, was not about to happen.

"The best part is still to come," Sarge said.

Charlie lowered his head. "I didn't race. I …" He gulped. "I drove across the Trout Creek trestle."

"You did what?" his dad said. He turned his back on Charlie, walked into the living room and kicked over the ottoman and a basket of magazines. "You are the stupidest person on this earth."

"Have you lost your brain?" his mom said. "You could've died!"

"What about my truck?" Dad yelled from the living room.

"The truck had to be towed away. It blew a tire. I don't know where it is," Charlie said, wiping his tears. "And I didn't die."

"Where are your cool friends now?" his mom yelled.

Charlie looked at his parents through his tears. “I’m sorry. I’ll fix everything.”

“Oh, you bet you will. And don’t even think about asking to get your license until everything is fixed and paid for.” His dad wrung his hands together and put them on top of his head so he didn’t strangle Charlie. “I’m tempted to send you to Rattlesnake Island for the summer, where there are no cool kids, just spiders and rattlesnakes!”

Sarge undid Charlie’s handcuffs and gave his dad directions on where to pick up his truck.

“Do you want to press charges?”

“What happens if I do?”

“He’ll go to juvenile detention.”

Charlie stepped back and looked at his parents. “Please don’t do this to me.”

His dad bit his lower lip as if trying to decide the right thing to do.

“Officers, we’re not going to press charges. But if he ever does anything like this again, we will.”

His dad shut the front door still looking livid. Charlie collapsed onto the sofa and closed his eyes, wishing it was just an awful nightmare. *I’m a fool, a stupid fool.* He opened his eyes and saw his family huddled together, looking relieved that he was still alive, which made him feel even worse.

On Monday, he was a hero at school. Everyone wanted to know what had happened to him. A crowd gathered around his locker asking, “Did you get arrested? What did your parents say?” Billy was at the front of the crowd waiting for the answers. But Charlie just turned and walked away.

CENTRAL & NORTH OKANAGAN VALLEYS

Kelowna © Mike Biden

Shuswap © Mike Biden

SHUSWAP REGION

The Shuswap is situated in south-central BC, between Mabel Lake to the West and Sugar Lake to the East. To the south is the upper Shuswap River. The four surrounding mountain ranges, including the Monashee Mountains, boast elevations of over 2,000 metres (6,600 feet). The highest summit in the area is Tsuius Mountain at 2487 metres (8159 feet).

The Secwepemc People, also known as the Shuswap, are a Nation of 17 bands in this area. The ancestors of the Secwepemc people have lived in the interior for at least 10,000 years. Through hard work they have established strong communities and many organizations such as the Shuswap Nation Tribal Council and Secwepemc Cultural.

The CP Railway, Trans-Canada Highway, (Highway 1) and Highway 97 make the Shuswap easily accessible from all directions. Shuswap Lake, one of the most popular recreational destinations in BC, offers 400 kilometres (250 miles) of shoreline. The surrounding mountains provide miles of trails for cross-country skiing, snowmobiling, mountain-biking and hiking.

North Shuswap has many draws for vacationers, with over 100 kilometres (60 miles) of natural shoreline. And just a short drive away, in autumn, is the world-famous Adams River Salmon Run. The North Shuswap is also home to many artists, craftspeople and authors. Their work can be found at numerous venues and local festivals year-round.

South Shuswap, "The Heart of Shuswap," is located on the Trans-Canada Highway. Summer and winter activities abound as a result of a very moderate climate and innovative entrepreneurs.

Salmon Arm is considered the Okanagan Valley's northern gateway, but also the Shuswap's center of commerce and government services. Outdoor recreation includes water sports, 18-hole golf courses, top-rated cross-country ski trails, back-country sleigh rides, snowmobiling, mountain-biking, and hiking. The arts, cultural-based programs, festivals, carnivals, and sporting events abound, and agriculture's roots run deep here.

Sicamous, whose name comes from the Shuswap Nation term for "narrow" and is known as "The Houseboat Capital of Canada," provides visitors with many vacation options from water activities, hiking and golfing in the summer to snowmobiling and ice fishing in the winter. During the month of May, it's actually possible to snowmobile, golf and houseboat, all in one day.

RETURN TO SENDER

Fern G.Z. Carr

"Neither snow nor rain nor heat nor gloom of night
stays these couriers from the swift completion
of their appointed rounds."
Post Office Motto

No snow, no rain, no heat, no gloom of night –
just good old-fashioned sunshine enveloped

the mail truck as it dog-ged-ly
grappled its way to the summit

passing conifers and homes nudged
slightly askew by their mountain host

on a glorious Okanagan morning –
flowers a-bloomin' and birds a-tweetin'.

The postmistress steered her van with one hand
while she sorted mail with the other,

experienced eyes darting back and forth –
road, mail, road, mail, road, mail

until the road got lost in the mail
and she found herself being returned to sender,

truck plummeting into the azure lake below.
A splash. Silence. Eternity...

Now she is but an anecdote stamped into memory –
local folklore shared with tourists on lazy summer days.

FIRESTORM

Fiction

William S. Peckham

As sweat rolled down his sides, soaked his shirt, and stung his eyes, Carl trudged across the yard to the front porch and the cool of the welcoming shade.

"God, it's hot again," Carl spat out. "Won't it ever let up? We need rain, and we need it bad."

Carl had worked hard the last few years digging and laying irrigation lines. He started in May and was finished by early July. Now, in August, the county said he could not irrigate, the lake levels were too low.

I'll lose everything I worked for my whole life if I can't get water to those crops.

He trudged across the yard towards the house. Seeing his wife Annie, Carl stopped in the shade of the old elm tree by the barn and watched her as she sat on the front porch and stared out over the withered and dying crops.

God, she's still as beautiful as the day I met her. Without her, all these years of work wouldn't count for anything.

He strode toward their house. "Hi, darlin'."

She sipped on an iced tea, sighed, and mopped her brow. "How much more of this scorching heat can the fields take?"

The result of two years of oppressing hot summers was evident in the valley. Where lush green grass, blooming fruit trees, and stately birch and ash once stood, now only crumpled, yellow grass and dying leaves covered the ground.

"I'm worried, honey. What'll happen to the farm if we don't get some rain?" Annie asked.

The faint, acrid smell of decaying vegetation from the fields assaulted Carl's senses. "There's your answer—look at the yellow fields and lawn. Even the trees are losing their leaves."

Carl didn't want to alarm Annie, but an unspoken fear plagued him—a wildfire just waiting to explode into a conflagration.

"Hell, we'll probably lose the whole crop," Carl said.

"It's that bad?"

"Yeah! We've gotta get some water or we're lost."

"If we can't irrigate, where're we gonna get water?" Annie asked.

Months of worry showed on her beautiful face.

Carl mopped his brow. “Don’t know.”

Across his fields, Carl saw stunted hay crops, dry and useless. The grapes hung like raisins on the vine, and the vegetables were withered and almost unsaleable. He shuddered at this all-to-familiar scene in the valley these last few years.

Carl watched as their son Tommy, who just turned eighteen, trudged down from the barn, sweaty and tired, his phone plugged into his ear, as usual.

Tommy neared and pulled out his earphone. “Just heard the weather forecast. Said there’s rain and possible thundershowers comin’. D’ya think we’ll get enough rain to do any good? The ground’s so dry a heavy rain’ll just run off.”

“Right, if it’s too heavy we could have flooding and erosion of the slopes above. Heaven help us if there’s lightning—could even start a wildfire.” Carl anxiously eyed the sky in the west.

Tommy looked up at the sky. “Those black thunderclouds piling up over there look pretty angry—with this wind they’re movin’ our way real fast.”

“Gettin’ blacker and angrier, too.” Annie pulled her jacket tighter around her. “It’s gonna be a violent one when it hits … don’t like the looks of it.”

They heard thunder and a loud crack of lightning.

“Better get the horses into the barn and bolt the doors behind you, son. Annie, get the chairs off the porch, I’ll secure the rest of the buildings,” Carl hollered.

“Where’s your sister, Tommy?” Annie yelled. “We’d better find her before the storm hits.”

Even at twelve, Tara was becoming her own person, strong-willed, independent, and very precocious. Her emerging personality could be frightening at times.

Carl cringed as he looked anxiously at the sky where the midmorning sun glinted off the pure-white tops of the clouds and gave the violent black underbelly an ethereal look. He knew that when the full impact of the storm reached their farm it would be packing a devastating wallop. The wind was wild—dry grass and weeds blew around the yard and glanced off the buildings, like a hockey puck off the boards. Carl’s eyes stung from the dust. A screaming wind tore at the two men as they frantically searched the out buildings for Tara.

“Dad, she’s not in the drive shed.”

“Not in the barn either,” Carl called back. “Here comes the rain. Let’s head for the house, see if your mom’s found Tara.”

The men struggled against the wind and reached the shelter of the porch.

They pulled the front door shut behind them.

"Where's Tara?" Annie cried.

"Isn't she here?" Carl asked.

Annie threw up her arms in dismay. "She's not in her room, and she's not in the TV room."

Worried looks spread across their faces.

"Tara, Tara!" Annie shouted.

Silence.

"Tara!" Annie screamed as fear edged her voice. "Where is she?"

Carl tried not to show his worry. "You look down in the basement, Tommy. Annie, you look on this floor, and I'll go upstairs."

Calling Tara's name, the three moved rapidly throughout the house.

"Not downstairs," Tommy said as he came up the basement stairs.

"Not on this floor either," from Annie.

"Not upstairs," Carl said as he ran downstairs.

The three just stood in the hall dumbfounded, looking at each other, worry in their eyes.

"Where is she?" Annie sobbed. "Where's my baby?"

"Maybe she's in the cabin at the pond."

Annie headed out the door, with Carl and Tommy in hot pursuit.

A blinding flash of white light lit up the yard. A bolt of lightning split the old elm tree in the yard, sending it hurtling down onto the barn.

"Omigod!" Annie screamed.

A crash of ear-splitting thunder announced the onslaught of a devastating storm. Dry leaves on the old elm tree began to smolder, then burst into flames. Fanned by the heavy winds, they soon engulfed the roof of the barn.

"Tara!" Annie started for the cabin.

Carl ran after her and grabbed her by the shoulders.

"Hold it, Annie. I'll go to the cabin. You call 911," Carl shouted above the roar of the storm. "Tommy, you get the hose from the shed."

Another flash of blinding white light, and the tinder-dry pine needles and cones on the slope above the house erupted into a line of yellow-red flames and licked voraciously at the edge of the clearing.

Tommy turned the hose on; water just dribbled out.

"Forget the hose. Go get your mother," Carl called frantically. "I'm headed for the cabin."

Carl faced the wind-fed flames alone. The ever-building inferno crept up the slope towards the cabin.

I've gotta get to the cabin before the flames. "Tara, I'm coming!" he bellowed.

He charged towards the all-consuming flames. Terror ripped at his heart; the adrenaline surged through his body. Carl grabbed a shovel and beat his way into the spreading flames. Smoke and searing heat tore at his lungs as ashes and pieces of burning tree limbs crashed around him. He plunged on, blindly scraping his shins on logs and rocks. Blood trickled down his legs.

"She's gotta be in the cabin. Lord, please help me save my baby," Carl implored of the God he worshiped every day.

His powerful shoulder shattered the flimsy panels of the cabin door. It flew open with an ear-splitting crash–door, frame and trim flying everywhere.

"Tara! Tara!" Carl screamed above the thunder of the all-consuming flames outside.

"Daddy," a frightened little voice whimpered.

She's alive! Thank God.

Tara was huddled in the corner of the cabin, arms around herself, her eyes wide with terror. Carl snatched her up and charged out the doorway just as a flaming pine tree hit the roof. A flood of flame covered the grass and candled to the top of the trees. The way to the bottom of the slope was blocked.

For the first time, Carl felt death lapping at his heels.

"There's gotta be a way down. There's just gotta be," he screamed.

With his daughter held tightly in his arms, racing against time, Carl headed for the all-consuming wall of fire. A tree crashed down, opening up a path, and he stumbled through it. As he charged down the slope, he stubbed his toes on sharp rocks and burned his hands on red-hot branches. They both coughed and choked on the smoke.

Carl stumbled through the swirling wall of smoke into the yard, Tara clutched tightly in his arms.

Annie was waiting for them. "Tara, Tara my baby! Are you all right?" she screamed. Hot tears ran like rivers down her blackened soot-smudged face. "Tommy, get the hose."

"But there's no water pressure, mom. I'll have ta get water from the horse trough," Tommy shouted.

Carl slumped to the ground with Tara in his arms. Tommy ran up with a bucket and dumped water on them. It was cold, but it doused their singed and smouldering clothing.

Annie frantically grabbed Tara and held her close, stroking her hair.

"My baby! Thank God you're safe!"

"Let's get the hell out of here," Carl wildly shouted over the sound of the inferno.

"I'll get the dog, Dad," yelled Tommy. "Then we can harness the horses."

"We'd better saddle them as well. We might need to ride them later. Put the blindfolds over their heads—we don't want them to spook. We'll tether them to the truck and lead them to safety," Carl shouted above the roar of the firestorm.

As the two men raced towards the animals, a wailing siren pierced the air. Flashing lights bounced and twisted as fire trucks hurtled up the road towards the farm.

Quickly, the family piled into the truck with the little caravan of livestock in tow. They wound their way down the slope, dodging debris, and waved as the emergency crews passed.

"You okay?" Captain Scott shouted.

"Yeah, but watch out! It's pretty wild up there. We were lucky to get out with our lives," Carl said.

At the bend in the road, the family stopped and looked back at their home. The feared wildfire was well underway. A swirling inferno engulfed the barn and drive shed and licked dangerously at the roof of the house.

Carl put his arm around Annie. "It'll all be gone in a few minutes."

"We'll build again, Dad," Tommy said, trying to sound positive.

Tommy has become a man today. Guess he's not my little Tommy anymore.

"I hope so, Tom."

His son looked at him. "Tommy is still okay, Dad."

With a deafening roar the propane tanks in the barn exploded. A ball of flame shot skyward and plummeted toward the little group.

"Omigod! Move it!"

As the trees above them roared into flame, the Emmersons raced down the road.

"I can't breathe!" Tara screamed as the oxygen was sucked out of the air by the holocaust above them.

Her mother grabbed a cloth and soaked it with some of the precious bottled water in her bag. "Put this over your mouth and nose. It'll help."

Burning trees, crackling with flames fuelled by the dry bark, thundered to the ground and tumbled onto the road.

"Look out!" Carl shouted.

Another tree hit the road just in front of them. Annie screamed and grabbed Tara.

"Hold it," Carl said. "We've gotta find a way around that one. Better leave the truck. I'm glad we saddled the horses."

The saddles creaked, as they clambered aboard the restless animals.

"Over here, Dad!" Tommy hollered.

Choking and coughing, eyes watering and feet burning, the little troop worked their horses around the root end of the tree and plodded on. With the intense heat and overwhelming noise around them, controlling the horses became increasingly difficult.

"There's the lake." Tara pointed to a shimmering body of water off in the distance.

A water bomber screamed overhead as it unleashed its load behind the motley crew. The flames were doused.

"Thank God for that. Let's get to the lake!" Carl yelled.

Annie pointed back to the wall of flame ravenously devouring everything behind them. "Look back there, it's the Tronsens' house! And over there, the Peters' place…all gone."

"Sure hope they got out," Tommy said.

The road was clear now, and the Emmersons steadily threaded their way through the city streets towards the lake.

"Looks like the city's been evacuated…not a soul in sight. It's eerie, downright spooky," Tommy said.

A cat shot across the street and up the alley, behind the bookstore. Papers and dust swirled and kicked up a storm on the street. The smoke that hung like a black, ominous cloud over the buildings threatened to burst into flame and obliterate the city below.

"Look at that." Carl pointed at the reflection in the window of the bank. "Just like a mural in living colour."

"Up there!" Annie shouted.

The family turned and looked at their farm. The mountain behind them was engulfed in leaping, spitting flames.

"The farm's gone," Carl cried in dismay.

As Annie sobbed loudly, Carl put his arm around her.

Four horses, a dog, and the bedraggled family slogged on.

"I'm thirsty," Tara cried.

"In a minute, baby," Annie said. "It looks safe here, Carl. Can we stop for a rest and a drink?"

"Sure. Tommy, let's tie the horses to that tree. Annie, you and Tara head for that bench in the shade. Take the dog with you."

The men secured the horses to a tree, and the family, tired and bedraggled, dragged themselves to a bench on the street corner.

"Ahhh, this feels better. My bum's sore from that saddle," Tommy said.

Carefully, Carl opened a bottle of water and passed it around.

"Just a sip—we need to conserve this for later," Carl cautioned.

The peaceful silence of the street was shattered by an ear-splitting screech of metal on asphalt, and the fuselage of a water bomber careened past them, flames spewing out of the engine.

"What the—!" Carl shouted.

"Daddy!" Tara screamed.

Behind them, all hell broke loose. There was a blinding flash; an ear-crunching explosion, and the plane disintegrated. Just a pile of molten, flaming metal rested near the City's fire station.

"What was that?" Annie shrieked.

"It looks like the fuselage of an aircraft, but it can't be," Carl hollered back over the din.

Security officers appeared from nowhere and charged down the boulevard. A few shopkeepers, who'd stayed behind to protect their stores, chased after them. Before the Emmersons could get to the plane, emergency crews pumped foam on the burning wreckage.

"Where's the pilot?"

"Put more foam around the cockpit area." Questions and orders flew hot and heavy.

Paramedics pulled a gurney to the site, then first responders used the jaws-of-life on the cockpit. They managed to free the charred body of the pilot, a tragic fatality of the firestorm.

"Daddy, what happened?" Tara asked.

The terror on her face told the whole story. The scene of destruction and death was something this family would carry with them—forever.

"Looks like the pilot lost control of the plane, then tried to land on the boulevard."

The wind blew smoke from the wreckage over the onlookers. The acrid, putrid smell of burning plastic, mingled with that of the charred body of the pilot, assaulted their senses.

"Mommy, I'm gonna be sick." Tara leaned over and retched.

"Here, baby, drink some water," Annie soothed her daughter. "Carl, we gotta get the children out of here and down to the lake."

"Right! The emergency crews have things under control, and we can't help, now."

Beneath the umbrella of smoke, falling ashes, and hot embers, the sombre line picked its way through fire debris to the sandy shore and the sanctuary of the cool water.

They all took a dip in the lake. “Wow, the water’s cold, but it feels great,” Tommy shouted.

“When we dry off, I’ll look for shelter for the night. There’ll be emergency shelters somewhere around,” Carl assured his family. He decided to go back to the boulevard and talk to the security people. He had to find food and shelter and a place for the animals.

Carl looked up at the mountain. His heart sank as he saw the smouldering spot where their home had once stood. A plume of smoke rose as a depressing reminder. This was a picture that would play in the theatre of Carl’s mind forever.

It’s all gone … all gone.

The sound of Carl’s cell phone jolted him back to the present. “Hello?”

“Carl, it’s Mom. Are you safe? Is the fire anywhere near you? We’ve been watching the television news. We’re so worried.”

“Whoa, Mom, not so fast. We’re okay. The fire started at our house with a lightning strike and all hell broke loose. Everyone’s safe, but tired and dirty. We’re in town, and it’s been evacuated.”

“Is the town on fire?” his mother asked.

“Not yet, but it’s like a ghost town. I’m trying to find food and shelter for the family. I’ll call you when we’re settled somewhere.”

“Carl, don’t hang up. Your sister Liz is flying one of the water bombers. I know you and she haven’t talked for three years, but maybe, after all this is over, you’ll look for her.”

“Liz is here?” Carl asked. His chest felt tight.

“Yes. I’ll give you her cell phone number when you call me later. Your dad and I are praying for you and the family. Love you, son.”

“Love you, too, Mom. Say hello to Pop for me.”

Carl disconnected.

“Who was on the phone?” Annie asked.

“It was my mom. She wanted to be sure we’re safe. She also said my sister Liz is piloting one of those water bombers screaming overhead.”

As soon as the words left his lips, his thoughts flashed back to the black and mangled body of the dead pilot.

Please, no.

The look in his wife’s eyes told him she shared his fear and dread.

“Carl, we’d better find out who was piloting that plane.”

“I’ll head to the boulevard and talk to security—see if they’ve identified the pilot. I want to be sure it’s not …”

“I know, darlin’. I know.” Annie lovingly squeezed her husband’s hand.

"And maybe they can also tell me where the emergency centre is located and if there's a shelter for the animals."

Carl started to leave, then stopped, and turned back to the family. "You guys wait over there in the shade. If anyone comes along, ask about an emergency shelter. I'll phone you when I have news."

Carl headed for the boulevard. His cell phone buzzed, again. "Hello."

"Hi, big brother. It's Liz."

He let out a breath of relief. "Liz…" Tears welled up in his eyes as he tried to choke back the overwhelming emotions he felt. "I'm sorry," was all he could manage.

"It's okay, big brother. I talked to Mom. Just wanted you to know I'm safe. Glad you all are, too. Where are you now?"

"Downtown on the boulevard. I…I…" he stuttered. "I thought you were in…"

"Thankfully, I wasn't, so don't worry, big brother," she said softly. "But, what a tragedy—the pilot who crashed had a wife and two kids. He was a good friend of mine. But you take care, I'll call you again, as soon as I'm able. And Carl … I'm sorry too."

FOREST FIRE

Kelowna, 2003

Fern G.Z. Carr

Sooty wads of cotton batting cling to the sky
as cinder snowflakes f-l-u-t-t-e-r
in the searing summer heat;

layers of ash enshroud sidewalks,
patios, cars and lungs with their suffocating filth

like living in an ashtray,

and haze wafts indoors permeating everything
with its brimstone stench.

A red-orange hole punched in the sky
casts an eerie glow transforming neighborhoods
into rows of sinister jack-o'-lanterns.

Power outages, contaminated drinking water,
shifting smoke, erratic winds – there is no mercy.

Airplanes and helicopters douse the inferno
with water bombs and fire retardants
but the dragon is out of control
refusing
to be captured,
defying the brave who confront the beast.

Pets and necessities are crammed into U-hauls
while a stream of traffic descends the mountain

in silence

with thousands more on alert.

Night approaches and hell pulsates with malevolent fury

as the raging firestorm slashes the horizon.
Ravenous flames blast skyward
with unchained pyrotechnic violence –
homes explode flinging their blazing embers

into oblivion

leaving nothing but the masonry from defiant hearths;
fire respects fire – a cruel master.

Yet Kelowna's communities band together
despite the devastation,
despite the trauma,
in their struggle for survival
in what has now become
a war zone.

THE CHOKERMAN

Creative Nonfiction

Denise S. King

"I'm setting up a trailer in the Monashee," Dad says. "Just a fifteen-footer. That's all I need."

Mom points to an area on the North Okanagan map near Cherryville in the Monashee Mountains, her mouth tight, her eyes tired. She lifts her cup of coffee and drinks. Each week for the last six months, Mom has been driving Dad to various spots along the highway so he can dig up dirt, his test buckets he calls them. He's searching for "the spot."

We sit in Dad's TV room surrounded by memorabilia from his glory days. A photo of Dad with four of his buddies up at the Bull River, a six-point bull poised between them. In the corner is the gun case holding his prized gun collection: a double-barrel 12-gauge side-by-side, a 30-30 Smith and Wesson, a Savage 308, and a Cooey 22. There is a painting of Pillar Lake hanging above the 1910 Sumter wall phone, which sits atop the Ranney Golden Oak ice chest from 1925. Both items were from Pillar Lake, a fishing resort Mom and Dad owned forty years ago. Two shelves, one above the other, hold beer steins, shot glasses, spear heads, chunks of quartz, agate, and jade, and a container with three nuggets of gold, each marginally larger than a grain of sand. Three sets of glass eyes form a 'V' on the other wall, mounts of a bobcat, a lynx and a coyote. The bookcase holds *Mysteries of the Unexplained, Never Chop Your Rope, Lost Bonanzas of Western Canada, Herman*, and many placer mining books. The room is a showcase of his past.

Dad pushes himself out of his easy chair to an awkward stand. He shuffles to the table, looks at me, and points to the map. "You and me, we drove too far that day and started looking too late."

A couple months ago I took Dad in search of "the spot." Mom needed a break. I drove with Dad sitting beside me in his flannel, quilted jacket and jeans bunching around his shrinking body. I had to adjust the heat constantly to keep him warm. We took the Vernon-Slocan Highway from Vernon to Coldstream and past Cherryville. In the 1860s, prospectors from California came north to BC and set up camp. Dad is convinced there is more gold to be found in that area. As we wound through the Monashee, a logging truck passed, fully loaded.

Dad scoffed, "Those aren't logs. Those are twigs. We used to leave bigger stuff than that behind." He leaned forward and turned up the heat. "I was a damn good choke setter. Steep mountains, slick logs, it didn't matter. Just dug in hard," he said. "It'd be colder than piss on a plate, and there I am wrapping this steel cable around a log. A cable thick, like my arm. And a real log," he said. "Not like those. Those are twigs."

I grew up hearing all of these stories. Back then, his voice would fill the room, and he'd spread his arms wide, showing the breadth of the logs as he slung the cable, standing on wood greasy from the water streaming from the sky. Back then I was on the mountain too. Now his words are forced and his voice raspy from years of smoking.

He continued, "I had to climb underneath the bloody thing and scale it to get the cable up and over. The rigging slinger gave the signal to the hooker, and I got the hell out of the way." Dad gazed out the passenger window at the mountain.

When Mom and Dad were first together that was his job—a chokerman. Mom was born in Denmark and grew up on a wheat farm with farmhands and gardeners and a maid. She spent time working in Sicily as a housekeeper and then returned to Denmark to train as a nurse. Ever the wanderlust, she decided she wanted to see America. Travelling with her girlfriend, they landed in California, but made their way north to BC in search of something. Much like the prospectors. While working at the hospital in Chilliwack, she met her future mother-in-law who invited her over for dinner, and that's where she met Dad. Mom used to say, "He was unlike anyone I had ever met."

Now Dad lowers himself in the chair beside the table. He speaks slowly, deliberately. "Joel and I found the spot."

Joel is my older brother, and a week ago he took a turn driving Dad.

Mom says, "The spot is down a dirt road full of pot holes and boulders and fallen logs. Joel had to get out several times to move them out of the way. Way too steep for my car. You'd never get a trailer down there."

"I can and I will, Ragna," Dad says. "Remember Bliss Landing."

When I was a kid, every spring break while my best friend got to go to Hawaii, I went fishing up the Sunshine Coast. It was a long journey from Penticton. First over the Hope-Princeton to Horseshoe Bay, on the ferry to Langdale, then a winding drive to Earl's Cove, where we boarded a second ferry to Saltery Bay and then drove to Lund where Highway 101 ends. Dad's mom lived in a bay called Bliss Landing and most people accessed it by boat. Not us. The road we took from Lund to Bliss Landing was full of rock steps and the lane so narrow the brush scraped the side of the van.

Trucks with four-wheel drive were recommended, but Dad drove the van in and out of there.

"But Dad," I say, "that was a long time ago. And things are different."

"Exactly," Mom says, "Have you forgotten that you aren't allowed to drive?"

Dad glares at her. "I don't give a shit about that. No cops out there."

Last year Dad had his license revoked for medical reasons. It happened when he was in the hospital for a month getting the fluid around his lungs drained. The letter came in the mail once he was home. Mom called me and explained, "He wants to pay the $500 to get his license back, but the doctor won't even sign off on the paperwork that allows him to take the test."

He was lucky to have kept his license for as long as he had, given the previous strokes.

"No license, bah." Dad snorts.

Mom and I share a look. "What will you do for power?" I ask. I can see him in his 1980s van pulling an equally old trailer up the winding Monashee, the whole unit drifting over the centre line as he coughs up a ball of phlegm.

"Generator."

"And gas for the generator?"

"I'm getting one of those 500-gallon tanks. Should last me the winter."

I thought back to our drive up to the area and the other makeshift homes. Dad had no intention of purchasing the land. He'd be a squatter.

"So, you're really going to look for gold up there?"

"It's the spot." Dad scuffles over to his walker and wheels his way out of the room, down the hall to the bathroom.

Mom whispers, "I just can't go along with this one." She sips her coffee. "Look at all this stuff." Her eyes move around the room. "And in the shed. Tools he never uses. He won't part with anything." She rubs her eyes. "All he can talk about is going up the Monashee. All I want is for him to walk up to his shed and pack a box. Neither are realistic."

At eighty-four years of age, Mom is ready to live in town close to grocery stores and the hospital. She's ready to downsize to a small yard so she can spend her time going to Sovereign Lake for cross country skiing and to Swan Lake for her paddling practices for Dragon Boat racing. Mom joined a team called Keeping Abreast after she lost her breast to cancer.

Mom does everything in the house: grocery shopping, laundry, housework, cooking, and dishes; she takes care of the finances and books all the appointments. The only thing Dad does is sleep, eat, watch TV, and walk from his easy chair to the bathroom. When they drive to the Monashee area, Mom even digs up the dirt, puts it in the buckets, and loads them in the back of the van.

I'm not sure who I'm angrier with, Dad or Mom.

Mom continues, "I've had it up to here with his crazy schemes." She lifts her hand to her eyes. "If I think about it too much, I can't breathe."

Dad huffs back into the room, hovers over his walker until his breath catches up to him, and sits at the table.

Mom goes to the kitchen to get Dad's breakfast.

Maybe I can talk some sense into Dad. "What will you do with all your things in this room?" I ask.

"I'll build a deck the same size and put it all there," Dad says.

"Doesn't it rain a lot up there?"

"Trailers come with awnings. It'll be fine."

"What about the black water? You won't be able to pull the trailer out to take the sewage to a sani-dump."

"It don't matter out there. It can just go on the ground."

I press on with my questions, despite the look of disdain on his face. "And garbage? Surely there won't be garbage pick-up out there."

"Burn it."

He is smug. He's thought of everything.

"Are you going to hunt too?"

"Of course."

Mom comes in and sets a bowl in front of him. Puffed wheat and bran that's been soaking in warm milk topped with raisins.

We both leave so Dad can eat. He won't eat with us because he claims we natter too loudly, yet he sits in his room with the news cranked.

Mom and I have our rye bread and cheese and fruit salad in the dining room. Mom heaves a sigh. It's only 9:30 in the morning.

Mom and Dad have been married for fifty-four years, and they have done a lot of different things. Mom liked owning Pillar Lake Resort the best. She would have stayed there, but they sold because there were a couple of car accidents on the road bordering the lake and people died. Dad couldn't stay there. He always said, "I keep imagining those bodies in the water. Can't shake it." They bought the fruit stand and orchard, but grew tired of working so hard for so little. With those businesses, they were both invested and they both worked hard. When they moved to Trout Lake, Mom took a job in extended care in the hospital, while Dad sat at home dreaming up money-making schemes. He was convinced there was a quicker, easier way to make a good living.

First there was the investment in a rabbit farm in Nova Scotia with a buddy of his. "A sure thing. Rabbit fur," he said at the time. "And rabbit's feet. People are stupid enough to think those feet are lucky. Not for the rabbit." He'd laugh.

I'd cringe. Poor rabbits.

I don't know how much money they lost in that deal, but Dad was determined to earn it back, so he tried counting cards in Reno. He began teaching himself. For weeks he studied a book and played cards with himself. When he was ready, he packed his bag and his $5,000, and got on a plane.

His belief in the card-counting system was infectious. "How can I lose?" he'd say while we sat at the table.

I watched and listened as he won hand after hand.

"It's just math," he said, "and memory."

Dad returned from Reno a week later and said, "I got some good tips on the stock market. That's where the real money is."

So began the pages and pages of recording stocks. For months, he tracked everything from penny stocks to pigs to wheat to gold to determine the pattern. Every morning he watched the news and noted down the stocks. When he'd correctly predict a raise in the stock, he would jump up and do a little dance and the drinks would begin.

Then there was the peanut farm in Costa Rica. At least Mom got a nice holiday out of that trip. Finally, he settled into making his own biodegradable soap. He used himself as a test subject for the soap, washing his hair with it, brushing his teeth. Mom washed clothes with it and used it for dishes. That soap product took up many years of his life. It was hard not to believe in him. His sense of the rising trend for environmentally friendly products was spot on, but competition in the soap market is tough and there was only so much money for investing.

In the late afternoon, the smell of spaghetti sauce fills the house.

"Go visit with your dad," Mom says as she hands me a glass of red wine.

I take it into Dad's room where he sits at the table studying the map. It's quiet in the room with the TV on mute.

I settle in at the table. "Getting hungry?"

He grunts, his focus not straying from the map.

"You know, Dad…" I start to say, but then he points at the map.

"This is it. I am sure of it." He leans back in his chair and rubs his hands together, his eyes bright. From beside his chair he brings up a Pilsner. "Keller Koldt," he says. "Tastes like piss but don't hurt my teeth." He takes a drink and sighs. "Used to need it ice cold. Not now." He clasps his hands over his stomach and says, "See, in the trailer I won't need to take up space in the fridge with beer."

"I suppose so," I say.

"Everything will be close. Even the shitter is just a few steps away."

I sip my wine.

After supper, Mom and I clean up. Mom goes into Dad's room and gets his plate. She sets it with a clatter on the counter. "If he would even just bring his plate into the kitchen," she says. "I don't understand why he can't just do that." Mom glances at the clock and looks into Dad's room. "He'll be heading to bed soon. I need to turn on his electric blanket and put out his pills."

She bustles off and I stand in the kitchen shaking my head. Dad may be the chokerman, but Mom gives him the rope.

OH DEER

Fern G.Z. Carr

September breezes nudge
arthritic arms of gnarled trees
against their will

Oh dear. Oh dear.

when branches capriciously caper away
prancing to their own primal rhythms
retreating from their arboreal camouflage

Oh dear. Oh dear.

atop the head of a swaggering Whitetail buck
in his once-familiar territory
on an anonymous Okanagan mountain

Oh dear. Oh deer.

where urban encroachment now bullies
forest ecosystems into involuntary
juxtaposition

Oh dear. Oh deer.

with monsters who mow *his* grass, sculpt *his* shrubs
and shine their headlights into *his* startled eyes
while he remains transfixed.

Oh deer. Oh deer.

THE SALMON RUN

Nonfiction

Sylvia H. Olson

BC may be known for its fitness craze, but we also have the salmon run. No, they don't have legs, as one CBC comedian from Toronto joked. It is a bit like an Olympic event, as it occurs every four years and looks like an enormous swim meet. There are smaller runs every year, but the big run every fourth year is known as the dominant year. More than two million salmon swim upstream to the rivers where they were hatched. It's an event that draws millions of visitors to BC during the month of October. During this time of year, the river is streaming with salmon, the trails are crowded with kids, and the parking lots are filled with cars and tour buses. This phenomenon draws visitors from as far away as Japan.

The salmon who survive the arduous swim upstream from the ocean lay their eggs in interior rivers, then slowly die. The eggs hatch, and the small fry grow to become smolts. They make their way back out to the Pacific Ocean, and in four years the cycle begins again. BC school children learn the life cycle of a salmon in the earliest grades and go on field trips in dominant years. In my area of Kamloops, the largest run is at the Roderick Haig-Brown Provincial Park at the Adams River, which runs into Shuswap Lake.

As an elementary teacher, I've visited the Adams River site with my classes many times. We usually book the buses for the beginning of the run in early October. Waiting till the end of the month could result in a very smelly field trip as many of the dead fish pile up along the shore. The students are always fascinated by the sight of millions of red spawning salmon covering the shallow river bottom. It's an awesome sight to walk the trails along the river's edge and see such a vast number of fish laying their eggs in the rocky nests. Wildlife Conservation Officers are always on hand to answer questions during the run. The area is festive, with many tents displaying the salmon life cycle as well as information on the flora and fauna of the trails.

One year, my class of eight-year-olds was all prepped and excited to go. We had completed the salmonid science unit, and they had learned about the different kinds of salmon: sockeye, coho, pink, and chinook. Some species of salmon look bigger than others and some differ in colour as well. Our area is home to the sockeye salmon, which turn bright red during the spawning season. The males are easily identified by their bright green heads and hooked beaks.

Each student was counted as they left the bus and placed in a group with a parent supervisor, then off they went to see their classroom lessons come to life. As we rounded the second bend of the river, we saw lots of children from other schools gathered all along the river bed. The trails were full of adult visitors as well. It was a busy place.

All of a sudden we heard a boy yell, “A SHARK, A SHARK!” Within seconds everyone ran in that direction. Chaos ensued. Even the adults went to see what was going on. When I arrived at the spot, I realized it was one of *my* students who was yelling “shark.” A conservation officer explained to the crowd that my student had spotted a stray coho salmon, and slowly the crowd dispersed. Then he asked the student for his teacher. I stepped forward and the officer gave me a disapproving look. He gave us both a short lecture on the difference between sharks and salmon.

My student was sent back to join his group, and then the officer asked me, “Don’t you teach this stuff in school?”

“Yes of course,” I answered, “But that was my new student. He just arrived yesterday from Saskatchewan.”

Sockeye Salmon, Adams River, photo © Murphy Shewchuk

MYRA CANYON

Fern G.Z. Carr

With a compulsive need
to discover glimpses
of breathtaking scenery,
we coaxed the car
to fight gravity
as it trundled up
a one-lane service road
to the Myra Canyon trestles

until we were *startled*
from our reverie

by the onslaught
of tortuous curves,
sheer drops,
and the slickness
of our snow-glazed path.

No winter tires,
no chains,
no spot w - i - d - e enough
to turn around
and head back.

We climbed.
Our hearts sank –

visions of sliding off
a precipice
plummeting
into the muffled silence
of a snowy ravine

undiscovered
until the spring thaw.

SWEET DREAMS

Fiction

Cheryl Kaye Tardif

I always hated camping—the strange lurking noises in the woods, the bloodsucking mosquitoes that voraciously drilled for blood, *the thin canvas of a tent that could be so easily slashed by a bear.* Then there were the shadows, pervasive and malignant, hovering in every corner. Of course, peeing in the woods wasn't my idea of a good time either.

When Justin, my husband, decided we were going on a camping trip with three other couples, I groaned and whined like a petulant child. But I knew that I couldn't escape fate. So reluctantly I packed up our tents, sleeping bags and Coleman coolers filled with more beer than food. Then we headed for Hunakwa Lake in BC's Shuswap region.

Justin told me that Hunakwa meant "echo" in the Secwepemc language.

During the monotonous drive, our newest friends, Margie and Burton, were ensnared in a deadly lip-lock. After ten minutes, I avoided glancing over my shoulder and decided that they just weren't interested in the antique store we passed. Or the three elk grazing in the ditch. And Margie and Burton certainly didn't give a hoot about the dead skunk lying in the middle of the road.

For a fraction of a second I thought about interrupting their spit-swapping contest.

Instead, I slept.

It was pitch black when we arrived at Hunakwa Lake. Carol, my dearest friend who was already on to her third husband, Fabio, had arrived an hour ahead of us. Fabio, the *Italian Stallion* with long black hair, was busy chopping wood. I caught a glimmer of his axe illuminated by the light of five lanterns. A small fire crackled and sputtered off to one side where Carol had arranged some folding chairs.

I confiscated a chair and sat down.

"Fabio's making stew for supper," Carol called out.

Justin approached, his new sapphire earring sparkling in the left ear. "Wanna beer, Lexie?"

Every word he said echoed in my head, and I shook my head. I was feeling fuzzy enough without any alcohol.

"We'll be back in half an hour," Burton said with a wink. "Gonna test the temperature of the water." His grinning mouth returned to suck the air out of Margie. Strangely, she didn't seem to mind.

I pictured them skinny-dipping in the mist-shrouded lake. Yuck! So much for spending the weekend swimming.

A van lurched to a stop by our car. Dylan Hunt and his latest acquisition, Blonde Bimbo, got out. Okay, I'll admit that's not her real name, but that's what we called her. The woman's name kept changing along with her face, but Dylan, my husband's boss, always managed to find a replacement that was unbelievably dumber than the last.

"Blonde Bimbo's going to break her ankle," Carol snorted in my ear.

We stared at the woman who thought three-inch spiked heels were a trendy fashion statement while camping in the woods.

"Dyl, honey, can you get me some wine?" Blonde Bimbo simpered. She stumbled toward a padded chair. "I'm parched."

Dyl, honey immediately stopped setting up their tent and pulled out a bottle of wine from a cooler. He passed the woman the wine and a corkscrew, and Carol and I had to look away for fear we'd burst out laughing when the woman stared, uncomprehending, at the alien metal object. When we glanced back, Blonde Bimbo was trying to hammer the corkscrew through the metal wrapper.

Carol nudged me with her elbow. "Now isn't *she* a keeper?"

Snickering quietly, I grabbed two flashlights and whispered, "I have to pee."

When Carol looked at me with that *Why are you telling me?* look, I shoved a flashlight into her hand. "You're coming with me. I'm not going into these spooky old woods alone. God only knows what's lurking out there."

"*Woooooooo*," Carol moaned, doing an Academy Award-winning ghost impression.

It freaked the hell out of me.

Peering behind us as we followed a trail, I watched Justin toss a log on the fire and then sit down next to Blonde Bimbo. He was laughing at something the woman had said. My fingers curled reflexively as the wildcat in me scratched to the surface.

"Oh, Lexie," my best friend said, patting my shoulder. "Don't worry about *her*. Justin isn't interested in airheads."

Swallowing hard, I realized Carol was right. Justin and I had been married for six years. Our marriage was strong. Wasn't it?

"Go pee." Carol pointed to a tall cedar. She sat down on a tree stump. "I'll wait for you."

I disappeared around the wide trunk of the cedar, wedged my flashlight between some branches and squatted, praying to God that I wouldn't topple over. Although my bladder was full, I couldn't seem to relax enough to do anything.

Come on. Pee, dammit!

"So tell me more about Margie and Ben," Carol hollered after a minute.

"Burton," I corrected.

"So?"

"Margie and Burton moved in down the road. Two months ago. They're nice enough people."

I heard Carol grunt. "Yeah, for a couple of leeches."

I laughed. "You should have been in the car for the ride up here. You wouldn't have been able to pry them apart with a crowbar. They were stuck together like Crazy Glue. I haven't seen anything like it since high school. And when they did come up for air—which was maybe once—they whispered stuff to each other like, 'You're the one, baby' and 'It's all for you, lover.' Oh my God! You should have been there, Carol."

"I'm so glad I wasn't. Now tell me, what's with all the ass-kissing between Justin and the head honcho?"

"Justin thinks it's his *job* to impress Dylan," I muttered. "I mean, Justin is a great employee. He works late, fills in when Dylan asks and then invites the big boss to come *camping* with us. And then he makes me find two other unfortunate couples to beg to come with us." I flinched. "Sorry about that."

When my friend didn't answer, I realized she was probably miffed at me. I had led her to believe that the camping trip was more for the four of us—that Dylan, Blonde Bimbo, Margie and Burton were just last-minute add-ons.

"I know you would have preferred—" A sudden rush of hot liquid poured onto the ground. When it veered off and began trickling down my right leg, I swore. "Oh, crap! I just peed on myself, Carol. Now I'm going to have to change my jeans. Who the hell decided to go camping anyway?" Without waiting for an answer, I let out a huff. "Oh, yeah. It was my darling husband."

Justin, I'm gonna kill ya!

"I mean, it was Justin's bright idea to come out here. I personally can't wait until the weekend is over. No offense, Carol. I really would have loved to have done something with just you and Fabio. You've been married for two weeks, and I haven't exchanged a simple conversation with Fabio. In fact, let's make plans to do something next weekend—just the four of us."

Silence greeted me.

"What do you think?" I called out.

The only response I got was the nervous chattering from invisible night birds that perched somewhere overhead.

Digging into my pocket for some tissue, I came up empty. *Some kind of camper I was!* Embarrassed, I hung my head, even though no one could see me. "Carol? I need some toilet paper. Did you bring some?"

Carol didn't answer. Was she pissed off?

"Okay, this isn't funny," I whined. "I need some paper – Kleenex – anything."

Something crackled in the bushes to my left. When I turned sharply, I lost my balance and one hand slid into the soil. The ground was damp and warm. Fresh pee does that.

"Shit!" Well, technically it was urine, but *shit* is what I muttered. "Carol?"

My friend was gone. She had left me stranded, alone in the heart-gripping darkness. I hastily pulled up my jeans, feeling a cold patch on the inside left thigh. Cursing under my breath, I stepped out onto the path.

Snnap!

In the dead calm of night the snapping branch sounded like a gunshot echoing in the air.

I moved cautiously along the path.

Crrraack!

Abruptly, the night birds stopped twittering. That's when I knew that something was coming for me. I could *feel* it.

A golden glimmer of light trickled through the trees and wound its way between and around the thick dense brush. As the light sinuously surrounded thick tree trunks and lush branches, every leaf and flower fell to the forest ground.

My heart pounded as the light moved closer, caressing the tree behind me. Frozen with fear, I held my breath and waited for the light to disintegrate my skin, but the eerie glow vanished as quickly as it had appeared. It was maybe fifteen minutes before I could make my legs stop trembling and force them to move forward. Carol wasn't going to be forgiven for leaving me behind. Not for a long while. And if I ever found out that it was Justin or one of the others out there with a flashlight…

When I reached the campsite, I stared in disbelief. Everyone was gone. The vehicles were parked by the side, the tents were pitched a few yards from the fire, and the chairs were empty. Fabio's axe glistened when my flashlight cut a path across its blade. It lay abandoned in the grass. Justin's beer can was jammed into the chair's cup holder. The tab hadn't even been pulled. Carol's sweater lay on the ground, trampled with dirt, moss and wine.

My stomach heaved and I struggled for air. "Justin?"

The only reply I heard was the oversized cooking pot boiling over. Carol had said Fabio was making stew. I peeked under the lid, partly from curiosity and partly to let the steam vent.

That's when I saw it.

At the surface of the meaty stew, a sapphire earring sparkled—still attached to Justin's ear.

"Juuuuustiiiiin!" I shrieked, feeling the air rush from my lungs. I fainted and hit the ground, hard.

I awoke abruptly as the air around me lurched to a stop. Opening my eyes, I realized I was in the car. Justin was driving, and it was pitch black outside.

"Sweet dreams?" he whispered with a smile, his earring dancing in the moonlight.

I smiled. "They are now." Relieved, I closed my eyes again. It had all been a nasty dream. My heart settled into a happy pitter-patter.

"We're here," he said a moment later.

A light flickered over a wood-carved sign. *Hunakwa Lake.*

Our campground was an identical echo of my dream. Carol, my dearest friend, greeted me at the campsite. When I saw Fabio, the *Italian Stallion* with long black hair, busily chopping wood, I gasped. I caught a glimmer of his axe, illuminated by the light of five lanterns. A small fire crackled and sputtered off to one side where Carol arranged some folding chairs.

It was all too familiar, and my heart dropped into the pit of my stomach. Confused and disoriented, I confiscated a chair and sat down. *What the fu—?*

"Wanna beer?" Justin asked, interrupting my thoughts.

I shook my head. I was feeling fuzzy enough without any alcohol.

"Gonna test the temperature of the water," Burton said with a wink. His grinning mouth returned to suck the air out of Margie. Strangely, she didn't seem to mind.

"We'll be back in half an hour," Margie called out.

Fabio's eyes narrowed as he watched them, and he licked his lips. "I'll get some wild game for a stew." He walked off toward the lake, the axe slicing through the air with each step.

Catching a glimmer of golden light swirling around Fabio's axe, I shivered. A ripple, some kind of déjà vu or simply an echo in time and space had already shown me how this would end at Hunakwa Lake.

"Echo Lake," I whispered, awaiting my inescapable fate … *my destiny*.

VISITORS TO OUR NEW SUBURBAN LOT

Kelowna, 2005

Dianne Hildebrand

They stood in a horrified row on the sidewalk
faces ranging from sober to alarmed
Gazing at us, their own flesh and blood
Heedless perpetrators of urban sprawl

No use trying to paper over
the horizontal tangle
Of giant Ponderosa pines
Which filled the pit of our new lot
Futile to deny the screech of the wood chipper
And the howl of the chainsaw, which echoed silently
Even after we hastily turned them off

We should build a small straw bale house
With geothermic heating, and R4000 everything
On a downtown infill lot
Or buy a camper van and tour about doing original things
Or just live somewhere cheap and green
and walk everywhere

And we thought about those things
tossed them around
Briefly in the late evenings as we sat
Night after night exhausted
Trying to make sense out of our lives

No doubt we are
Contributing to the greenhouse and every other
Negative effect
In spite of all our prayers and dreams
We don't seem to know
What else to do

NATURE'S PRECIOUS GIFT

Nonfiction

Shirley Bigelow DeKelver

It was late and we were exhausted. We had left Calgary after work, eventually arriving at the turn-off to our cabin at White Lake, a few miles west of Salmon Arm. We drove up the dirt driveway leading to the backyard, our headlights slicing through the darkness, highlighting the silhouettes of the huge cedars, hemlocks, and firs. The cabin came into view, and we noticed the yard was buried under waist-high grasses and thistles. A light fog drifted through the underbrush, creating an ethereal ambiance.

All of a sudden, a doe, lying hidden in the shadows, jumped up and stepped into the path of our car. Don slammed on the brakes. For a few seconds, the startled deer stared into our headlights, then she veered sharply and disappeared into the trees. Thankful she was not injured, we drove the last few feet to the cabin, unpacked the cars, and went to bed.

The next morning, before anyone in the house had stirred, I went outside to enjoy the panoramic view of White Lake and Queest Mountain, which rose loftily in the background. Our porch, located on the second floor, looks directly down onto our front yard. Out of the corner of my eye, I noticed a movement in a pile of logs and dead-fall. At first I couldn't *s*ee anything but dense foliage, but a slight disparity in the shape of the undergrowth made me peer closer. A young fawn was watching my every movement! It was so well camouflaged I had not noticed it. When the rest of the family awoke, I quietly showed them my discovery. The doe we had startled the night before was more than likely the mother, and was probably somewhere in the vicinity.

Throughout the day, we pulled the thistles and mowed the grass in the backyard, which helped to relieve the incessant horde of insects pestering anyone venturing outside. At the top of the lot close to the tree line, we discovered a bowl-shaped cavity. There was a good possibility the young fawn had been born on our lot, and we had found the doe's nest. If the mother was observing our movements, we assumed she would eventually come out and tend to her baby.

But that was not to be the case. The temperature soared into the high thirties, and for three anxious days, we kept a worried vigil. There was no sign of the mother. How long could the fawn survive without her protection and nourishment? I recalled reading an article about animals implanting on humans, which was enough of a deterrent for us to not interfere or touch the abandoned baby.

To keep my granddaughters occupied, although they would have been perfectly happy sitting on the porch watching the fawn, we took them to Herald Beach to swim in the tepid waters of Shuswap Lake, and as a reprieve from the intense heat, we hiked down the canyon path leading to Margaret Falls.

Whenever we returned to the cabin, we spotted the fawn hidden in the dead-fall. There was no sign of the missing mother. We were not sure how long it could survive, and we worried about its well-being. The long weekend went by far too quickly, and we were returning to Calgary the next day. I wondered if I should contact the closest wildlife centre and ask them for advice. Before going to bed that night, I decided I would call first thing in the morning.

As was my routine, the next morning I rose early. I was staring out the kitchen window when I spotted a deer lying in the nest we had discovered earlier. She didn't seem to be in distress.

After what seemed an interminable amount of time, she stood, entered the forest, and walked cautiously through the underbrush bordering our lot, until she arrived at a huge cedar. I was not sure how the fawn knew, but there must have been an unspoken bond between them as it leapt up and raced straight toward her. The doe sniffed her baby, gently butted it a few times, and turned so that it could nurse.

By now everyone in the household was up. Six happy faces gawking out of the kitchen and dining room windows did not seem to concern the doe. Although she was attentive to the fawn, she continued to stare into the trees. We presumed she was watching for any unexpected danger that could cause potential harm to her baby.

We were completely unprepared as to what happened next. We watched in disbelief when a second fawn emerged. Not only had we been unaware of its existence, it had been concealed so well in the trees and undergrowth, we had not detected it or noticed any movement in all the time it was there.

The second baby was smaller than its twin. It shakily approached the mother, who greeted it in the same fashion as she had her first baby, and soon it too was feeding hungrily.

Over the years, we often thought about the doe and her little family. Why did she hide her babies so close to the house? Maybe a larger animal was in the area and was a threat to her defenseless offspring. Or was she training them to survive on their own? We like to think she returned to feed them while we were away during the day, or while we were sleeping, leaving them there for safekeeping. We can only be thankful that matters turned out as well as they did.

Years later, my husband and I retired and moved to White Lake. Deer, bears, wolves, coyotes, and other wild animals often walk through our lot on their way back from the lake.

Last year in late June, I spotted a doe in the backyard. I recognized her, so I kept a watchful eye as I thought she might try to eat the flowers growing next to the house. She stood rigidly for the longest time, then she cautiously walked towards our garden. We have a deer fence surrounding it, and knowing that deer do not like it touching their skin, I realized this was not normal behaviour. Something was wrong. She was agitated, and suddenly I realized why. She had a fawn, and it had wandered into the garden and had somehow become tangled in the deer fence. Anxiously, I watched as it struggled, and sighed in relief when it eventually freed itself. Unfortunately, it was inside the perimeter of the garden and could not find its way out. I called Don, and by the time he arrived in the kitchen, the fawn was nowhere in sight. Luckily, I had watched as it had tottered into the tomato plants, and knew it was hiding in the leaves.

Don went outside and stood on the porch. The mother watched him, then turned and looked at the garden. He walked down the steps, then slowly headed towards the garden, all the while keeping a close watch on the doe. He found the baby huddled under the leaves, then he picked it up and carried it out. The mother backed up and headed towards the trees, staying visible, never taking her eyes off the fawn. Don laid the baby in the grass at a spot next to the garden and closer to the tree line. He thought it could not have been very old as it was quite small and weighed no more than five or six pounds.

It took the doe close to three hours to work her way over to her baby. During all this time, the fawn remained motionless, never once lifting its head. Although it was quite young, the mother had trained it well. We were relieved when she accepted the baby without hesitation.

Deer often return to where they were born, and I like to think we have a trusting rapport with the deer that frequent our lot. At times they frustrate us when they eat our flowers, vegetables or fruit, but they will always be welcome.

THOMPSON & NICOLA VALLEYS

Balance Rock, Kamloops Lake, BC. © Murphy Shewchuk

THOMPSON – NICOLA

The Thompson – Nicola region, a rugged and diverse area of BC extending from the Fraser Canyon in the west through the Shuswap in the east, is part of the vast Thompson Okanagan region. The Cascade Mountain Range extends northward from northern California to the confluence of the Thompson and Nicola rivers at Lytton. The northern part of the range reaches to Lytton Mountain.

The Thompson and Nicola Valleys are surrounded by the massive Monashee and Cariboo Mountain Ranges. Within Wells Gray Park, near Clearwater, there are wondrous high mountains, deep canyons, volcanic cones, old-growth forests, and white-water rivers.

The region has numerous beautiful provincial parks, including Wells Gray, Shuswap, Mount Robson and Monck. Wells Gray Provincial Park has many waterfalls, but Helmcken Falls, at 141 metres (463 feet), three times the height of Niagara Falls, vies for the title of BC's greatest.

The native Nicola Valley tribe, as well as the Nlaka'pamux Nation tribe of the Thompson and Stl'atl'imc of Lillooet area, and more, travel to and also host the colourful and lively Powwow. This includes dancing in traditional regalia and singing. Powwow singers are very important figures. Without them there would be no dancing. The songs are of many varieties, from religious to war to social. This is a great event for all to enjoy.

Cities and municipalities in the Thompson – Nicola region include Kamloops, Merritt, Chase, Clearwater, Logan Lake, Barriere, Ashcroft, Cache Creek, Clinton, and Lytton.

D.F. Barrett

NICOLA WIND SURFERS

Howard Baker

Merritt, BC

…for Howard Williams

We all hang up sails and
Venture onto an unfamiliar element,
Courting a wind that may
Pull us for a time.

We choose our courses and
Look for a path with no markings,
Hoping to skim like beads
Tipped down a mirror.

We all have our afternoon chances to
Unlock a treasure of rainbow-gold droplets,
Slicing brave trails that the ripples
Promptly cover.

Some sail home, some paddle home,
But all of us return to shore,
Admitting that at sunset there is only memory left,
A day's fading record of how we dared, fell,
And climbed back up;
Only a map written on water,
Read and read again by those who love us the most.

THE SILENCE OF THE FOREST

A personal narrative

Keith Dixon

Anxiety gnaws at the beauty of the valley. I follow highway 5A as it winds its way amongst the mirror lakes of the Nicola Valley, north from Merritt.

"Get gas before heading up in the mountains to the monastery," I was warned. The smooth faces of the nude grey hills are marred by wrinkles. Traffic is sparse. I feel alone. I love that feeling, but I fear it at the same time. I am heading into mountain wilderness trusting totally on my van to get me there and back. What if I have a flat tire? What if I careen off the road on one of these sharp curves?

The barren beauty fascinates me, and I think of taking photos. But I must keep moving. Anxiety urges me on. I am an old man alone in a converted Dodge Caravan with a power chair in back and crutches nestled beside me. Winter snow is just ahead. An accident waiting to happen. Sure, I have travelled the world alone, but always surrounded by people. Now I head into the wilderness alone … really alone. If I get in trouble, how long will it be before anyone even notices?

The sign reads Roche Lake Road. That is my turnoff. The monastery lies fifteen kilometres up in the mountains from that intersection. Gravel winding road. Mud holes big enough to bathe a moose. Steep inclines. Rare signs of human habitation. Am I crazy to keep going?

Canadian-born Abbot Ajahn Sona had made it sound so tempting to visit his forest monastery during his talk in Penticton last month. Silence and simplicity intrigued me. I had studied under Tibetan lamas for many years and had visited Buddhist temples in New York State, France, India, Nepal, and Tibet.

Berkin monastery belongs to a different tradition than the familiar Tibetan Mahayana monks and lamas. At the Berkin monastery, I am entering a Theravada realm. They follow the same Buddha but choose unique rituals and practices. That fascinates me. The mountains and forest fascinate me. The lure of stillness fascinates me.

Why am I so anxious?

I arrive at a parking lot. My anxiety eases. Avoiding puddles, I walk across a courtyard to a large brown building and struggle up a flight of wooden steps to the front door. I knock. A young Asian woman opens the door, greets me warmly, and identifies herself as Delani. She asks if I would like a tour before settling in my room. I fear impossible steps and stairs. Delani has read about my disability in my emails.

My room, just down the hall, has an enormous window which lets in the afternoon sun. Outside is the courtyard. Beyond that are aspens and spruce as far as the eye can see. Bamboo roll-up screens provide room dividers. A single bed has a foam mattress and a stack of bedding. Blankets for making up your own bed. A broom and dustpan stand in a corner. Delani explains all this, checking anxiously to see if I am okay with each expectation. No roommate. It already feels like my very own room.

Down the hall is the shrine room, called the *sala*. It is enormous. A life-size white Buddha sits on a high platform at the middle of a wall-size window. Out the window is dense forest. The Buddha meditates in the silent forest. This feels exactly like what I have come to explore.

Outside, an array of solar panels collects energy. The building has just one wood stove. The rest of the heat comes through large windows, open during the day and shuttered tight at night. All lights in hallways and stairs are linked to motion detectors. TVs, radios, cell phones and computers are banned because retreats are all about experiencing silence. Nirvana is clearly a location off the grid. This eco-technology is distracting. I need to focus on just being present.

Back in the sala, the floor appears to be concrete slabs polished so highly that with a coat of glossy black paint they reflect like a mirror. They are so beautiful I hesitate to walk on them. Delani wears just socks on her feet, and doesn't seem the least perturbed that I am violating the "No shoes" sign at the entrance. She tells me the Abbot has waived that rule for me. Walking with shoes while everyone else walks barefoot gives me mixed feelings. For 65 years I have been "different" and do not enjoy it being made more obvious. On the other hand, no one seems to notice. Each one is absorbed in his own silence.

Guests routinely join the staff for kitchen and cleanup duties. Delani broaches the subject of meals and chores and asks me what I want to do. The monastery is built in a most inhospitable way for those who have trouble with steps. She suggests that I can stay exclusively on the main floor and she will carry up my meals. I would be excused from chores.

Before making a decision, I ask to see the stairs. Good sturdy railings on the flight of stairs to the kitchen encourage me. I can manage them. The lower flight, to the dining room make descending possible, but there is no left hand railing for getting back up. I ask Delani if there is an external exit from the dining room floor. She says there is, but looks dubious. At tea time we finally go down to the lowest level. I find the Abbot has posted a sign on the exit saying "Do not use this door." Delani ignores the no exit rule, so I pretend I don't notice it either. I walk up an outside path leading to the main floor. Problem solved.

In the dining room, benches are built into the wall on three sides. Individual slabs can be pulled from the benches to hold food or books. Traditional raised cushions for the monastics are at the centre of the room. At tea time (5 pm), we make our own tea and think up questions to ask the Abbot. His answers are lengthy, so we do not get through many questions. He speaks of playfulness blossoming from living in the moment. Here deep thoughts are always counterbalanced with laughter. I am surprised but also relieved. I relish both silence and laughter.

I suspect that Delani's regular job is to manage the office. I have become an extra duty. There are two meals a day. Breakfast at 7 am and lunch at 11:30 am. Both are hearty meals. Vegetarian, in keeping with Theravada tradition. Self-serve is normal practice, but Delani is at my side offering to help if I want it. Meals are taken in silence, with no socializing. Eating is considered a meditation practice. Delani offers me the use of the solarium beside the kitchen as my eating space. She brings a folding table and an over-flowing plate from the buffet table and joins me, silently, for most meals. Another staff person sometimes joins us.

A dozen lay people are present for the weekend. Some notice that I have accessibility problems and ask if they can help. I decide that this offer could solve my problem with the stairs to the dining room. I suggest to Delani that I need two sturdy volunteers. She comes back with two guys who lift me bodily up the stairs. I could get used to indulgences like this.

Delani asks me if I want to book an interview with the Abbot. She explains that it is informal. One space is available Sunday afternoon. Tibetan lamas grant personal interviews routinely. Is it the same here?

Other interviews I had were always formal. Questions about meditation practice. Requests for guidance. And always the white envelope with a gift of money to be left behind. I ask Delani about Theravada protocol. She fills me in. Interviews are very informal. Any topic is fair game. And no, they don't use the white envelope, except as one leaves the monastery. They have no fees for anything. They function solely on volunteer labour and freely given gifts (*dana*). I am eager to meet this Abbot who has created an amazing sharing community.

I spend half an hour with Ajhan Sola Sunday afternoon. I have no idea what I will say to him and start by telling him that I knew intuitively at the end of his talk in Penticton that I had to visit his monastery. I tell him about my years of involvement with Tibetan Buddhists, and I even whine a bit about how their fight over selecting the true reincarnated Karmapa had soured me.

Theravada teachers aren't strong on reincarnation. Ajhan Sola promptly makes a joke about it. In the playground of life, reincarnation is not a big thing with him. It doesn't matter one way or another to him if others choose to embrace that belief. It is just another playground game. He doesn't take games very seriously, though he admits they are an essential ingredient for living a full life. We ramble on into overtime, and he makes no move to end the interview. I know someone is waiting outside the door for his turn, so finally I thank Ajhan Sola and leave. I smile a bit sheepishly at the guy outside the door as I pass him.

On Monday, I have my noon meal then leave right after cleanup duty. On arrival at Berkin, Delani showed me how to label my tea mug. It then sat on a plate and bowl on a kitchen shelf with "Keith" written on a green sticker. Everyone did the same.

After I have eaten lunch, I peel my name off the mug I have used all weekend. Delani comments, "It is always a sad time when it comes to taking off the green name tags." It is. I suddenly feel the sadness of leaving, and it feels more intense than most farewells. She smiles. She understands those sad things about a silent retreat and is pleased that I am experiencing them.

A bit later, when I am back down in the Nicola valley, I am struck by the beauty of the landscape. Hay bales stacked with geometric precision. White swans preening themselves in puddles of sky. Flashes of incandescent yellow leaves reflecting in Nicola Lake. These things and more pull me to stop…to record their colour and breath-taking stillness. It doesn't dawn on me until I get home and reflect on what has happened to me at the retreat that I am in a state of heightened awareness. Colours are more vivid. Sounds are more intense. Heat and coldness are more immediate. Feelings flow more quickly. Those things are the result of living the silence of the forest. The monastics see them simply as pleasurable side effects. For them, this sharpening of the senses is just training the mind to notice subtle ways the universe changes and works.

But I am happy with just the side effects.

'53 INDIAN

Chris Kempling

She was black
The colour God intended
Eighty cubes of snarling steel
A throaty rumble burbling
From fishtail pipes
Deep skirted fenders
Swooping demurely
Man, she had lines.

Chief's head scanning
The dark road ahead
Darting deer, soft shoulder
Oh the pain, the pain
Busted leg, shredded shins
Mangled front end
Death of a legend.

Auntie's barn a dusty crypt
Scuttling spiders spinning
Gossamer webs on
Handlebars and spokes
Twenty years on
Farm's on the block
"Get that piece of junk
outta my barn."
"Jimmie, loan me the flatbed."
Ten hours later
Rusted memories stand tall again.

Roadside diner, great for pie
Good ol' boy sidles up
"Whatcha got there?"
"'53 Indian, wrecked."
"Give ya 10 large, as is."
"Tell you what.

I'm goin' in for pie.
If you're here with 10 grand
When I come out,
She's yours."

Spitting gravel and dust
Chevy pickup tears off
Each mouthful of cream pie
Comes with a memory
Carving the corners
Arms locked around my waist
Breasts soft against my back
"Slow down! Slow down!"
Barely audible
Over twin pipes' roar
Showed them friggin' Harleys
Who was boss
Damn she was fine.

Back at the flatbed
Lookin' her over
Wounded, but proud
Twenty-year-old mud
Still smearing the chief's face
It's all right, babe
Resurrection day's comin'
Chevy pickup in a four wheel drift
Guy waving a big wad out the window
"Take good care of her, hear
Or I'll come back
And kick your sorry ass."
Seeing the shine in his eyes
Made the parting easier.

Ain't nothing like
A '53 Indian.

CAPTIVATED BY WHITEWATER RAFTING

Nonfiction

Bernie Fandrich

The beauty of the Thompson River can astound you—and its power can zap you in seconds.

The azure Thompson converges with the larger, silty Fraser River at Lytton BC. The First Nations and early explorers referred to this spectacle as "the great forks" or "kumsheen."

Forty years of my life and livelihood are interwoven with this majestic river. I have travelled its rapids, hiked its shores, marvelled at it from the highway, and studied its history.

My first rafting trip was journeying eight miles from Spences Bridge to Goldpan Provincial Park on June 10, 1973, at high water. That year, as spring flowed into summer and the water level receded, I saw a new river emerge. When the water level lowered and warm water replaced the melting snow, boiling rapids disappeared and fresh torrents surfaced.

In the fall, the rapids morphed into the most amazing stretches of whitewater imaginable—stunning in every respect. The river hosted millions of salmon, hundreds of anglers, and myriad birds and wildlife. I was smitten.

In mid-summer 1973, I decided to make my first run down the lower Thompson and the river's biggest, wildest rapids. I recruited several Lytton friends and we launched, slipping down the river, bouncing from rapid to rapid.

When we entered the Jaws of Death Rapids, the bottom fell out of my world. We plunged eight feet and a huge, towering wall of water surged above us, smashing down into our raft. Looking up, on that hot, hot day, I could see sun shining through the crest of the wave. It struck with such force, I didn't know if we had flipped, crashed, or been jettisoned overboard.

Crazily, we popped through the other side. The raft was awash, but we were intact and right-side-up. We had conquered the Jaws of Death. From that day forward, I was hooked on whitewater.

In 1973, Bernie Fandrich and friends conquer the Devil's Gorge of the Thompson River for the first time.
Photo Credit: Kumsheen Rafting Resort

THE CACHE

Elaine Durst

He came from the Cache Creek hills
Footsore weary to circle the camp.

He watched from half-closed eyes.
His coyote muzzle shone silver
When tilted towards the morning sun
And caught the aroma of salami in the sand.

Meals were few when slowed by age.
He had to take chances.
Rising he hobbled,
In diminishing circles towards the cache.

My camera caught each stalking pose.
He moved away then warily returned
Driven by hunger
Licking his snout.

His furry blur across the desert
Flushed out nearby birds.
He claimed the cache.
I missed the picture.
The cache is gone.

Drawing by Elaine Durst

UPPER FRASER VALLEY AND BRIDGE RIVER VALLEY

THE UPPER FRASER VALLEY AND THE FRASER RIVER CANYON

The mighty Fraser River separates the Cascade Mountains from the Coast Mountains. The Fraser Canyon is an 84 kilometre landform of the Fraser River where it descends rapidly through narrow rock gorges in the Coast Mountains en route from the Interior Plateau of BC to the Lower Fraser Valley. During the Fraser Canyon Gold Rush of 1858–1860, 10,500 miners and various other settlers populated its banks and towns. At Hell's Gate, near Boston Bar, the canyon walls rise about 1,000 metres (3,300 feet) above the rapids. Fish ladders help salmon migrate up the Fraser River to spawn. Seven tunnels were built along the Fraser Canyon from 1957 to 1964, between Yale and Boston Bar, as part of the Trans-Canada Highway project. Municipalities along the Fraser Canyon include Lillooet, Lytton, Boston Bar, Yale, and Hope. The town of Lillooet often vies with nearby Lytton for the title of "Canada's Hot Spot" during the summer months. The canyon actually continues to extend north to the Chilcotin River.

THE BRIDGE RIVER VALLEY

Head west from Lillooet or north from Squamish and Pemberton and you'll come to the Bridge River Valley, with its ghost towns of Bralorne Mine and Pioneer Mine, which were both thriving gold-mining company towns for many years. Pioneer Mine ceased production in 1960, and Bralorne closed down in 1971. A handful of people still live in Bralorne, and more in nearby Goldbridge. Gun Lake, a nearby volcanic lake, provides a cherished summer home for a number of people with cabins on its shores.

Fraser Canyon from Jackass Mountain, photo © Murphy Shewchuk

SNOWY STILLNESS ABOVE THE FRASER CANYON

Creative Nonfiction

Ross Urquhart

In the late '70s, I helped out on a cattle ranch along the Fraser River between Lytton and Lillooet. It was one of those mutually beneficial relationships that people with a few skills and not much else go looking for. The memories are the most valuable things I came away with, and some of those arrived unexpectedly.

One early winter's day, Arne asked for help to retrieve the chainsaw we'd left up in the mountains. When we had chased the cows up to the high range in the spring of that year, it had turned into a mess. Windfalls had come down on the winding, narrow trail and the cows got jammed up trying to climb over them. We were hollering and cursing and the dogs were barking at their heels, so when a bunch tried to go around they ended up going off in the wrong direction. We had to fight our way through the dense jack pine and turn them back, but they kept splitting up and heading off in too many directions. There were only four of us, Arne, his two young daughters, and me, and we were moving over a hundred head. The horses were good and the dogs were old pros, but the cows just set off at random with every opportunity. It took us longer to push them the last mile up and over the ridge than it took to move them ten times that distance from the ranch. When we finally made it over the top, everyone agreed this was a problem that needed fixing.

A couple months later, Arne and I came back with the right tools loaded on a pack horse. We cleared the trail and built some drift fences on the switchback corners. It was a long hard day, but we got most of worst areas finished. Arne thought he might come back in a few days and sort it out even better, so he hid his chainsaw in the bushes. Few people used that trail and the saw was so beat-up it blended right into the forest floor. As it turned out, things got busy around the ranch and he didn't get back up to that particular trail until the fall.

The first snowfall on the high ridge usually starts the animals on their way home. The herd matriarchs point their noses toward the ranch and begin a gradual journey down into the high valley and, from there, along the road and further down into the Fraser Canyon, complete with their now-sturdy calves following behind. The last to leave are the bulls, and they don't want to. Usually we have to go up in late October or early November and badger them out of some lush little hole where the grass is still tasty and the sun still hits the right spots at the right time. The bulls are too arrogant to come down on their own and if we don't chase them over the hump, before the snow is deep on the ridge top, they can be trapped and starve as the grass is buried under snow. This year it took so long to find them and chase the ornery creatures back on the safe side of the mountain, we were worn out. We had planned to pick up the saw that day, but it didn't happen.

By late November, all the animals were finally back at the ranch, the hay cut and stacked, the irrigation put away, and the fences around the feeding areas checked and mended. The winter routines were firmly in place, but Arne was still without his saw. It was a handy little saw too. Just big enough to throw in a pickup or tie on behind a saddle without being in the way—and it wasn't as if he had enough money to go and buy another one when the one he had worked perfectly well. It was a pain in the ass, but Arne figured he really needed to go and get the damned thing.

The days were getting very short down in the bottom of the Canyon. We already had six inches of snow on the ground at the ranch from a couple early storms, but we knew it would be twice that a few thousand feet up. Arne asked me to come along for support and dangled the possibility of picking up a mule deer in the process, so I gave in and agreed.

Arne was the rancher. I was just a sometime helper who pitched in when I had the time. My wife and I had a deal with him where he looked after our horses and provided us with the space and "fixins" for a large vegetable garden and, in return, I helped him do chores, especially around branding and cattle drive time. It became more, of course. It became a long-lasting friendship.

Arne was a big, brash Dane. He was born in rural Denmark in the '30s and grew to his mid-teens under Nazi occupation. After the war he travelled a bit, looking for work and, he admitted, out of pure curiosity. Europe was devastated and it showed.

He and some friends emigrated to Canada on a Canadian Pacific program that supplied workers for prairie farms, and after a while he learned he could get a dollar an hour building tunnels in Kitimat, British Columbia, so off he went. He worked a few years in logging afterward, then construction on the Duffy Lake Road, until finally he had earned enough to go back to his first love, farming—or as we call it here in the West, ranching.

The day arrived to get the saw. I went out around dawn and caught my horse, Trig, and saddled him, ready to go. It was only a few degrees below freezing at the ranch but dark overcast, and it would be colder up in the mountains. I had dressed warmly in thick long johns, wool pants, sweaters, felt-lined boots, and a heavy coat with a rifle slung across my back. Arne was dressed about the same, except he had on his fur-lined Russian peasant hat with the fuzzy earflaps. I said he looked like a Ukrainian cowboy, and he laughed.

His horse was high-spirited, so there was trouble loading her on the truck, but we finally managed it. My old fella loaded without a fuss, and we headed out about the expected time. As we drove up into the high valley, the snow got deeper and fresher and we realized we wouldn't be able to off-load the horses as close as we wanted. The main valley road was plowed, but the entrance to the old logging road had a high snow bank in front. Normally we could gain a couple more miles but not this day. It was already nine o'clock by the time we were in the saddle and dark would be setting in around four, so we were forced to take a tricky shortcut straight up the mountain. The easier winding-road route could be used on the way back down. Even if it got dark the old tote road would be visible with the snow cover. Besides, the horses knew their way home on that road. They would get us back.

The shortcut was clear but steep, and tough on the horses. Arne's horse was younger and in better shape than mine, but Trig had a better temperament and was much more square and muscular, which suited me. The deep dry snow muffled their hooves, so in the still air the only sounds were the loud creaking of saddle leather and the rhythmic, labored breathing of the horses. Both horses worked up a lather, and when we stopped to rest them, they just stood in a rising cloud of steam, blowing thick frozen air from their nostrils like smoke from fire-breathing dragons.

When we emerged from the dense timber to where the grazing land started, it was still uphill but the footing was better and we felt less claustrophobic. It was one o'clock and we were making good time, so we stopped, poured some coffee from a thermos, and took in the scenery. We had arrived at the "flats," which weren't anywhere near flat but were closer to it than the mountainous surroundings. The landscape was a series of gently rolling meadows dotted with stray bunches of poplar and alder, and all of it was ringed by thick timber and rock bluffs. The dense, dark clouds hung just above our heads, but we had a clear view down into the Botanie Valley below and could even see the Fraser Canyon off in the distance. The top of the highest ridge was where our cattle trail ended. From there, we could look down on either the Thompson or Fraser Rivers. The entrance to the last timbered section was now only a few hundred yards away.

The snow was a blanket of fresh powder about twelve to fourteen inches thick, and we weren't sure what was under it for traction, so we decided to switchback—angle across—the last open steep slope. Two-thirds of the way, Arne's horse started to lose footing but regained it quickly and kept going. Trig got to the same spot and began to slip too. The problem was that one of Trig's front hooves had split years before and never healed, so we kept shoes on him to keep it from getting worse—and the shoes weren't fitted with "calks" for winter traction. They were just the raw steel, and on the icy slope under the deep snow they couldn't find anything to grab hold of. Trig began to slide sideways down the slope picking up speed. I tried to hold his head down and turn him into the slope as he frantically pawed and stumbled, but all of a sudden he came up against something solid under the snow and began to pitch over. I had kicked my feet out of the stirrups when he started to slide, so I managed to throw myself off on the high side as he went down. I landed on my back in the deep snow and just lay there stunned for a few moments, mentally checking to see if anything was noticeably wrong. My back had a sore spot but that was from landing on my rifle. Everything else appeared to be in one piece—and functioning. When I sat up, Trig was at the bottom of the hill but up and shaking like a dog to get rid of his snowy overcoat.

Arne heard the commotion and turned and looked as I bailed off. I waved at him to keep going and hollered that I would meet him at the bottom of the hill when he got back from fetching the saw. I told him I would go for a ride around the meadows in the meantime. Trig waited for me as I slid the rest of the way down the hill, and I led him around a bit to see if he was all right. He didn't seem to have any tender spots. It took a while to brush myself off and clean the snow from my neck and pockets. Every nook and cranny of my rifle was jammed with snow, but it was none the worse for wear. After brushing Trig down, I got back in the saddle and went for a ride around the Flats. Trig moved easily through the deep fluffy snow just kicking a little cloud of ice crystals ahead of each step. The only tracks were animal tracks, so I guessed we were the only people who had been here in weeks.

The air was frosty without a hint of movement while the dense dark cloud ceiling touched the tops of the big firs that lined the open meadows. It was a soft, padded landscape with stumps, boulders and drooping tree limbs cloaked in a foot of fluffy snow, so quiet I could hear the whoosh of a small bird's wings as it flew by. The surroundings had a magical quality to them, like walking through Mother Nature's cathedral. The day was getting on, so Trig and I reluctantly turned around. Halfway back I ran into Arne, who had tied the saw onto the back of the saddle and come looking for me. He greeted me in a whisper, so I realized that he, too, was impressed with the fairyland quality of this winter scene. We rode back to the head of the down trail without speaking and stopped at the viewpoint overlooking the valley below to drink the last of the hot coffee. A chill was seeping into both of us so we started down the mountain on foot, leading the horses at a jog-trot until we had worked up some body heat, then climbed back in the saddle. We made it to the truck just as it got fully dark. Both horses loaded easy this time. It was a quiet drive back to the ranch.

In the years that followed, we never did say much about the ride. After all, it was just about fetching a battered old chainsaw many people would have left until spring. Still, for me, and I think for him too, it represented more. At the time, we were just two working men, relying on fading skills passed through who knows how many generations, but for a short while we were given the opportunity to appreciate a level of natural serenity and extreme beauty offered rarely—and only to people who live the life we live, in the place we live it. Nothing earth-shattering, but all the parts combined to create something special. Maybe that's how it's supposed to be.

SNOWSTORM ON JACKASS MOUNTAIN

Memoir

Loreena M. Lee

My family made several trips through the Fraser Canyon from both Wells and Prince George to Vancouver during the early '50s. I don't remember much about most of them because I suffered from motion-sickness. The narrow, winding roads were bad enough, but the ubiquitous smoke from my parents' cigarettes made my discomfort infinitely worse.

One trip in particular was unforgettable. It was January, and with three small children, aged eleven, two, and nine months, a seasonally unemployed husband, and three feet of snow covering the landscape, Mother contracted a case of cabin fever. So they packed up our large-size Oldsmobile, and we started down the icy roads through Prince George and across the bridge to the highway. By early afternoon the grey day turned to black, and the delicate snowflakes became heavy clumps that splatted against the windshield like snowballs. The car slipped and slithered along the shoulderless road. The headlights illuminated little else besides the swirling snow, and I had no idea how Dad could see the road, much less stay on it. I didn't have time to be sick; tension tightened my tummy and worry about how we would safely make the trip consumed my every thought.

A slender, two-lane trail, the road had been gouged out of the Coastal Mountain range. It wound through the steep granite canyon above the Fraser River, which raged below on its way to the sea. Normally a nail-biting ride, in winter it became the worst of possible driving conditions.

At last we came to the most precarious section, a steep, winding hill called Jackass Mountain. This spot was aptly named. Anyone attempting to scale the steep slope in the dark of winter during a heavy snowfall with icy conditions was a momentous jackass. I had heard it said many times. And yet there we were.

The hill was named for a mule-train that during the gold rush in the 1800's didn't make it over the bluff and the men and mules all fell to their death in the river, a thousand feet below. That was before the Cariboo Road, as it was called then, was built in 1862. Since then many travellers, teams of mules and oxen, and perhaps even some camels that were used for carrying the miners' equipment, perished on the precarious trail. Later on, cars, RV's and trucks met their fate there. I prayed we wouldn't be another statistic.

Dad put his head out the window and squinted. "The plow's been through and only one lane's been cleared, but it looks pretty good."

"If someone comes down from the other way," Mother said. "We'll both be in trouble."

"Naw, that won't happen," Dad assured her. "Nobody in their right mind will be out in this storm." I waited for Mother to use that opening to question his sanity, but for a change, she was silent. After all, this was her idea. "Besides," he continued. "The plow was just here—it'll be fine."

If sure-footed mules couldn't make it, I thought, what chance do we have? Dad gunned the engine and we surged upward, but the tires lost their purchase before the first turn. He backed the car down and took another run at it with the same result. He tried again and twice more. Each time he became angrier, his big hands guiding the car into the skid until the tires spun, then pounding the steering wheel as he gave in and backed down.

Dad finally subsided and lit a cigarette. Mother sat quietly, tight-lipped, holding my baby sister, Shirley. In the back seat, two-year-old Elaine and I held on to each other. A big sister at eleven, I was expected to give a good example. Willing with every fibre of my being to help achieve our goal, I concentrated so hard that I forgot the black abyss below. I tried not to picture the churning waters of the river claiming the big car with us inside, undiscovered until spring thaw.

Mother finally broke the silence. "Looks like we'll have to wait for the plow to come back."

"Who knows when that'll happen," Dad growled. "We could be sitting here for hours. We'll either run out of gas or freeze to death." I steeled myself for another of their arguments, but he subsided, and Mother became unusually quiet. There was nothing else to be done.

We waited at the foot of Jackass Mountain, enveloped in swirling snow and stillness, and before too long lights appeared high in the blackness. The plow truck came slowly toward us, snowflakes dancing in the headlights. Dad got out of the car and an arm-waving discussion with the plow driver ensued. After some maneuvering of the vehicles on the narrow road, we were hooked up and towed to the top, able to continue on our way.

Dad was not pleased that he had to be assisted up the steep hill. He took it personally, gripping the steering wheel, his lips white and thin, jaw moving as he ground his teeth. That road was as sly as the devil in his opinion, and he wasn't going to let it get the best of him, ever again. He vented his wrath in both English and Ukrainian for the next several miles.

Mother sat silent, which she did when she agreed with him. Besides which, as previously mentioned, this trip was her idea, and she likely thought it best not to comment until we were safely at our destination.

We forged onward into the night without further incident, except for a heart-stopping skid or two. Eventually, the snow turned to slush, then to rain as the bright lights of Vancouver came into view.

Fraser Canyon, BC, old photo

THE BLOCKADE

John Arendt

The morning sky was grey and heavy, threatening rain, as I sat at a booth in the Cariboo Café, finishing my coffee and watching the traffic along the Gold Rush Trail. The highway began in Lillooet, nearly 100 kilometres to the south, and continued to Barkerville, another 400 kilometres north and east. It was Friday, almost the end of Spring Break, and I had far too many hours left to drive before I got home.

"Connor? Is that really you?"

I spun around, wondering who knew me in this coffee shop, in a town where I hadn't lived for more than two decades.

"I thought I recognized you." The woman was around my age, tall, slender and attractive, with long, dark hair. She was wearing a pine green waterproof jacket and carrying a large stainless steel travel mug.

It took a moment before I recognized her. "Megan! I didn't know you still lived here."

"I don't. I'm just up from the Coast for a few days," she said with a smile.

Most of the people from my high school days were distant memories, but I hadn't forgotten about Megan. A grade ahead of me, she had a reputation as the school's do-gooder, the champion of all causes.

When I was in Grade 9, she organized a downtown garbage clean-up for Earth Day, to show us how much we threw away. There must have been others involved, but it was her initiative. It was the first time the town had done anything for Earth Day.

At the end of the day, with dozens of garbage bags lined up in front of the school, she called the paper and asked for a reporter to come down and take a picture. The picture and the story made that week's front page, and the editorial praised the clean-up effort.

The next year, she spearheaded a talent show to raise money for a school and orphanage in Africa. Once again she got front page coverage.

In high school, I had idolized Megan. She was confident, decisive, articulate, and popular—everything I wasn't—and when my family moved to Abbotsford after Grade 10, I missed her more than anyone else in town. I was too shy to get her number, so we lost touch. It was something I regretted for a long time.

The last I'd heard, Megan had gone out to Vancouver Island one summer, joining more than 11,000 people who were gathered at Clayoquot

Sound to protest the logging of an old growth forest. As I sipped my coffee, I asked her about the protests that summer.

"I wouldn't have been able to live with myself if I hadn't at least tried to help, tried to make a difference," Megan said. "What about you, Connor? What are you doing these days?"

"I'm a middle school teacher, up in the Peace Country."

"You're a teacher? Seriously? Would've never believed it." She shook her head. "All I remember was how often you were in detention or in the principal's office."

I was about to reply when a phone rang. Megan took it from her jacket pocket, checked the number and answered it. "Sorry," she said, her voice now brisk and businesslike. "Just bumped into an old friend. I'll be a bit late." She put her phone back in her pocket.

"I better let you go," I said. "It's been nice seeing you."

"Hey, why don't you come along? I want to show you what I'm working on."

I glanced at the clock above the café counter. It was almost 9:30 and I still had a full day of driving ahead of me.

"Sorry. I don't really have a lot of extra time."

"At least have a look, okay? It's not too far and you don't have to stay long if you don't want."

Outside the coffee shop, Megan unlocked an old, rusty Toyota and started it. I followed her, noticing the Earth First! bumper sticker on the left side of the hatchback and the Cherish Aboriginal Culture sticker on the right. She had a small dreamcatcher hanging from the rearview mirror.

Megan pulled off the road at a wide spot at the base of a mountain. A few cars and trucks were parked nearby and a crowd of half a dozen people, dressed in rain gear and reflective vests, sat on camping stools and fallen logs nearby.

"There's the access road," she said, indicating a rough, steep dirt trail. "They want to put a cell tower up there, on top of the mountain. We can't let it happen."

I remembered many afternoons and evenings spent wandering the network of trails alone when our family still lived here. It had been my place of solace, my place to go when I needed to be alone. But why did Megan care about this mountain, especially if she lived at the Coast now?

Maybe she and the other protesters wanted to make sure the mountain was protected as park land. That would make sense, especially with the Earth First! sticker. Or maybe she knew about a First Nations burial site or heritage site here.

"Is that band land or something?" I asked.

Megan shook her head. "No. Nothing like that," she said. "We've got to stop that tower from being built. Microwave radiation coming off these towers, it's a huge health risk. Cell towers, phones, even a home Wi-Fi network—those things are bad for you. I could show you studies. Medical journals."

I remembered the call she had taken at the coffee shop. "But you've got a cell phone, right?" I said. "That doesn't make sense, not if you believe they're not safe."

Megan shook her head. "I don't just believe," she said slowly. "I know."

"So why do you use a cell phone?" I asked again. "I mean, if those things are as bad as you say."

Megan looked at me, her expression sad. "I know, right?" she said. "You probably think it's kind of hypocritical, but you've got to understand. I do this kind of stuff all over BC—speaking to city councils, writing to the B.C. Utilities Commission, organizing demonstrations. My phone's the only way I can keep in touch to do that job. The health hazards, that's a risk I've got to take."

I nodded but said nothing.

"Anyone call that guy from the paper?" Megan asked the protesters.

"Yeah. This morning," said a bearded man, his grey hair pulled back into a thin ponytail. "Said he's going to show up around noon."

The people at the blockade all looked perfect for the part. There was an aging hippie, a hipster university student, a couple of young moms, and a few early retirees. And of course there was Megan, ready to speak on behalf of them all.

Megan took a few steps away until she was just out of sight of the other protesters. She pulled out her phone and made a call. "Newspaper guy's showing up around noon for a picture. We need some more people at the blockade. Thanks."

I checked the time. Almost 10:30. It was time for me to resume the long drive home. I started for my car.

"Leaving so soon?" Megan asked, jogging after me.

"I've got to get going. It's a long drive and there's a lot of classroom prep for Monday, now that Spring Break's almost over."

I opened the door of my car.

"I still can't believe you're a teacher now," Megan said, shaking her head. "Never would have guessed that one."

I turned to her. "You know, you were a big part of the reason why I went into teaching," I said. "Something you talked about after Earth Day and again after that talent show for Africa."

"Really?" Megan asked. "What was that?"

"Every time there was a big event, you'd talk about how we needed to make a difference, be the change we wanted to see in the world. I clipped the stories out of the paper. Still have them somewhere." I paused. "A couple years after grad, I decided the best way I could make a difference was to teach, to work with kids who weren't doing well in school, so they wouldn't have it as rough as I did."

"Wow. Just..." Megan began.

"Anyhow, I've got to go. It's been nice seeing you again."

As I drove back to town, the image kept replaying in my mind. There was Megan, out with cell tower protesters, talking on her phone.

The first raindrops started when I reached Main Street. By the time I turned north onto the highway, the rain had turned to a steady drizzle. The clock on the dash of my car showed 10:50. In a little more than an hour, Megan and the other protesters would meet with the newspaper reporter, who would get a picture and a few comments for a story.

Once again, she'd be the voice of a cause, just like when we were in high school, and she'd speak out passionately.

She might even end up on the front page once again.

Lillooet, BC. Photo © Kim Lawton

Bridge River Valley, photo © Murphy Shewchuk

A CHILD GONE MISSING

Creative Nonfiction

Jodie Renner

I grew up in neighbouring remote mining towns, Pioneer and Bralorne, in the Bridge River Valley in BC's Coastal Mountains. One dark, cold, snowy January evening in 1964, when I was thirteen, my sister Linda and I were at the kitchen table doing homework when the phone rang. Everybody was on party lines back then in Pioneer Mine, so we had to listen to the rings to find out if it was for us or one of the neighbours. It was two shorts and a long, our ring, so I answered.

It was Mrs. Smythe, our neighbour. She sounded like she was having trouble breathing. She asked in a strained voice if any of us had seen her youngest child, Leo, since suppertime. I called Della, who was seven like Leo. Della came out of her room carrying her Barbie doll. I asked her if she'd seen her friend, Leo. She said they had played together outside in the snow after school with their friend, Terry, and then they all went home for supper.

Back on the phone, I told Mrs. Smythe, "Della hasn't seen Leo since before supper."

She asked, in a shaky voice, "Is your dad home?"

I called Dad, who had just got back from Cub Scouts, where he was the leader.

Dad came into the kitchen, a quizzical look on his face.

"It's Mrs. Smythe. She's looking for Leo."

He frowned and picked up the phone. "Hello, Murphy here."

I could tell by his side of the conversation that Mrs. Smythe was asking him if Leo had made it to Cubs. "No, he wasn't there tonight," Dad said. "I asked the other boys, and they hadn't seen him. Why? Isn't he home?" His eyes grew wide. "Could he be at someone's house? … Don't worry, we'll all get out there and help search for him."

By this time Mom had come into the kitchen, and we were all listening intently to the conversation.

Dad hung up, looking worried.

"What's the problem?" Mom asked him.

"Leo Smythe's mom said he didn't come home after Cubs, so his parents and sisters have been phoning everyone and knocking on doors to see where he went. They didn't know he wasn't even at Cubs tonight. Nobody has seen him, and he's not at any of his friends' houses."

"Oh, no! Where could he be?" Mom asked. We all looked at each other in concern. I stood there, biting my nails.

"I hope he's all right. It's dark and cold out there, and he's just a little boy." Mom pulled Della, the baby of the family, in for a hug.

I squeezed Della's hand. Her eyes were round as she looked up to Mom, then to me.

As we started to look for flashlights and get organized to go out, the phone rang again. This time it was for someone else on our party line. The phone didn't stop ringing that night as word spread.

Still all in the kitchen, we heard a loud, urgent rapping at the front door. Mom was looking for flashlights and Dad was by the back door, putting on his winter boots, coat, tuque and gloves, so I went to answer it.

As I headed to answer the front door, I glanced out the front window to try to see who it was. All I could see was snow in piles everywhere and at least a foot deep on all the rooftops—typical for January in the mountains. I turned on the porch light and opened the door. A blast of cold air blew in.

It was another neighbour, who stepped inside and quickly filled us in. "Little Leo Smythe is missing, and his parents are frantic with worry. We're forming search parties now to start looking for him."

Mom had come up behind me. "Murphy's on his way out with a big flashlight to search for him. Our two older daughters will help, too. Too bad our sons aren't still living here at home."

"Great. We're also looking for some volunteers to provide warm-up stations, with coffee and hot chocolate for the searchers. Can you help?"

"Sure," Mom said. "The door to our basement is on street level. It's warm, and they can come in there without having to take off their boots. I'll make some hot drinks for them."

"Thanks. Leo was wearing a red parka and a blue tuque when he headed out to Cubs after supper."

We all bundled up in thick sweaters, then donned our boots, parkas, tuques, and gloves and headed out into the cold. We started searching in the dark with flashlights, calling Leo's name over and over. Everyone was worried sick about him. Maybe he had broken a leg or a foot and was stuck somewhere? We had to find him before he froze to death!

One of the neighbours brought his German shepherd over and gave him Leo's socks to smell. Someone noticed that the snow had slid off the roof of Leo's house, and they sent the dog there. He started sniffing around the snow, but Leo's mom said that was a waste of time. She'd sent him off to Cubs, so he wouldn't have been playing around the house. Nevertheless, some men located long poles and started pushing them down into the deep piles of snow beside the house, to see if they hit a body under there. No luck.

We kept searching. Every hour or so, shivering from the cold, we came back to our basement, grateful for a chance to warm up a bit before heading back out into the frigid darkness.

The biggest fear was that little Leo had fallen into the raging river, misnamed a "creek," that ran through town. Many of us searched along both banks of the river, shining our flashlights into the rushing water partially encrusted with thick ice and snow, calling his name, over and over.

We didn't find him that first night, so shifts were organized to keep searching. The mining company instructed the miners going on midnight shift to go out and search for Leo instead of reporting to the mine. They didn't find him by morning, so the dayshift miners continued searching, with pay, instead of working in the mine. Wearing hip waders, they started downriver and worked their way upstream, breaking up the ice floes on the river to see if his body would wash down.

All that day, they and everyone else continued looking everywhere and calling, but there was no trace of him. All in all, the mining company paid for three days' work by the miners, as they kept breaking up the ice floes in the river and searching the whole area, to no avail.

By the fourth day, people started wondering whether he'd been abducted and began asking about any strangers recently seen around town. Our remote village only had a security officer, so the RCMP were called in from outside. They brought a search dog and gave it a piece of Leo's clothing to sniff. The dog picked up his scent around his yard, but then lost it. The police also questioned lots of people. When they questioned my little sister, Della, she answered and then began to cry. They didn't turn up anything new.

This went on for weeks, speculation increasing as to what might have happened to little Leo. One neighbour even pulled out her Ouija Board and asked it where Leo was. The Ouija Board spelled out an address in Kamloops. Leo's distraught parents, grasping at straws, tried to follow that up, but of course the address did not exist in Kamloops.

Leo's dad went back to work and his sisters went back to school, looking drawn, with dark circles around their eyes from sleepless nights. It was hard to know what to say to them.

Finally, several months later, on a mild April afternoon, with snow melting everywhere, Leo's mother was hanging clothes on the line when she noticed something red peeking through the snow. Heart pounding, afraid to think the unthinkable, she hurried through the snow to investigate. She pushed aside more snow, then more. The red was Leo's winter jacket, and he was still in it, frozen solid. She started screaming. Hearing her screams, others came running.

The news spread rapidly, everyone expressing a mixture of deep sadness and relief that at least now his family knew what had happened to their beloved youngest child. The weight of the ice and snow that had fallen on him from the roof had broken his neck, so at least he'd died instantly. Somehow the men with the long poles had missed him.

Everyone came out to the funeral. The whole town was traumatized by the death of this lovable young boy, a tragedy that had brought us closer together as a community. Over fifty years later, I still remember the details vividly.

HIGH-GRADE GOLD IN HONEYMOON HOLLOW

Memoir

Clayton Campbell

In 1948, Bralorne Gold Mines started sinking a shaft and needed experienced shaft miners. My father, Pops, answered the call. We drove from Northern Ontario to Lillooet, BC, then rode the Gas Car, a train with a flat car, to Shalalth, BC. Finally, we drove up the steep, scary, switchback Mission Mountain dirt road to Goldbridge, then the final mountain road to Bralorne.

Just before entering Bralorne, we stopped at the Mines Hotel. Mom and Pops had a beer at The Big Stope, which is what the beer parlour was called. The hotel was operated by the Branca family, related to Angelo Branca, the prominent BC criminal lawyer.

Carved out of the wilderness on the side of a mountain, Bralorne was an impressive company town, which accommodated 1000-plus people. Downtown Bralorne included the company store, a soda shop, bank, and the cafeteria for the many single mine workers who lived in the bunkhouses. There were four townsites for the manager and senior staff, the mid-level staff, and married steady workers. The town had a church and school, and recreation facilities included a baseball pitch and a curling/skating rink.

The mine mill and the tunnel entrance were located farther down the mountainside below the main townsites.

Photo from *Bralorne-Pioneer: Their Past Lives Here*

Some private homes had been built, mostly by mineworkers, in Honeymoon Hollow, a small valley off to the side of the main Bralorne tract. We rented a house there, an old shack built on the side of a fairly steep hill. The back of the house rested on a dug-out area of the hill, with the front supported by stilts. Entry to the house was by a set of stairs up to a porch on the side. The owner of the shack was McGregor, a stope miner who had lived in it before purchasing and moving into a better house across the road, easily visible from our porch.

As my father was the only shaft miner with a house, the shaft crew, when not drinking at The Big Stope, descended to our home most weekends, drinking, playing cards and partying. They often joked about high-grading gold, which we kids found out meant stealing gold from the mine.

High-grading gold was a concern to Bralorne Gold Mines. The mine manager offered a $1,000 reward to anyone who identified a high-grader.

In the summer of 1949, I had just turned seven and Hugh was eight. The weather was great, and there were lots of kids to play with in Bralorne.

One weekend, the kids from Bradian, an upper townsite of Bralorne, challenged the Honeymoon Hollow kids to a Cowboy and Indian fight, with them being the Indians. We foolishly accepted. When they arrived, there were many more of them and they were bigger and wore scary war paint all over their bodies. We didn't stand a chance.

Hugh and I and a Smith boy from the Hollow snuck away from the slaughter back to our stilt house, hoping to find some comic books. We looked under the house, which had just dirt and boards, and saw a high dirt ledge. We couldn't see if there was anything on the ledge, so I climbed onto Smith's shoulders, and with a lift, I was on the ledge. It was dark and I couldn't see, so I crawled and felt around for a few minutes.

Then my hand felt something. It was a big heavy bag. I dragged it to the edge of the ledge and passed it down to Hugh. Then I climbed down and we took the bag out into the light and opened it. Inside were heavy rocks with golden spots and golden veins. We knew right away we had found gold. We hooped and hollered with excitement.

We took the bag of gold up to the kitchen. Six or seven of the shaft crew were seated at the kitchen table drinking, smoking, and gambling. It was a pretty intense game. Hugh and I showed the crew the bag we had found and pulled out the gold rocks and passed them around. Frenchie the hoistman, who was dealing, didn't say anything. Nor did Pops or Black Mike. One-eyed Jack McMaster said, "You know, I think this could be gold," but Haywire John said, "Na, this is just fool's gold." And they went back to their card game.

So we took the bag of gold out to the cowboys and Indians. We were generous and gave the gold rocks to all the kids as gifts to take home. We all agreed this was real gold.

A few days later, a couple of police officers from Lillooet, accompanied by the Bralorne cop, came to our shack. They asked Mom what she knew about the bag of gold and when we had moved into the house. They then asked Hugh and me where we found the bag. We told them and showed them. The police took photos of Hugh and me below the shack where we found the gold.

Then the police went to the McGregors' house across the road. They were there for hours. Mom was a hawk. She never left the porch, watching every move of the cops at McGregors', and providing an ongoing report of the activities. The cops searched the garage and all around the home, even digging in the garden beside the house. Mom noted that one of the cops picked up a canvas lying on the ground, looked under it, then threw the canvas to the side of the yard. Some time later, according to Mom, McGregor picked up that canvas and placed it back in the exact spot it had lain.

An alert cop took notice. He lifted up the canvas again, then started digging in that spot.

"They found something! They found something!" Mom shouted. And indeed they had. The constable had struck gold. High-grade gold was found in a bunch of large cans buried in McGregor's side garden.

McGregor was arrested and held. He hired Angelo Branca as his defence lawyer. Mom met with Angelo when he visited Bralorne. She was very worried we would get implicated in the gold theft. She was scared of court. Angelo told her not to worry, but she couldn't help herself.

There was constant talk at our kitchen table with all of the neighbours about the high-grade gold. What would happen to McGregor? Bralorne Mines wanted an example to be made of McGregor to deter other high-graders. We heard that the manager wanted McGregor to be locked up and the key thrown away. A newspaper reporter came and took photos of Hugh and me and Smith below the shack pointing to the ledge where we found the gold. Our photograph was on the front page of some newspaper, which we kept for a while.

The McGregor matter was set for a court hearing in Lillooet. Hugh and I got subpoenas to attend court. Mom, Hugh and I were driven by Sid, the know-all taxi driver who constantly wore a leather driver's cap.

When we arrived at the Lillooet courthouse, Angelo Branca was standing on the steps in a dark suit, his arms folded over his chest. The cab stopped in front, and Mom rushed to Angelo. He put out his arms and greeted her, and they talked as he walked her back to the cab. She kept asking, "Are you sure they don't have to testify?"

He repeated, "Don't worry, it's all done. You can take the boys home." We had the back window open. Angelo leaned down and said something like, "Look after your mother." And then it was over.

McGregor, I was told, was sentenced to nine months' imprisonment or so, but he was released after several months.

Back in Bralorne, Mom was sorry for Mrs. McGregor and spent some time with her. I felt guilty as McGregor was a pretty good guy.

Mrs. McGregor moved out of her house shortly after, and we moved into it. Hugh and I found a box of chocolates she had left for us, perhaps to let us know she didn't think it was our fault.

Angelo Branca continued his distinguished career. He was awarded the honorary title of King's Counsel, appointed to the Supreme Court of BC, then elevated to the BC Court of Appeal.

As a practicing lawyer now, I suspect that Angelo Branca plea-bargained with the Crown Counsel. McGregor would plead guilty to the lesser charge of "Possession of Stolen Property" and receive a much-reduced sentence than if found guilty of theft of the high-grade gold.

Some questions linger.

Mom always wondered what would have happened if McGregor had not replaced the canvas in the same spot that it had previously lain. Would the Police have found the buried gold anyway? She thought not. She thought McGregor cooked his own goose.

Hugh and I wondered which of the cowboys or Indians had parents smart enough to recognize the rocks we gave their children were indeed high-grade gold? And who received the $1,000 reward that we should have received?

CARIBOO – CHILCOTIN

Chilcotin – Horse and Itcha Volcano © Murphy Shewchuk

Chilco Lake Looking North © Murphy Shewchuk

CARIBOO – CHILCOTIN

The vast landscape of the Cariboo – Chilcotin stretches from the wildness of the Pacific coast to the rolling Cariboo Mountains. And set in between is Tweedsmuir Provincial Park – BC's largest park. Abundant with various wildlife, this is moose country at its finest.

This region, with a past rich in the spirit of adventure, has a strong Aboriginal culture. Amongst others, the Nlaka'pamux nation has deep roots in the land. In the 1800s, it was settled by early entrepreneurs and explorers. The Gold rush of 1862 boomed as a result of the Fraser River and Bridge River Gold rushes. The journey took prospectors across the prairies and over the Rocky Mountains to Tete Jaune Cache, then onward to Victoria to obtain mining licenses or down the Thompson River to Fort Kamloops.

Now the Cariboo Chilcotin is supreme ranch land. For visitors, there are many guest ranches, historic sites, studios, and galleries. There's the Gold Rush Trail and cowboy history in the Cariboo to explore. This region has hoodoos and volcanic mountains in the Chilcotin, and deep fjords on the Pacific Coast. Minerals such as copper, gold, and jade are still found here.

Cariboo – Chilcotin cities & towns include: Williams Lake, 100 Mile House, Anahim Lake, Clinton, Quesnel, and at the southern end, Lillooet. There's ranching throughout. And, of course, there's the annual Williams Lake Stampede.

D.F. Barrett

CABIN FEVER

Fiction

Herb Moore

The year was 1944 and I was fifteen. I had just gotten myself a winter's feeding job on a ranch up in the Cariboo. Gotta remember this was during the Second World War, and young men were away fighting. That's why young kids like us were put to work, regardless of our age or inexperience. I'd taken a bus from Cache Creek to 100 Mile House, where I was met at the depot. The rancher eyed me and the other fella up and down. "You two young cowboys think you can handle living in a line shack for the winter?"

"Oh yeah."

"You sure you know what's involved in looking after them three hundred head for the next four months?"

We nodded our heads. "Yep. Yep."

"They'll be calving come late February, and I 'speck you to be able to handle that too."

More head nodding.

"We try to get out there every two weeks with supplies, but sometimes if we get a heavy dump of snow it could be longer. So make sure you don't eat up all the grub. Keep some back just in case we can't get through."

I looked over at George, and he looked back at me. What he saw was a tall, slim young fellow of fifteen years trying to look older and confident I could hold up my end of the job. I saw this medium-height stocky fellow, probably a couple of years older who, like me, was probably wondering if this wasn't a big mistake.

We left the ranch headquarters early the next morning. I drove the team of percherons hitched to a hay wagon, on which we'd loaded a sleigh that we'd need to haul hay when the snow came, our few clothes and other possessions, saddles and bedrolls, and assorted tools. As I looked the tools over, the realization of what they meant started to settle in. Axes for chopping wood and cutting through the ice so we and the cattle and horses would have water, and bale hooks for throwing hay bales around. Best not to dwell on it, I decided.

The rancher and his wife were driving out in the ranch truck loaded with supplies to stock the shelves of the line shack. George was riding one of the saddle horses and ponying the other. The horses seemed to be in good shape and pretty well broke.

Our arrival at the shack late that afternoon was a further awakening to what we'd signed on for. Situated near a wide creek, it was a weather-beaten structure sheathed in shiplap, which had been haphazardly covered in tarpaper. It had a board and batten door that didn't look too secure and a small window with a cracked pane. A rusting stove pipe stuck through a roof of curling cedar shakes. When I walked in the cabin, the first thing I noticed was a strong smell of packrats. I could see several places that the floor would need patching to keep them out.

We checked out the stove. It seemed in good shape. We threw our gear on the bunks, one on either side of the ten-by-twelve room. George pointed out the rickety table that had pulled away from the wall where it had been attached. The two chairs appeared to be okay. We took stock of the supplies heaped on the counter and floor, then headed out to inspect the corral and the huge pile of good-looking hay. It was easy to see where the rancher's priorities lay—the corral was also in good shape.

The cattle would arrive in a couple of days, so we used the time to try and get the place into some kind of order and set up a schedule for cooking and for feeding the horses.

George had brought an apple box of his possessions, and when he unpacked it, out came a small portable windup gramophone and a few records. He set about building a shelf, then set the gramophone on it and immediately placed on it what he told me was his favourite record. After he wound it up, I was treated to Hank Snow singing a song I'll never forget. It is burned into my brain forever: "Over the hill, down by the stream, soon I'll be back where I can dream, back in my old prairie home."

The days went by in a steady routine. Get up, feed and water the horses, hook the team to the wagon or sleigh depending on the weather, haul hay out to the cattle, make sure the water was open to them, which meant chopping ice, sometimes twice a day if it was real cold, and don't forget cutting firewood and stacking it. The rancher impressed on us we were to leave the same amount of firewood at the end of our stay as there was when we got there.

George and I got along fairly well, both pulling our weight. The days were full of work, and then we took turns cooking our limited menu. In the evenings, I liked to read. Fortunately, the rancher's wife kept me supplied with books. After our supper we'd fill the gas lantern with white gas, pump it up with air, and light it, being careful of the mantle. When the pressure dropped and the light became dim, it was bedtime.

George would play his records over and over, in particular the one of Hank Snow singing, "Over the hill, down by the stream, soon I'll be back where I can dream, back in my old prairie home." I had to bite my tongue not to comment on the repetitiveness of the song and create a problem. We had to share this small space and work together in harmony.

It was along in the spring and calving was in full swing, which meant you were up most of the night checking on them. It seemed to me I had barely shut my eyes from spending the night helping a couple of first-time heifers calf out, when I woke to the sound of—you guessed it—Hank! I wanted to bury my head under the pillow to stop the noise, so I could sleep some more.

George, busy making our standard fare of oatmeal mush and feeling in need of song, had wound it up to listen to as he was bent over the stove stirring the pot of mush. That's when cabin fever struck!

I reached up above my bunk and lifted down my 22-calibre carbine from the pegs on the wall. I sat up, brought the butt up to my shoulder and thumbed back the hammer, took careful aim at the revolving record, and squeezed the trigger. The room echoed with the flat crack from my gun. The record shattered in pieces.

George jumped and spun around from the stove, glaring first at me as I replaced the gun on its pegs and then at the pieces of his favourite record scattered on the floor. We glowered at each other for seconds, but spoke not a word. I lowered myself down in my bunk, and George turned back to his stirring. Over the next weeks while we finished the calving, we didn't have a lot to say to each other. George would stare at his gramophone and finger the groove in the felt of the turntable, shake his head, and mumble a few cuss words in my direction. The incident was never discussed between us.

When we moved the herd back to the home ranch I collected my pay, ready to head home to hot baths, clean clothes, and mom's cooking. I found George, mumbled an apology, shook his hand, and offered to pay for the record.

He just shook his head and said, "Blame it on cabin fever."

Chilcotin Cowboys © Chris Czajkowski, wildernessdweller.ca

CHILLED IN CHILCOTIN

Alan Longworth

I was headed out Chilcotin way
Couldn't take the city for one more day
Too many folks and automobiles
Where no one gives a damn 'bout how you feels
All around there's a constant din
How I yearned to be in the quiet again.
I make a stop in Williams Lake
Got me a meal – two eggs and steak.
While in town I asked around
About any ranch jobs round there to be found.

In the hotel pub an old fellow sat
Looked like he was eighty, wore an old cowboy hat.
He must have heard me asking about
So he called to me with a wavering shout,
"Young feller," he says, "maybe I can advise.
I think I can give you a word to the wise.
There's a spread in Chilcotin, it's a long way in
It's the biggest old ranch out in Chilcotin.
They seem to have trouble keeping cowboys
The young fellers these days want big city toys
It's so far from town they don't stay very long
The cowboys today want wine, women, and song.

"So if you desire a cowboy's life
And you're not tied down with a doting wife
The Triple Bar X might just suit you
And I hear that they often hire new crew.
But try to stay warm whatever you're totin'
A man can get chilled out in the Chilcotin."
I thanked the old fellow for his advice
Bought him a beer, I didn't think twice.
I went out and fueled my trusty old van
Put extra gas in a red jerry can

I left Williams Lake and headed due west
Find the Triple Bar X. This was my quest.

As I leave Williams Lake town far behind
Welcome peace drifts into my mind.
It's lonesome country way out here,
A place of peace for man, cows and deer.
Along the roadside are fields of baled hay
Through open rangeland I make my way.
I've been driving now a good few hours
Close to the hills I run into rain showers
It kind of catches me by surprise
When I see the Bar X sign before my eyes.
I leave the road and drive up the track
A few miles up I spot a shack
Built of logs many winters ago
Its roof is sagging from the weight of deep snow.
I can tell it's the bunkhouse by the hanging tack
And the smoke curling up from a sheet metal stack.

So I enquire of the boss, a man named Sam Boone
"He's up at the big house," comes a voice from the gloom.
"If yer lookin' fer work yer not a minute too soon
For two young cowboys quit workin' today at high noon.
They left for the high life up in Prince George.
We're short a wrangler and a man for the forge.
Anyway, stranger, go see the boss
You might tell him you knows how to nail shoes on a hoss.

I walked to the big house, it too made of logs
On the front porch lay two big mangy dogs.
They showed me their teeth as I rapped on the door
From inside, I heard boots crossing the floor.
It swung open wide with a squawk of dry hinge
Big Sam stared at me. I thought I might cringe.
"I'm lookin' for work and was directed to here."

"I don't take on hands that can't live without beer
Or won't stay with me for at least a year.
I've got work a plenty for the right man

Those are my rules, or you can leave in your van."
It was plain that Sam was a man of few words
"You can start in the morning riding the herd.
Go find Ron Gillis. He's my top hand
He'll fix you up with the lay of the land.
I pay two fifty the month and all found
Plus an extra fifty if you're working the high ground."

It was plain big Sam would say no more
He stepped back inside and slammed the thick door.
It seems I'd been hired with little being said,
So I returned to the bunkhouse to check out my bed.
Brought in my gear from out of the van
The top hand walks in, drawls, "So you're the new man.
There's work round the ranch or out on the range
What I really need is a good cowhand
I've got cattle to bring down here to low land.
The Chilcotin winters can get awful mean
If bad weather traps 'em, it's a pretty bad scene.
When you pack your gear put a warm coat in
You can get mighty chilled here in Chilcotin."

"If it's a cowboy you want then I'm your man
I've been away for a while, but I'll soon catch on."
"My boys will be leavin' just after dawn
To get into the high country before daylight's gone.
You do realize being the new man
They'll put you in charge of the old frying pan."
"Don't worry boss, on that particular score
I know the rules, I've cowboyed before."

It's getting quite late so I hit the sack
Next thing I know cooking smells fill the shack
"It's dawn!" the top hand says, "it's time to get goin."
He gives me a pony, a strawberry roan.
There's frost on the ground, the ranch is all white
There's a fall of fresh snow on the hills to the right.
I saddle my pony, put on my warm gear
I feel the cold nipping at both of my ears
At last we are off, eight of us in all

"At noon we'll split up," top hand says in his drawl.

By noon we'd reached the first powdery snow
The wind it had risen, the temperature, raw.
Cow tracks abounded where they had foraged for feed
By dusk we camped and made the fire we would need.
I cooked up some bacon, coffee and beans,
All the while the cold bit my legs under my jeans.
With our bellies full, on our ground sheets we lay
With our heads on our saddles. All this for low pay?

Under my blanket I froze all night through
I wondered what I'd got myself into
My hands were frozen, so were my toes.
Mucus had frozen inside my nose.
I kept the fire going but it didn't much matter
It didn't stop my teeth of their constant chatter.
Through it all for some warmth I was hopin'
I got awful chilled here in Chilcotin.

Of course I was up first to cook for the boys
The same grub as last night, we hadn't much choice
For coffee water I had to use melted snow
If you've ever done it you know the process is slow.
Well we worked on the mountain for several days
The snow kept on falling like a soft gentle haze.
The boys separated to search the ravines
As the wind and the frost became even more keen.
I rode the roan into a deep rocky draw
Following the sound of a yearling cow's bawl.
By the time I found the mother and son
Daylight in the canyon had totally gone.

It was plain to me that I couldn't go on
It was much too dark for the roan to safely walk on.
The way I saw it I had to do what's right
I'd have to bed down here, for a dark freezing night.
I let the roan loose to forage for food
While I tried to get comfy as best as I could.
My one tattered blanket was awfully thin

I wrapped myself in it up to my chin
No way I could sleep, the words kept coming in
You can get awful chilled when you're in Chilcotin.

Not a moment too soon arrived the long-waited dawn
I saddled the roan and soon we were gone
I chased the two beasts down to the main herd
One cowboy rode up. "Can I have a word?
When you didn't show up, we thought you'd gone a courtin'
If so, you should know, you can get chilled in Chilcotin."

I laughed at his humour through my frozen cheeks
I figured when I thaws I will probably leak
By the time we had got a thousand head down
I was beginning to wish I had never left town.
Top hand figured the herd had come to no harm
But all of the time I never got warm.
When the herd was settled in on the bottom land
I began to rethink about being a cowhand.
Around the bunkhouse stove, the cowboys were talkin'
"Man, you can surely get chilled, when you work the Chilcotin."

THE FREEDOM ROAD

Nonfiction

Sterling Haynes

The people of the Chilcotin Plateau are tough as Jack pine knots. Living in a sparsely populated mountainous area west of the Fraser River and Williams Lake, B.C., they're known for their independence, determination, and self-reliance. They have to be resourceful—they live on a high, remote plateau that is snowbound for seven or eight months of the year. In the '50s and '60s, when I was a doctor in the area, most of the hardy inhabitants of "the chilly Chilcotin" were multi-talented First Nations people, ranchers, loggers, big game guides, mechanics, cat drivers, and road builders.

Feeling cut off from the world and with the high cost and difficulty of transporting goods in and out of the area, early residents of the Chilcotin would often talk about ways to reach the outside world more easily.

In the 1860s, gold miners used the Indian "Grease (Eulachon) Trail" to seek the gold fields at Barkerville. In the 1930s, "Expedition Polar Bear" surveyed a road from Anahim Lake to Bella Coola, but it didn't get built because of the outbreak of World War Two.

By 1952, the men of the West Chilcotin at the high end of the mountain pass were determined to build and complete the Freedom Road from Anahim Lake, 200 miles west of Williams Lake in the Chilcotin Plateau, through the vast, mountainous Tweedsmuir Park to Bella Coola on the Pacific Coast, a distance of 135 kilometres (84 miles). It would be a lifeline connecting the mountain ranchers and loggers with the Pacific Ocean and the rest of the world, and would also help Bella Coola, which at that time could only be reached by boat.

Provincial authorities declined to fund the project, citing the expense and the difficulty of the terrain, so the locals decided to build the road themselves. They enlisted the help of the people of the Bella Coola Valley to build the lower end.

In 1953, the Board of Trade in the Bella Coola Valley, led by Cliff Kopas, decided they would build the road. They leased a D6 caterpillar tractor and hired an engineer, Elijah Gurr, to start work. Then they added a "powder crew" and a T18 International bulldozer and started from the bottom end of the mountain pass. The provincial government's Highways Department refused any more funding for the final push to complete the road to Anahim Lake.

In the Chilcotin, with supplies bought on credit and a labour force that only had the promise of being paid, the Anahim Board of Trade and the community supplied a "powder crew," led by logger, rancher, catskinner, and road builder Alf Bracewell, to complete the top end of "The Freedom Road."

After over a year of backbreaking work, dynamiting rocks, and clearing the road, the two cat drivers met "bang on" in September 26, 1954. Mrs. Jerry Bracewell took an eight mm. movie of her husband, Alf, building the road and the meeting of the two cats.

Both the upper and lower road workers received very little pay for their dangerous work. The road was completed, not through government funding, but due to the guts and pioneer determination of the local people of the West Chilcotin and the Bella Coola valley. All supplies necessary were put on credit and billed to these dedicated men.

Despite the lack of government funding for the project, Flyin' Phil Gagliardi, the flamboyant B.C. provincial Minister of Highways, wanted to be in on the glory when the road was finally built. He arranged an entourage of exalted politicians in fancy government cars to attend the celebration of the opening of the Freedom Road at the start of Heckman pass.

Setting out from Williams Lake, the group were greeted by a huge sign at Alexis Creek. The sign said: THIS ROAD IS NOT PASSABLE, NOT EVEN JACKASSABLE. Many miles farther on the gravel road, the local residents had arranged a detour along the dusty road. The road, Highway 20, was closed by the rancher's detour sign and directed Flyin' Phil's entourage into a quagmire of mud and swamp and mosquitoes close to Chilanko Forks.

After the politicians spent hours trying to get out of the mud holes, the local ranchers took pity on them and dragged the government cars out of the mud with a team of horses, then lifted their falsely placed detour signs. The independent people of the Chilcotin had made their point: "Who needs Flyin' Phil and the B.C. Department of Highways?" The politicians did, however, make it to the grand opening of the "The Freedom Road." The local people had a good laugh and the story is continually retold and embellished with more jokes in coffee shops along highway 20 to the present.

Six years later, I met Alf Bracewell, rancher, guide, cat skinner, and road builder when he checked into the gray, dilapidated War Memorial Hospital at two a.m. Alf had a tree fall across his moving "cat" that landed on his right collar bone. Alf had driven himself to Williams Lake, about a five- or six-hour ride, with his arm in a sling. I was the doc-on-call that night.

"Sorry to get you up so early, Doc, but I had a jack pine tree kick back and fall on my shoulder while I was cat skinning. I think it may be busted bad, Doc."

"Looks like your clavicle may be broken, Alf. There's a lot of swelling and bruising, too. Have you any numbness or loss of feeling in your right arm?"

"It was kinda numbed up at first, but I got good feeling in my arm now and good strength too."

After determining there was no nerve or vascular injuries, I called Vi, the X-ray technician to X-ray the right shoulder and clavicle. While we were waiting, I gave Alf a combination of drugs called HMC#1 by IV injection. HMC was a potent drug consisting of large doses of Hyoscine, Morphine and Carbitral (a barbiturate). Within minutes Alf was snoring, but he woke up while Vi took his X-rays.

The clavicle was splintered and pushed downward, but by manipulating his shoulders with my knee in his back between his shoulder blades and pulling up with my fingers around the break, I managed to reduce the fracture. Using extra-large Kotex pads to cushion each axilla and four large tensor bandages, I immobilized the fracture and held it in alignment in a figure-of-eight splint. With giant dull safety pins, I secured the tensor bandages over each massive shoulder as a solid support.

It was after 5:30 a.m., and the hospital morning cooks had made us breakfast of Elk T-bone steaks, eggs, pancakes, and coffee. After breakfast, Alf remarked in a laconic way, "You know, Doc, did you mean to stick the huge safety pin through my hide? It seems to hurt worse than my fractured collar bone."

"Sorry, Alf. Let me change that damn safety pin. Take these 292 tablets three or four times a day for pain. See me in a month, and leave the splint on but change the 'pit pads' now and again."

After three months the collarbone was healed and Alf was back at work. When I ran into him and asked him about it, he said, "Thanks, Doc. The fracture healed okay, but them 'pit pads' were diabolical—and smelly too."

BELLA COOLA BUREAUCRAT

Creative Nonfiction

Ken Ludwig

I had been at Anahim Lake in the Chilcotin for five or six weeks in the spring of 1969, Michigan a fading memory, when I decided it was time to get my driver's license and truck registration taken care of. The nearest place to do so was in a little coastal fishing town called Bella Coola, about eighty-five miles west and down "The Hill." I had been hearing references to The Hill from time to time, but hadn't paid much attention. Now I wanted to know more.

I began asking people about The Hill, and each gave me the same answer. They would smile knowingly and say, "You'll find out." I figured the joke was going to be on me again, but when I looked at my map from the Queen's Printer (I loved having a Queen, especially one with her own printer), I saw that the road to Bella Coola dropped 5000 vertical feet in a short, rough stretch. The Hill.

Anahim Lake, where I was, is at an elevation of some 5000 feet above sea level. Bella Coola, on the other side of the Coastal Range of mountains, is at sea level. Building a road that would never have much use had encouraged highway engineers to seek the fastest way down Heckman Pass, hence the steep drop.

I never found out what Bella Coola meant. I assumed it was an Indian name. The natives who lived there were the Bella Coola Indians, but there was the possibility that the town was named by some Italian hipster whose slang was ahead of his time.

I set out for the coast in the old truck on a cold morning in May, snow blowing across the road, puddles crusted with ice. This was still winter to me, no different than March in Michigan. The road would take me through Tweedsmuir Park, a spectacularly wild and unspoiled wilderness, three times larger than the State of Rhode Island, more than two million acres in the Rainbow Mountain Range. I would go down The Hill and out the narrow Bella Coola River valley to the village of Bella Coola at the head of the fiord. The trees in the park were as dense and forbidding as those outside it. I travelled through them, rising toward the summit of the pass. The day was fine, so I figured eighty-five miles wasn't far to go, even on this road.

I reached The Hill and began my descent. I plunged down the steep, narrow, dirt track, passed the first switchback, and continued on. As I progressed fearfully on my hair-raising journey, I noticed the foliage changing with the altitude. I reached the second switchback and crawled around it, clutching the steering wheel, trying not to think about being wedged between a sheer, steep drop to my left and a wall of earth carved from the mountain on my right. Everything was going by at what seemed like tremendous speed, though I was going no more than ten or fifteen miles an hour around the turn. I glanced at the wall, and in that brief moment saw a ptarmigan etched against the reddish earth, its plumage mottled, stark white and dull brown, in mid-change from winter to summer colors.

I careened on down The Hill. At the final turn I came around a blind corner, my heart pounding, sweating from the concentrated effort of keeping myself from driving off the cliff into oblivion. There, in the middle of the road, standing stock still, was a doe and her fawn. I hit the brakes as they jumped and disappeared into the woods.

The foliage near the coast was very different, the season far more advanced. New growth was everywhere, buds and leaves, even a few flowers, all bright and lush. I had, in the space of a few miles, traversed from winter to spring, from high-altitude coniferous forest to coastal rain forest.

I reached the valley below and pulled off the road at a small clearing next to the river. There were ferns here and trees of great size and power. I walked to the river's edge and looked out. Across from me lay a fallen tree. On the dead branch hanging farthest over the river sat a pair of adult bald eagles. I felt as if all this had been arranged for me. That morning was etched into my memory by its beauty and by the adrenal rush of the wild ride down The Hill. I walked back to my truck and continued on to the village.

As I drove a little farther down the valley, still inside the park boundaries, the steep hillsides changed from lush marine forest growth to the mountains of the moon. Someone had clear-cut both sides of the narrow and beautiful valley. It looked as if a giant electric razor had shaved the side hills naked. I found out later this was a tactic of the timber company with logging rights in the park. These rights predated the establishment of the park. The province wanted to trade other timber rights elsewhere to protect the park. The timber company wanted more land than was being offered and, in order to force the issue, demonstrated how it could destroy the park. As I recall, they got an extra million acres for their trouble.

I reached Bella Coola. The village was small and lovely, with low buildings, homes and working places, spread along the river, nestled between the steep climbing mountains. The Indian fishing fleet was moored safely in the harbor, and the smell of the sea was in the air. I quickly found the motor vehicle place and parked my truck.

I anticipated major problems with my disorganized documents so I went on the offensive. “Good Morning. I’m going to spoil your day with impossible problems,” I said to the starchily erect, thin-mustached civil servant behind the counter. “I’m sorry to have to bring down this trouble on you, but this is the only place I can do this business.”

“What’s the trouble?” he asked, with no change of expression from the polite and distant air he had exhibited when I walked in. I proceeded to babble about the huge mess of my license, title, and registration. My New York driver’s license had finally expired, and I was now driving an illegal California tagged truck, with the wrong Michigan registration.

He held up his hand to stop me. “Go down the street to the Mounties’ office and have them clear you for a driver’s license. Have a cup of coffee and be back here in fifteen minutes. I will have taken care of the other papers by then.”

“But you don’t understand—everything is wrong. It’s a mess. It’s impossib—”

“Please go.”

“But—”

“GO!”

I went. I returned. My papers were ready, all in perfect order, all legal, all done. He issued me a driver’s license when I presented the Mounties’ approval slip and wished me a good day.

I said with wonder, “How did you do that? It was impossible.”

“You really do not need to know,” he said with a small, barely discernible smile of complete and perfect satisfaction.

THE GRIZZLY BEAR WHISPERER

Creative Nonfiction

Kate McDonough

Whenever anyone from "outside" comes to visit residents of the West Chilcotin, sooner or later the conversation gets around to bear stories. I'm always a bit embarrassed by this bragging. It's usually intended to impress the listeners with the courage of the storyteller, but it can also intimidate or humiliate someone, implying greenhorn status or urban ignorance. Not always, however. I too am guilty; telling these stories around a campfire or backed up to the woodstove on a winter night is just too entertaining, too much fun.

I'm not afraid of bears; it's rare to see them after all, especially grizzlies. They have their habits and their trails, sometimes used for eons, ways of getting from the high mountains to the river valleys, and after a few years in the country you get to know where they are. Sometimes, however, you find out too late.

In the summer of 1977, my husband, Mike, and I, along with our two young children, were moving into an old homestead near Kleena Kleene, a small, widely dispersed community of cattle ranches, outfitters, and trappers. Two hundred and fifty kilometres from Williams Lake, the nearest real town for supplies, our new home at the old Swedelander homestead was five kilometres from the nearest neighbour. When we first inspected the run-down old log cabin, it was a real "packrat hotel." Torn paper feedbags lined the walls, and a pile of smelly trash lived six feet high in the middle of its one pitiful room. The rats had chewed up everything in sight, including a faded once-velvet burgundy sofa, a grossly stained mattress, and an army-green stuffed chair, as well as most of the feed-bag wallpaper, transforming the cabin into a disgusting nest.

We'd spent the last month hauling the nest and other junk to the dump, tearing the paper off the logs, scrubbing the walls where the packrats had left their marks, propping up the rotten floor, laying fresh-cut pine boards, and adding a new roof. Oh yes, and attempting to deodorize the place in a variety of ways. We hadn't quite finished the job but decided to move in anyway. There was no door on the cabin.

"We'll get to that right away," Mike said, "just as soon as we get all moved in. In the meantime, it's good ventilation, eh?

The first pickup load included six gallon-sized jars of fresh, raw milk from our Jersey cow. The cow would come later, as would the propane refrigerator that held the milk for the children, and for the butter, yogurt, and cheese I would make later. It was hard to know what to do first. We found a large muddy puddle full of recent rainwater ten feet from the open back door of the cabin and stood the jars in that, lids on tight, hoping to keep the milk cool until the arrival of the next load of our belongings.

“Are you sure this will work?” I said, the hesitant sceptic.

“It’ll have to. Anyway, we’ll be back in less than two hours,” Mike said, the confident optimist.

Several hours later we returned, the truck overflowing with furniture, boxes, and the fridge, our faithful dog perched on top of the load, doing her job as scout. An excitable border-collie, her nose went up and she barked twice, flew off the truck, and disappeared into the woods. As we backed up the truck to the doorway, we could hear her bash and crash through the timber. Minutes later, she burst back through the soapberry bushes and stood growling at the edge of the rain puddle where the milk jars were supposed to be cooling, hackles raised on her neck, tail straight up. I jumped out of the truck and noticed what concerned her.

Hey,” I shouted, “the milk jars are empty! The lids are all off! What the—! They’re not even broken!" I walked around, studying the ground. "There’s a huge bear track in the mud.” I moved in closer. “This track is as big as my head! It’s three times the size of a black bear paw. It must have been a grizzly!”

How on earth did an animal manage to take off screw-top lids without breaking the glass? I imagined an enormous, humped grizzly sow sitting on her haunches, milk moustache, beard, and bib, delicately twisting the jar lids with soft paw pads and sharp claws, picking up the jar, careful not to spill the heavy yellow cream on top, tongue in the jar, licking, smacking, now drinking, tossing the empty behind her as she reached for another full jar. Even though I have a good imagination, I doubted the reality of this hypothesis.

Despite our amazement at this development, we had things to do, so shrugging our shoulders, we picked up the empty jars and lids, unloaded the truck, and moved into our new home. I did, however, keep a wary eye on the bushes by the rain puddle, checking over my shoulder at the dog guarding it.

A loud honk announced the arrival of an old, familiar pickup truck clattering up to the cabin, spilling children, our two and three more, their parents, and another load of our stuff. The last one. I sent my son to chop kindling after we had unloaded the truck and marvelled again at the milk jar phenomenon. He was only six, and he whined, "But Mom, there's no good wood and I can't find the ax."

"Well, pick up some little sticks then. We have to make a fire to cook supper."

And so he did, and we ate pancakes with Rogers Golden Syrup and yesterday's yogurt. Soon the ever-present mosquitoes began their own late afternoon meals, piercing skin and sucking our blood, with no door to keep them out. The five children were sent outside to play, so they could at least run away from the pesky bugs, but not before the warning:

"Don't go too far, now, and take the dog with you. She'll let you know if that old bear comes back."

The men sat smoking, their feet up on boxes. We women cleared the table and piled the dishes in the basin, then poured hot water from the kettle over them, so they wouldn't get too hard to wash later. I stirred down the grounds in the old tin coffeepot on the back of the cook stove.

"Well, the bear drank all the cream, so it will have to be black coffee," I said. "Are we going back to the old place to milk Buttercup tonight?"

"No, I left the calf on her. We can milk her in the morning. I feel like going fishing. Want to go, anybody?"

Our friend Pete said sure, then after lingering over their coffee and smokes, the men left, taking the fishing rods and the old blue truck. As they drove through the gate, I watched the dog race alongside, barking and begging to go. She must have thought it was time to go home, not understanding that this was her new home. The truck stopped and she leapt aboard. Off they went, down the bumpy narrow drive, the dog leaning way out over the edge, nose in the air, in a cloud of dust.

I glanced at the two rifles and the shotgun leaning in the corner of the kitchen by the nonexistent back door. In this country, everyone kept their guns near the door, on the safety setting but loaded, not to defend against people, but to protect livestock and themselves against predatory animals. Like bears. Taking a gun to go fishing didn't make much sense, so I was glad to see the guns, just in case…

A one-room affair, this old cabin held a double bed at one end, a kitchen at the other, and a sleeping loft just the right size for two children. Above it, we'd added a skylight that opened for ventilation. We'd taken the broken-down windows to the dump and had cut a big new hole in the log wall for a picture window. A friend had given us one, salvaged from an old brewery in Edmonton, which we'd installed. Now the cabin was more window than wall, which suited me fine. We'd have to put plastic over it in winter; I could see that coming. Fifty below is no joke, especially in an old shack like this, with the chinking between the logs all gone, used by packrats and mice for nests. We'd worry about that when the time came. It was only June. First the door.

One child, then another, wandered in the open doorway, slapping and complaining about the bugs and wanting a story, and then they were all inside the cabin. Settling them on the double bed with my friend Ginger, I found a book in one of the boxes for them to read.

I washed and dried the dishes, then put them away in the new cupboard above the sink. Feeling very tired from the move, I listened to the story as Ginger read out loud to the five children. It had been a long day. The sun was sinking and the mosquitoes made an audible whine inside the cabin. I rummaged through the boxes in the middle of the floor, found an old red blanket, and nailed it up over the open doorway. It was a little crooked and there was a bit of a gap where it didn't quite meet the doorframe, but it would do. Pausing, I admired my work. As I turned away, I saw a flashing movement over my left shoulder. Crushed close to the wall by the doorway, I pushed the blanket aside an inch with one finger, not wanting to be seen.

She sat like a giant rabbit, paws lifted in front of her chest, not ten feet from where I stood on the other side of the useless blanket, a blond grizzly, just as I had imagined her. Her massive piggy-eyed head swung slowly left and right like a searchlight in the night, her nose wiggling, sniffing the evening air, aiming for the source of her curiosity. She was huge, at least the size of a rhinoceros. Definitely not a teddy.

No men, no dog, no door. I waved frantically, soundlessly, at Ginger, pointing up at the loft and mouthing "GO!" Not one of the children let out a peep, and they were quickly up in the loft, wide-eyed. I grabbed the 30-0-6, the biggest rifle.

I hate guns. I've had a hundred lessons, can shoot a bull's-eye on a target, but one week later I can't remember whether the safety is here or there or whether it's on or off. Hands shaking, I grabbed and nearly dropped the big gun. I knew it was loaded—the guns were always loaded—but I couldn't remember if there was a shell in the chamber or if I had to do something before it would go off. I didn't want to shoot, didn't want to breathe, didn't want to look out the gap in the blanket. I took hold of the knob-thing on the bolt, figuring out that I'd better make sure there was a bullet in there, and slid it back as silently as I could. Click, clunk, the bullet jammed, in there all right—stuck.

She was still there, and I could tell she had heard my noises with the gun as I peeked through the crack beside the blanket-curtain. Her nose pointed straight at me. I didn't dare look her in the eye, even though I knew grizzlies didn't see well. She smelled awful.

I very slowly reached for another gun, the shotgun. Fat chance, I thought, but I'd heard of people killing bears with shotguns, even though they were best for hunting birds or ducks. You just had to hit the right spot—but where was it? This gun didn't have a bolt, or whatever you call it. How did it work? Pump it, pump it; now I remembered. There was a familiar sound—my second pump had jammed this gun too. My heart was thumping, my hands shaking, and my breath shallow and fast.

One rifle left, a pitiful little .22. I figured that a .22 was really a lost cause, but I tried it anyway and sure enough, it was indeed a lost cause, jammed tight. I stopped moving, put the useless little rifle down, and a strange calmness came over me. My breath slowed down. I looked over at the group huddled in the loft. The skylight was open. Thank goodness, I thought, they could get out that way if they had to, up on the roof. Expectant, poised to move, silent children and mother stared back. They did not look frightened, surprisingly. I took a breath and then another deeper one. It didn't occur to me to join them in the loft. Hoping that the bear could not see me through the small window, aware that I was not on very solid ground here, but not in a panic, I surrendered.

I began to talk to the bear in a soft whisper but the voice I heard was not exactly recognizable as my own:

"It's okay. Look here now, Mother Bear, the milk's all gone. You've had it all, my gift to you. There are children in this house, and mothers too. Mothers with children. We will protect our children, just as you would. With our lives. I want you to leave, leave us alone. There will be no more milk, nothing but trouble for you here now. Leave. It's all right, dear, we understand you are just looking for more milk, so sorry. But you have to go now, it's over. Please leave peacefully, Mama."

I went on like this for what seemed like ten minutes but probably wasn't. With curiosity and an odd feeling of respect and awe, I inched the blanket aside, revealing myself slightly to her. (When did this bear become a "she" to me?) I kept on whispering to her.

She was motionless, sitting like a curious but confused dog, front paws on the ground in front of her, head cocked to one side. I swear she was listening. Her chest hairs were matted and dirty, milk-sour. Her squinty little eyes met mine for less than a second, I took a deep breath, and she was gone, blond rump rolling like a field of grain in a gust of wind, vanishing into the thick timber.

She visited us many times in the next few years, but we never actually laid eyes on her again. She bit holes in the plastic water pipe from the spring; she stole plastic buckets from the shed and chomped holes in them too. We saw her tracks everywhere. The children rode their horses and played in the meadows and woods, walked down the road to catch their rides to school, and we weren't afraid. We had a truce, I suppose, to stay out of each other's way, and we finally caught on to the fact that we had moved right into the middle of her ancient trail to the river.

I get much more excited, almost fearful, telling this story around the campfire, you know, than I was when it actually happened. Then, I was amazed at my response to this bear, but I never really doubted its most certain outcome.

Grizzly bear photo © Murphy Shewchuk

CHILCOTIN CRASH

Creative nonfiction

Sterling Haynes

Over fifty-five years ago, I had just started practicing medicine in the small, frontier town of Williams Lake, in central British Columbia. I was fresh from a residency in California and still green, but keen and enthusiastic.

One Tuesday morning, a call came in: a light plane had crashed at One Eye Lake in the Chilcotin, an area of jack pine, swamp, stump ranches and Indian reservations, about 130 miles west of Williams Lake on a plateau between the Rocky Mountains and the Coastal range.

Being the junior man of the four practitioners, I was "elected" to go on the mercy flight. I had been on call all week. It was supposed to be my day off.

I phoned my wife from the hospital to tell her I'd be gone again and collected the equipment I'd need: emergency room bag, a frame wire stretcher, bottles of dextran and saline, needles, and Thomas splints. I had trouble loading everything in my VW Beetle. The stretcher ended up partly in the back seat and partly out of the window. Off I went in a cloud of dust (there being few paved roads in Williams Lake at the time) to find my pilot, Colonel Joe.

Colonel Joe was an American, a Southern gentleman who had flown with the Flying Tigers under General Chenault in Southeast Asia. He was now working as a bush pilot, flying his Cessna 180 in the rugged central BC wilderness.

I finally found him at the float plane wharf on the East Side of Williams Lake, using a hand pump to fill his plane with gas from a forty-five-gallon tank.

We started loading the equipment but couldn't figure out what to do with the stretcher. Then we hit on it: we'd lash it horizontally across the front of the pontoons. We threw the bags, dextran, and splints into the plane. I closed the passenger side door, and Colonel Joe pushed off and paddled out onto Williams Lake. The prop eventually caught and we taxied down the lake. As we turned into the wind, I nervously wondered if this "white knuckle" airline would be able to get me to my destination and back again with the patients. Colonel Joe had only a vague idea where One Eye Lake was, and I had none.

We took off and flew ever-widening circles around the lake to gain altitude for the journey west. We passed over the Fraser River at about 1500 feet and followed the road up the Sheep Creek Hill. At the top of the hill, the Chilcotin lay veiled before, us covered in smoke. A massive forest fire was blazing. The smoke obscured the roads, so the lakes were only hazy blotches beneath us. Flames shot up about three hundred feet, the sparks shooting even higher. The heat was so intense and the smoke so dense that we had to climb higher. This added to my nervousness.

After circling for what seemed like hours in that droning machine, we spotted Puntzi Lake and the U.S. airstrip at the Puntzi Mountain early warning system. At Colonel Joe's request, I fumbled around the tail of the plane looking for a topographic map. I found the one we wanted. The map section with One Eye Lake was missing. Colonel Joe didn't seem worried.

"We'll look for the lake all day if we have to," he said. "Or until we run out of gas."

The smoke was starting to disperse in the west, and Colonel Joe dropped lower until we were skimming the tree tops, trying to figure which of the many lakes in the area might be One Eye. Suddenly we saw a lodge and a man waving. Then we heard two shots from his side-by-side shotgun. This was the lake.

We circled the area, looking for log snags and a safe place to land. "Don't want to put a hole in one of the goddamned pontoons," said Colonel Joe. "Then we'd be in a hell of a fix. You can swim, can't you, Doc?"

The landing was smooth, and Cappy, a retired British officer, met us at the wharf. We unloaded the equipment with the help of two young Chilcotin natives.

The downed plane was in a field about a quarter of a mile away. The pilot was dead. The man in the seat beside him was alive, but barely. A frightened young boy, sitting among some sleeping bags in the back, had only injured his ankle. The sergeant medic and a corporal from the U.S. base at Puntzi were at the site, trying to pry open the passenger door of the plane to get the injured man out. The prop and engine had been driven into the mud, making the door extremely difficult to budge.

We managed to pry it open and slowly lifted the injured man onto the wire stretcher. His curled up position and seat belt had saved him. He was semiconscious and in shock from multiple fractures. His scalp had been torn off. I looked around, found it by his seat and wrapped it in a lunch bag. He was obviously having trouble breathing, so I cleaned his mouth with my fingers, removed bits of broken teeth with gauze, and inserted an oral airway. I searched for a large vein without a fracture around it and started dextran. We splinted the fractures as best we could. With dextran running in each arm and the two young natives carrying the bottles, the four of us started through the woods for the plane.

The patient began to scream. We stopped and I gave him two milligrams of IV morphine. A bad mistake. Within a minute he stopped breathing. The combination of shock and morphine had totally depressed all respiration. I had to intubate him in a mud hole with flexible rubber endo-tracheal tubes and only a small portable oxygen tank. After twenty minutes, the patient started screaming again. Thank God. We continued moving.

Back at the lodge, we sent the two medics back to get the boy with the injured ankle. Colonel Joe proposed we strap the stretcher to the pontoons, covering the man with a canvas tarp to prevent him from getting too wet. I vetoed that idea. It was Cappy who suggested we use his radio to contact the RCMP detachment at Williams Lake to see if they would fly in with a larger plane.

After much static and crackling, Cappy managed to get through and they agreed to fly the "Beaver" down from Prince George. Colonel Joe decided to fly back and notify the hospital that we'd follow with the two patients.

By the time the plane arrived at noon, the normal saline and dextran were almost used up. The patient's vital signs were present but his blood pressure was very low. We moved the seats to accommodate the basket stretcher, and with IV bottles strung from light switches, we reached Williams Lake. The plane taxied to Colonel Joe's wharf, where we were met by the mortician, who doubled as an ambulance driver, and the hearse, which doubled as an ambulance. We loaded the patient into the hearse and were off in a cloud of dust.

I was exhausted, but stayed with the patient for twenty-four hours. We pumped blood, sewed lacerations, resutured his scalp, and applied plaster splints. Thirty-six hours later, the Air-Sea Rescue arrived from Vancouver to transport him to the Vancouver General Hospital, where he was to stay for the greater part of the next three years.

Thirty years later, I was on a locum in Nakusp, a southeastern town in B.C. about three hours from anywhere. Another emergency, this time a man with acute myocardial infarction. We transferred him by air to Kelowna. Monitors, life packs, nitroglycerine, a lidocaine drip and IV morphine were set out in a well-equipped ambulance, which rushed us to an airstrip on the outskirts of town. A small jet with state-of-the-art stretcher and equipment were waiting there.

We were off in a matter of minutes, and minutes later we were in the ICU of Kelowna General Hospital. The cardiologist was waiting. The patient was dozing and comfortable.

Cessna 180 float plane, old photo, public domain, Wikemedia Commons

THE LAST LITTLE NIGHT MUSIC

Memoir, Anahim Lake, Chilcotin, 1969

Ken Ludwig

I stepped outside the cabin, isolated by more than seven miles from the nearest neighbour, into the frozen night. The stars glinted by the thousands, with a hard, pure light. The deep, powdered snow absorbed every sound. As I stood in the silence, I began to be aware of the sound of my heart beating, the blood pumping through my arteries on its journey to supply the cells of my body. There were no distractions, no murmurings of external sound, not a rustle, not a hint of movement anywhere except inside the bag of my skin.

As I immersed myself in the sound of my own pumping life, another noise began to intrude on my awareness. A faint susurrus of static quietly but insistently became the background to my heart sound. I puzzled until I deduced that this new instrument in my internal orchestra could only be discharges of electricity across the synapses of my nervous system. I felt, not different from the star pulses above me, but the same. In those moments, I absorbed both the sounds within me and the quiet surrounding me and created a place in the depths of myself to which I have ever after returned, for solace, and connection, and calm. But I hunger too, for the perfect external silence that I have never found again.

I had with me, in that small log cabin, the last cabin on the Bella Coola Road, a battery-operated record player. When the silent, stunning moment had passed, I fetched the record player and a record. I placed the little red machine, a toy really, on a stump in the dooryard, then carefully set the record in place, gently moved the arm over it, and lowered the needle into contact with the record.

The opening chords of Beethoven's Fifth Symphony rolled out into the perfect silence and filled it. Every nook, every space between every molecule swelled and ripened with the roiling waves of music. The symphony played on and on, washing over the surrounding hills, moving like the tide through the trees and swelling inexorably toward the stars. When the last chord sounded, a more perfect silence descended. Now it held the memory of music, which defined it as the pallet upon which sound must paint.

The dog, Tybalt, who, at five months old, was already fifty pounds, wolf grey and yellow-eyed, one small step away from wild, lay calmly at my feet during the night's events. A few dozen heartbeats after the music ceased, as the silence grew and stretched, he sat up on his haunches and began, from deep inside himself, to howl. His voice carried into the wild with no less majesty than had the symphony. He went on and on, his reasons his own and unknown to me. And soon, from a distant ridge, came the Gregorian response of the wilderness. A pack of wolves took up the cry and hurled their voices, some six or seven, back to Tybalt. Whether they were challenging or acknowledging a brother, or singing to applaud the music, I did not know. I did not care. All the beasts howled and moaned and yipped until, finally, they were done. And so to bed.

Within a month, the settlement's new diesel generator arrived. The storekeepers wanted electricity and what seemed to them, civilization. In a week it was installed, and its chunking sound obliterated the deep ocean of silence forever. And with it, the wilderness.

DRIVING SOUTH FROM PRINCE GEORGE

Dianne Hildebrand

An eagle pierces the snowy mist with flashes of brighter white
Ten paints flow up the unfenced gully, tossing their manes,
Free as longing.
The wide river, sides still winter-bound, wends it slurried way
Through the uplands towards the sea.
By the side of the road, a large fox, silvery, pauses on its limping way
Watching us through the snow.

Southward, the pines lose their grip on the landscape,
marshes push cattails
through a torn blanket of snow
The winding creek reflects blue, and only
A clean, elegant ribbon of ice on its edge
Marks where winter has been.

Drawing by Dianne Hildebrand

AGREEMENT AT BEAVER CREEK

Fiction

Anita Perry

"No, no, no!"

Sarah sank up to her knees in the stinky black goo that had replaced the dry grass around the creek. She wind-milled her arms to keep her balance and would have succeeded if Fly hadn't come charging past her. The mere brush of the border collie's tail was just enough impetus to push her backwards into the mud.

"Shit." She stared up at the cobalt sky and cursed the beavers that had caused her recently purchased acreage to become flooded. The newly made swamp already reeked of decay and now so did she.

Sarah tried to push herself into a sitting position, but each attempt resulted in her hands sinking into the muck. As well, the mud encased her lower legs like concrete.

Okay. No need to panic. She could think herself out of this. People didn't just die because they got stuck in mud. Did they?

She suppressed a nervous giggle as she imagined the news item:

RCMP in 100 Mile House verified they have found the remains of former corporate lawyer, Sarah Thomas, in a bog just east of the city. Ex-husband Michael Thomas confirmed the 35-year old had indeed chosen to live off the grid in Lone Butte, in B.C.'s Cariboo region. "Yeah, she pretty much was an old stick in the mud. Figures she'd go this way." RCMP are currently investigating the possibility of foul play in the blonde's death, although the local constable is not ruling out the possibility of an extreme game of hide and seek...

Fly trotted up to her, panting heavily, dripping with mud.

Great. Now both of them were going to stink to high heaven.

"This is all your fault, you know," she told the dog sternly.

Fly whined and licked her face.

Sarah grabbed a nearby stick and waved it enticingly. "Tug of war!"

Fly gave an excited bark and clamped his jaws around the piece of wood. He backed away, trying to wrest the stick from her, but Sarah held on with both hands, allowing him to pull her into a sitting position.

She grabbed onto a scraggly bush and hoisted herself to her feet, but when she tried to lift her leg, she succeeded only in removing her foot from the boot. It took three attempts at carefully rocking her boot back and forth before the clinging mud released her.

When she had finally extricated herself from the mire and made her way to the safety of drier ground, she looked around and sighed. In the three short months she'd been there, the area had changed from a pleasant gurgling waterway to a swamp. Without a current to keep it clean, the stream was now choked with debris and algae.

Bev at the Three Corners Market had shown little sympathy. "Beavers. They're a nuisance, to be sure, but there's not much you can do about it. They got more right to be on your land than you have."

"Are you serious?" Sarah's jaw had dropped. "But they weren't there when I bought the property. They're squatting."

Bev had shrugged as she scanned Sarah's purchases through. "If you can prove they're a threat to your home, you can get 'em removed. But if I was you, I wouldn't go near 'em. Call Jack. He's the only trapper who deals with the C.O. 'round these parts."

Trapper Jack. No doubt some grizzled old-timer who looked like Yosemite Sam. But if he was the only guy the local Conservation Officer would deal with, then he'd have to do. All the same, it irked Sarah that she had to call on yet another man to help her out of a fix. And it was infuriating that when she'd called this famous Trapper Jack, he'd made a vague promise to drop by "sometime." Well, when the hell was that?

Sarah wiped the sweat from her upper lip with the back of her hand. The air was oppressive, as if yesterday's storm had never happened. Vancouver rarely raised the mercury above 26 or 27, but here it was a sizzling 34. She lifted the hair on the back of her neck and fanned her nape.

"Come on, Fly," she called. "Let's see if today we can get that motor started on the first try."

She continued her precarious way to the creek edge, careful to test the path for stability. The agenda for today was getting the water-pump going to fill up her reserve tanks by the trailer, then doing something about those beavers on her own. She was sick of having to play helpless princess. She could take care of herself. She didn't need a man. She was a strong, capable woman, and she sure as hell wasn't going to let some buck-toothed rodent run her life—definitely not part of the agreement.

But when she reached the outcropping that had only yesterday been high and dry, Sarah was dismayed to see the pump was now half submerged in the murky water. There was no way it was going to start. She'd have to get it up to higher ground to dry out, and god only knew how long that would take. It wouldn't be an easy job—that sucker had to weigh at least fifty kilos. It was going to take all her strength to pull it up the bank.

"Shit!" Because of those stupid rodents, she was going to have to rethink her entire strategy for getting water up to the trailer and cabin site.

Being a corporate lawyer was a piece of cake compared to this.

Sarah pinched her lower lip. She'd have to unscrew part of the now-submerged walkway to make a temporary platform on higher ground, then drag the pump onto it, then figure out how to raise her existing structure.

She strode towards the pump, reaching in her work belt for her screwdriver. She didn't see the sapling that had been gnawed through and abandoned on the wooden path.

She did, however, trip on it.

It wasn't so much that she winded herself when she went down, or that now her front sported as much mud as her backside. No, it was the fact that her favorite screwdriver, the one her father had given her, went flying out of her hand and right into the creek.

The first breath she managed to drag into her collapsed lungs was used to utter a colourful expletive. She then pulled herself up and crawled on her hands and knees to the soggy creek edge. The screwdriver glinted dully in the cloudy depths.

"Damnation."

She thrust her arm into the cool water. Even sinking up to the point her ear touched the surface, Sarah couldn't reach the tool. She took her arm out and glared at the screwdriver lying tranquilly in the muck. With a muttered curse, she took a deep breath and plunged her head into the scummy water.

Opening her eyes in the murk was out of the question, so she groped in the silt. To make matters worse, the bank was starting to give way under her weight. Her hand scrabbled frantically while she imagined the newspaper item:

Blonde found drowned in creek clutching screwdriver. Sources say she was always a bit screwy...

Her fingers closed around the familiar handle just as a clump of bank crumbled under her. She wrenched her torso out, hair plastered over her face and shirt completely soaked.

"I s'pose that's one way of panning for gold."

The male voice startled her, and Sarah jerked into a sitting position. She swung her head around, sodden hair whipping her cheeks.

A man stood a few metres from her. One thumb was looped through his belt while the other hand scratched Fly absently behind the ears. The worn cowboy hat was pushed back, revealing laugh lines around blue eyes, while a faded T-shirt and jeans hugged his lean build.

"Trifle unorthodox, though." He looked amused.

Sarah pushed back her dripping hair and stood, slipping the screwdriver into her work belt. The fact that Fly was sitting submissively at the stranger's feet told her she had nothing to fear from him. Still, she didn't like the idea that anyone, especially an unknown male, could just waltz onto her property.

She gave him her coldest, most intimidating courtroom stare. "Excuse me, you are...?"

"Jackson," he said, unhooking his thumb from the belt and extending his hand to her. "Garnet Jackson. You called me about some beavers."

This was Trapper Jack? Not quite the Yosemite Sam look-alike she was expecting. After a moment's hesitation, she took his hand. It was warm and hard, the palms dry and calloused. "Sarah Thomas." She was suddenly aware of the picture she must present and felt her cheeks heat. "I wasn't sure when you'd arrive, Mr. Jackson." Or *if* you'd arrive.

The corner of his mouth lifted and the eyes crinkled. "Call me Jack," he said. "Was in the neighbourhood. Thought I'd stop by."

Sarah found herself wondering how many women had been swept off their feet by the boyish charm of that smile. Fortunately, her divorce had cured her of all desire to flirt, so she was completely immune. And even if a quick glance at the hand playing with Fly's ear revealed an absence of a wedding ring, she wasn't interested. Not one bit.

Jack nodded at the pump. "Might want to have that raised a couple of feet. Don't think she'll run in the water."

Sarah ground her teeth and swallowed the sarcastic *Oh really?* that bubbled to her lips. Still, she couldn't help retorting. "Well, it wasn't in the water when I brought it down last week."

Surprise registered on the rugged features. "*You* brought it?" He strode to the pump. "That thing's pretty heavy." He gave the metal frame a shake. It barely moved. "How'd you get it down here?"

Sarah's temper rose. Clearly, he didn't believe she'd been able to do it herself. "I had it air dropped by an Amazon drone," she snapped. "What do you think? I dragged it."

He chuckled. "You and what army?"

She clenched her fists. Trapper Jack was showing his sexist stripes.

He squatted to look at the now-submerged pump platform. "You get Rob to do this? I'm surprised he'd take a job under water."

"I built it myself," she ground out stiffly.

He glanced at her, eyebrow raised. "Is that right, eh?" His voice dripped with disbelief.

She opened her mouth to retort and then closed it again. Blow him off and she'd find herself without a trapper and a mess of beavers that were ruining her property. She swallowed. "My dad was a framer," she said evenly. "When he had to babysit me, he'd drag me along to his worksite. He worked, I watched."

"A man don't babysit his own kids. He cares for 'em."

The blue eyes were looking at her with a singular intensity that made her heart skip a beat. In an effort to hide her emotion, she folded her arms. "At any rate, I'm going to have to add a metre to that platform."

He stood. "How high was the creek yesterday?"

"A good foot lower than it is right now."

Jack whistled. "How 'bout you show me that dam?"

Without another word, Sarah led the way through the tall grass that was now most definitely a marsh. Her boots squelched noisily in the mud and mosquitoes swarmed around her face. She was hot and sticky, and her stinky mud-encrusted shirt clung heavily to her skin. She hoped this guy would get rid of the beavers asap so she could get back to fixing her pump and trying to make a new life for herself.

The dam was on the opposite bank a few metres from the pump's location and looked for all the world like a pile of sticks. Sarah pointed an accusing finger at the structure. "There."

Jack stood beside her. There was something about him, a kind of rock-solid steadiness that was strangely comfortable. For a moment, she allowed herself to wonder what it would be like to be with a man who was at ease with himself, someone who didn't have to resort to belittling her to prove his masculinity.

Jack jerked his head in the direction of the structure. "'Fraid that's not a dam. It's a lodge."

Sarah turned to him. "Does it really make a difference? It's made by beavers, it's blocking my creek, and it's turning my property into a swamp. Just do something about it."

He rubbed his chin. "Well, you'll have to get the permits before I do anything."

Sarah put her hands on hips. "Permits? What do I need a permit for? It's my land and they're trespassing." When he didn't respond, she continued. "Can't you just tear the dam—lodge—apart? Don't you have a gun or something? Shoot 'em!"

Jack raised an eyebrow. "Can't do that," he drawled. "Not legal. Feds won't allow it."

Frustration surged over her. "How—"

"Shh!" He put a hand on her arm and pointed. "Look."

His palm was warm on her sweat-cooled skin and very distracting. Sarah had to will herself to follow his outstretched hand.

A beaver swam from the lodge, effortlessly cutting the water. Two smaller versions of the rodent trailed behind paddling valiantly to keep up. The parent pulled itself onto the bank and began to chew on the nearby cattails. Eager to mimic, the little ones likewise tried to pull themselves up. One succeeded, but the other couldn't seem to find a purchase on the slippery bank. The large beaver called a series of rising tones, and with this encouragement, the kit pulled itself onto land. The trio then waddled farther into the grass and was lost from view.

It was a touching moment and Sarah was aware that she had witnessed something rare. All at once she felt as if she was the intruder. Granted, the beavers had moved in after she had, but this was their environment. Who was she to throw them out?

She turned and found Jack studying her.

"Kinda puts a different spin on things, don't it?" he said.

She nodded and slapped at a mosquito. Then again, the beavers were making a mess of her plans. She didn't want to have to draw her water from a stagnant pond, and she didn't much care for the insects that were breeding in the still water.

Jack stared out at the lodge. "Saw where you put your trailer," he said. "Nice spot."

"Thank you," she said crisply. "I'm going to build my cabin there."

"Uh-huh."

Sarah could hear disbelief behind the bland tones and drew a breath to retort.

"If memory serves," he continued, plucking a piece of grass and twirling it between his fingers. "I think there's an even better location over yonder." He nodded his head downstream.

The nerve of the man. First he intrudes on her solitude, then he tells her where to build her cabin. As if she didn't know the best location on her own property. It took every ounce of willpower to take a calming breath instead of telling him to stuff his ideas someplace dark and inaccessible.

"If memory serves?"

His cheek lifted and the eyes softened. "Used to swim this creek as a kid. My folks live just up a ways."

Sarah blinked. It was strange to think that this man hadn't moved away from the place where he'd grown up. Did people here just...stay?

He was looking at her steadily now. "If you built there, you'd be downstream from the beavers."

Sarah gazed back, sinking into the depths of his blue eyes. "I guess..." Okay, she hadn't really explored all of her property; she'd just basically gone with the suggestion of the real estate agent regarding locating the cabin. Downstream, the creek would run freely and the water would be fresh.

She sighed. "Just where is this spot of yours?"

"Round that bend and along a ways," he said, inclining his head. "I think I remember some kind of rough track leading to it from the road." He started off through the grass. "Could probably get a truck down it."

They walked in silence along the reedy bank; the only sounds were the wind in the grass and the deep buzzing of a dragonfly as it flew past. She vaguely recalled this area from when she'd searched for Fly on the first or second day she'd arrived. She realized now that she probably should have scouted her whole property before starting to make her nest.

Jack halted abruptly, and she almost plowed into him.

"What do you think?"

She followed his outstretched arm to where the creek curved gently, hugging a stand of poplars. She could hear the gurgle of water and noticed a tiny waterfall splashing into a pool enclosed by grassy banks. A trio of spruce trees invited the placement of a picnic table or bench, and the gentle breeze that blew past carried no trace of decay. It was a lovely location and Sarah was humbled that it was hers.

Jack gestured to a clearing about twenty meters from the creek. "I'd say that would be a sweet spot for a little cabin. 'Course, you'd have to move your pump," he continued. "But just until you put in your well."

Move your pump? Dragging it up the bank was one thing, but getting it all the way over here was quite another. Air-dropping it would be about the only solution. She envisioned the item in the Interlakes Bulletin:

Residents were astounded to see a drone barely skimming the surface of Horse Lake carrying what looked like a water pump. "Poor lil' thing was all tuckered out, totin' that load," old-timer Herb Watson said. "Near ran over Shorty Biggar and his son while they was fishin'..."

Sarah took a deep breath. "It's a very nice location, but there's no way I'm going to lug that pump all the way here. Besides," she continued looking him in the eye. "I've done a hell of a lot of work on my present site, and I really don't feel like starting over."

Jack folded his arms over his chest. "Truth be told, I'm not much for killing critters, 'less it's for meat or pelt."

Sarah's jaw dropped. "You're a trapper and you don't like killing crit—animals?"

He shook his head and looked out at the creek. "Even relocating 'em's a gamble. They usually don't take to their new surroundings and wind up as cougar fodder." He scratched his forehead. "So, I'd be mighty motivated to prevent something like that."

"You would, would you?"

"Yes ma'am. Why, I might even see myself helping a neighbour out with moving a heavy pump or digging a foundation."

Sarah stiffened. She could see where this was going. Help the damsel in distress, worm into her bed. This was exactly why she'd left Vancouver. "Thank you, Mr. Jackson, but—"

"The way I see it," he interrupted, "moving your cabin site'd save me a heap of trouble. Won't have to fill out papers or get permits."

"Right." She folded her arms across her chest.

"Reckon if we used my winch, it'd probably take an hour to move that pump, whereas it'd take at least a week to get those beavers gone."

"Are you kidding me? A week?"

He nodded towards the cabin site. "In a week, we could have a nice little foundation ready and set up your trailer snug and cozy."

We? Seriously? Who did this guy think he was? Even if this location was much nicer and more picturesque than her present site, did he really think she'd let him call the shots? Did he expect her to let him into her life so easily? She took a breath to retort.

"There'd be a price, mind you," he said.

Aha! Negotiation—something she was familiar with. Would any of his terms include dining? Dancing? Romancing?

"Price?"

The corner of his mouth lifted. "Yes, ma'am. You don't get something for nothing out here."

She raised an eyebrow. "Of course."

He pushed his hat up on his forehead. "Well, it's like this. I have a little wild animal sanctuary—a rehab centre, you might say."

Whatever she was expecting to come out of his mouth, it certainly wasn't that. "A rehab centre?"

"Yes, ma'am. Got a little bear cub named Stubby that near starved after his mama got shot. I have a crane with a broke wing, and a fawn that was just left for dead at the side of the road. Folks find 'em and bring 'em to me."

"A rehab centre?" Was he serious? A trapper with a wild animal menagerie?

He nodded. "Now, problem is, I don't have enough hands to muck out the cages, bring in fresh bedding, and make sure the water's filled. That's where you'd come in."

Sarah stared at him. "You're serious."

"Dead to rights. I even got a beaver kit. Taking care of that young-un would be a good way to get to know your new tenants."

Sarah pinched her lower lip. It wasn't first time she'd been surprised by the opposing side's offer, but definitely the first time cleaning out animal cages had been presented as a term. "How would you determine an equitable exchange?"

Jack rubbed his forehead with his thumb, then pulled down the brim of his hat. "I'd say equal time. If I put in an hour, I'd expect the same from you."

It sounded reasonable. Sarah looked around the idyllic site. More than reasonable. At that moment, Fly came galloping out of the grass and made a beeline for Jack, tail wagging happily.

The trapper crouched down to scratch the dog behind the ears. "Let me know your decision. Meantime, I'll get started on the paperwork. Have to warn you though, the C.O. might not approve. Trapping season's long over."

Sarah's gaze rested on Fly, panting up at Jack with adoring eyes. Maybe it was time she stopped looking at every male as someone she had to prove her worth to. If she could manage this agreement and maintain her independence, then she would have proved to herself that she wasn't a helpless princess.

And at the same time, maybe she could teach a certain trapper that Sarah Thomas was a force to be reckoned with.

"No, don't bother," she said, looking into his clear eyes. "Your terms are fair, and I can certainly see this is an ideal spot."

Jack rose and extended his hand. "So, we have an agreement?"

The corner of her mouth lifted and she took his hand. "We have an agreement."

WEDDING CRASHER COUGAR

Creative Nonfiction

Chris Kempling

The large bride, who was eight months pregnant, moved across the dance floor in a stately way, a BC Ferry cruising into port. The spindly groom tenuously grasped her poufed shoulders, not quite able to get a good grip, looking like a parenthesis against a marshmallow. Being invited to a wedding for someone I barely knew was not my idea of a good time, but I thought I would settle in and do some serious people watching.

The hall was not large, but the only one available in the small Cariboo community. The DJ was pumping out country tunes, the obligatory chicken dance song, and Bob Seeger's "Old Time Rock 'n' Roll." I was desperately hoping to hear the "Too Fat Polka" (*I don't want her, you can have her, she's too fat for me, Hey!*), but didn't think it would go over too well.

Little boys in crooked bow ties chased one another around the edges of the hall until they bumped into the mother of the bride and got screeched at by several tipsy matrons. A too-tall flower girl did a stiff-legged "waltz" with a boy half her size, pausing occasionally to reach behind and lift a hand sliding surreptitiously below the waist. Her partner would then cast a mischievous grin to his buddy at the next table and initiate his next attempt to cop a feel.

The tobacco addicts headed out to the covered entrance to escape the heat and nurse their beers while sucking squinty-eyed on their smokes. The talk ranged from the high price of hay and the low price of steers to the lousy condition of the roads and the friggin' idiots at the regional district office.

Back inside, it was time for the bride to throw the bouquet. All the unmarried lasses gathered for the traditional foliage fling, giggling at one another, but with determined glints in their eyes. The first toss went directly into the low ceiling, so a second attempt ensued. The next throw sailed over the heads of everyone and landed in the lap of the mother of the groom. Everyone roared with laughter. Toss three resulted in a wild dogpile of taffeta and lace and ended with a victorious bridesmaid brandishing her trophy like the Statue of Liberty, a displaced tendril of hair dangling indecorously over her left eye.

A loud squawk at a table across the hall was followed by a string of curses as the bride's uncle dumped a full glass of red wine down his wife's pale yellow party dress. A gaggle of women swooped down, clucking and dabbing, then hustled her off to the ladies' room for more determined cleaning efforts. Uncle Wilf looked uncertainly at his glass, at the knot of women at the door of the ladies' room, then wobbled over to the bartender for a refill. No sense crying over spilled wine, eh?

While that little drama played itself out, an older woman dressed in tight jeans wandered in the front door. Apparently she was from the trailer court across the road and couldn't sleep with the big party going on at the hall. Nobody seemed to mind the wedding crasher. She headed over to the bar and got a drink, but it was clear she had already had a good head start before she came across the road. She stood at the edge of the dance floor, drink in hand, eyeing the dancers, cowboy boot tapping to the tune.

The few dancers left on the floor were dodging the bride and her father, who were vigorously stacking the chairs of the guests who had already headed home. The wedding crasher spotted the groom and headed over to ask him for a dance. It was a surreal scene, as the cougar snuggled up with the groom on the dance floor, while his enormously pregnant bride in full wedding regalia tipped over tables and snapped the folding legs shut, seemingly oblivious to her new husband's dance partner. As the music faded, the cougar reluctantly released her prey and wandered off into the sultry heat of the night.

Uncle Wilf's stained wife emerged from the ladies' room and ripped into him with unrestrained ferocity. He slowly got up and weaved unsteadily for the exit, pursued by his enraged wife, who did not appear to have inhaled since the beginning of her diatribe.

Was I just in a Fellini movie? As I crossed the parking lot, the click-clunk of bride-stacked chairs punctuated the night.

TRUE NORTH STRONG

Fiction

Katie Marti

The wind howls and I wish I was home, warm under my grandmother's quilt watching soap operas with her and my sister. I wish I was anywhere but where I'm at, which is the Tim Horton's parking lot beside my school, waiting to fight Cody Simon. The crowd is way bigger than I thought it would be—maybe forty or fifty kids all bundled up and huddled together because it's late November and feels like snow. There's even kids here who don't go to our school, kids I never seen before in my life. Some of them are from the reserve and some aren't, but none of them give a shit why me and Cody are fighting. They just want to watch and be part of something so they can talk about it later and say they were there. They're all texting and taking photos and one of them's wearing a Tim Horton's uniform, probably on his smoke break. I blow into my hands because they're already stiff and I don't want my skin to crack and bleed once we get going.

Cody called my sister, Mikayla, a whore. He said she went all the way with him and now she's pregnant. I know it's true, but I told him he was a liar, just like his father. I told him he would end up dead, just like his father. That's when he told me to meet him here after school, to see who would end up dead.

Everyone knows Cody's father killed himself. It's not a secret. It's not even that interesting, really. He was in debt and got caught stealing from the band council is what I heard, but who ever really knows what's going through a person's mind. I do know that Cody's mom left the two of them a couple months before his dad died. No matter why or how a mother leaves, things always go to shit when she's gone.

Cody's here now and he's breaking through the crowd until he makes it to the inside of the circle on the other side from me. His eyes are wild and huge, but I can't tell if they're full of hate or fear. He throws his chin toward me and I nod back. That means it's on, but neither of us makes much of a first move except for hopping around and spitting on dirt so cold it may as well be pavement. The crowd won't have it, though. They start yelling, phones in the air. Everyone wants to see a good fight, especially the kid in the Tim Horton's uniform. He's calling me a pussy, so I guess he's on Cody's side.

Fighting is 90 percent wrestling and 10 percent punching. I'm a decent wrestler because I'm pretty big, but I hate punching. Punching hurts. A few years back, my mother's boyfriend came home drunk when she was working and went into my sister's room. I burst in and hit him so hard I shattered his eye socket and broke three of the bones in my right hand. It took a whole month before I could hold a pencil. Last I heard he was still blind in one eye, and far as I'm concerned, he's one lucky bastard. I don't actually think of myself as a violent person, but I would have killed him in that moment if my sister hadn't pulled me off of him and hit me in the face herself.

This is what I'm thinking about when I feel Cody on top of me and the ground underneath me. It's a swirling mess of stale smoke and fresh weed. Cody's arm is across my throat and I can't breathe, but then, somehow, I'm on top of him and I'm punching him, hard. I try to stay away from his eye socket but it's impossible because he's thrashing around, trying to get me off him. We trade top and bottom a bunch of times. It's exhausting—neither of us is in very good shape, but the crowd is screaming so loud I know if I stop fighting I'll never hear the end of it. I'd say Cody probably wins in the end. He gives me a black eye and a fat lip, plus my hand is already so swollen I can't even make a fist. I got him good a couple times too, but his face looks pretty much the same as it did when we started.

The only reason it's over is because our gym teacher is here now, running and yelling and jumping in the middle of everything.

"HEY!" He hollers as he grabs my arm, yanking on me. "Break it up, boys! BREAK IT UP!"

We act like we're still fired up but I think, secretly, we're both pretty glad he's here. I mean, we showed up and we fought so there's nothing to be ashamed of. I think it was a pretty decent fight. Cody and I swear our faces off and give each other the finger as Mr. Peters stands between us with his arms stretched out like a traffic cop and tells us that the principal will be calling our parents. I say not to bother calling Cody's dad because he's dead. Someone nails me in the back with a can of Coke and it fizzes like a firecracker when it hits the ground.

The trailer smells like moose stew and wood smoke when I get home. My grandmother's crockpot is sitting on the kitchen counter, and I take a peek inside, lifting the sweaty lid and breathing through my nose. The steam makes my face wet.

"Eh!" she scolds from the living room. "Keep it closed!"

She's sitting in her chair, rocking and doing beadwork with her legs crossed at the ankles, and Mikayla is asleep on the couch, curled up in a tight ball like she always is. She sleeps a lot lately. I know it's not right, but I leave everything about my sister's situation up to my grandmother because it scares the shit out of me and I don't know what to do. I have to walk right through the living room past both of them in order to get to my bedroom, so I pretend to scratch my head as I pass by my grandmother, trying to hide the black eye but also knowing she'll see it anyways.

"What's this?" she asks me. "Were you fighting?"

I keep walking down the narrow hallway to my room, running my fingers along the ridges of fake wood panel. *Thwap. Thwap. Thwap.*

"Eh!" she calls after me. "Don't you walk away from your grandmother, Alexander Paul!"

I sigh and stop in my tracks, chucking my backpack, so it crashes against my bedroom door. My sister is awake now and I walk over to sit on the armrest of the couch, picking at the rust-coloured fabric where it's all worn out.

"Start talking," my grandmother says.

"Nothing to say."

"You have a black eye and your lip is fat, but you have nothing to say?"

I shrug, still picking.

"You get kicked out of school?" she asks me. She always asks if I got kicked out of school.

"They don't kick people out of school," I remind her, finally looking up. She's still sewing and staring me down at the same time.

"Well maybe they should," she replies. "What was this fight about? Was it Cody Simon?"

"It was nothing," I tell her.

Then I make the mistake of looking at my sister, and we all know what the fight was about.

"He's a fucking asshole," my sister says, laying her head down and closing her eyes again. Her long hair is greasy. I can smell it. She used to be so proud of her looks, always wearing too much makeup and taking forever in the bathroom.

My grandmother puts her sewing in her lap and waves me over. She takes my hand, pulling me down to kneel on the floor in front of her old leather rocker. I wince when she squeezes my swollen knuckles, so she lets go and touches my face instead.

"Your mother would not want this."

I nod with my head bowed low, but she lifts my chin, and I have to look into her small, dark eyes. They're my mother's eyes. You don't forget your mother's eyes.

"I understand fighting," she tells me. "We are all fighting, Alex. But strength is not power. You are strong, sure. Such a tough guy. But tell me, will your knuckles bring your mother back?"

I bow my head again.

"Look at you," she continues, swatting me on the top of the head. "You can't even hold an old woman's hand."

I smile because my grandmother's hardly an old woman. She had my mother when she was nineteen and my mother had me when she was twenty. Her hair is still as black as mine. She touches my face again and, as I stand up, I kiss her on the cheek. It's round and smooth, and it smells like Noxzema.

"I'm sorry," I say. It's mostly true.

The theme music from the end of her soap opera fills the living room, and my sister gets off the couch, holding onto her stomach even though she hasn't even started to get big yet. Maybe she has, I don't know. She wears the same sweatpants and hoodie every day. I watch her shuffle into the kitchen and begin setting the table.

"Wash up for dinner," my grandmother says. "And change your clothes. You're filthy."

In the bathroom I clench my teeth and swear under my breath when the hot water hits all the tiny cuts on my skin. I look into the mirror, past the streaks and splashes at my own face, into my own eyes. They are my mother's too, even the black one. Especially the black one. I feel bad for upsetting my grandmother, but I'm not sorry for fighting Cody Simon or for saying what I said. I won't apologize. I'm not a liar.

I change into clean clothes right down to my socks and head back toward the kitchen where my grandmother is scooping stew into bowls and my sister's piling slices of bread on a plate. I stand in the living room watching TV until the next commercial break, then turn it off and take my seat at the head of the old wooden table we still set for four.

NORTHERN BRITISH COLUMBIA

Northern BC's vast wilderness is twice the size of the United Kingdom. The mountain ranges, which dominate the northern landscape, were shaped by volcanic fire. The rugged, heavily forested valleys between them were carved by glaciers. Much of Northern BC is preserved and protected by provincial parks and nature reserves. The stunning landscape features turquoise-coloured glacial lakes, alpine meadows, hot springs, volcanic cinder cones, and a miniature Grand Canyon.

Many of the pristine wilderness areas are accessible only by horseback, charter plane, or on foot. The Great Bear Rainforest and other parks of the region are known for their magnificent freshwater and saltwater fishing, paddling, hiking, skiing and snowmobiling. Parks provide habitats and sanctuary for wildlife small and large alike.

Northern Native Peoples speaking Cree (Ne:hiyawe:win), Sekani and Dunne-za, among others, are thriving in this lush farm country. The vast and highly productive plains here are known as "Canada's Bread Basket."

Cities & towns include: Dawson Creek, Fort Nelson, Fort St. James, Fort St. John, Houston, Kitimat, McBride, New Hazelton, Prince George, Prince Rupert, Smithers, Stewart, Terrace, Tumbler Ridge, and Vanderhoof.

Dawson Creek is "Mile Zero" of the historic and picturesque Alaska Highway, which was constructed during World War II for the purpose of connecting the US to Alaska through Canada. This highway, which opened to the public in 1948, goes north through Fort St. John, Fort Nelson, Stone Mountain, Muncho Provincial Park, and Liard Hot springs to mile 1500 (2414 kilometres) at Watson Lake, Yukon.

D.F. Barrett

Punchaw Lake, south of Prince George, photo © Murphy Shewchuk

PRINCE GEORGE, HOUSTON, SMITHERS, TERRACE, FRASER LAKE, HAZELTON AREAS

BIG CITY HUNTER

Creative Nonfiction

Denise Little

Sometimes you can't *wring* the city out of someone.

My dad was a big city boy. He grew up in Toronto during the Big Band era and danced his weekends away in the ballroom of the Casa Loma, wearing a canary yellow zoot suit replete with extended watch chain looped nearly as low as his knee.

He was a gifted dancer, a fact that I can personally attest to, having had the father-daughter dance at my own wedding. We twirled, spun and covered the floor like we had been rehearsing for months. By contrast, my newly minted husband, Richard, and I looked like a couple of ill-trained circus bears caught rocking from one foot to the other, more or less in time with the music.

Anyway, the point is, Dad was a guy who grew up revelling in the city life and kind of out of the loop with respect to earthier pursuits—hunting, for example. On the other hand, my dad was also the kind of guy who liked to take on new and exciting hobbies, interests, and passions, and so it came to be that—since a move to my mother's hometown of Prince George obliged him to adapt—he kitted himself out for hunting in the bountiful woods of Northern British Columbia's vast interior forests, Gerry style.

To go hunting, Dad prepared by donning his typical hunting attire. He wore leather dress shoes. He had no option but to wear his preferred dress pants, having never owned a pair of blue jeans in his life. Rather than the ubiquitous hunter's mackinaw, Dad chose a dress shirt, an argyle sweater, and no tie. He had a warm jacket, and on his head he wore a fluorescent orange hunter's cap, so that another hunter would not mistake him for an animal and shoot him by mistake.

I was privileged to have been invited to hunt with Dad a few times over the years. The car I best recall going hunting in was Dad's Chrysler New Yorker. He loved that car. We would head out of town on a highway, and then eventually turn off onto a forestry road. We'd follow the forestry road and then finally turn onto an inactive logging road. That is when the work of hunting *really* began.

Dad would slow the New Yorker to a crawl. He would smoke Matinee cigarettes with his left hand perched out the driver's side window and listen intently for the sound of wildlife. My job was to remain silent. His 306 rifle, safety on, was propped between him and me within handy reach, should a moose chance to cross our path.

Dad sloooowly traversed the labyrinth of old logging roads and occasionally pulled to a near complete halt in order to deliver a moose-call. With hands cupped around his mouth, he called loudly, "mmmmmmMMMeh!" or "mmmmmmMMMah!" out the window of the New Yorker.

Other than the rifle and the fluorescent cap, I can't think of a single other thing Dad carried that would come in handy, should he shoot and kill a big game animal. No knife. No tarp. No rope. No flashlight in case darkness fell while we were dressing our quarry with our bare hands. Nothing.

The very first time my big brother, Ken, set out to go moose hunting without our Dad, he bagged a moose. Dad could hardly believe Ken's great luck. "Those things are practically extinct around here!" he assured us all.

You would be excused for believing that Dad never did shoot a moose of his own. Especially since, as keen as he was, he never did.

Big game hunting, it turned out, was not Dad's strong suit, and it is kind of amazing that he didn't get shot at more often.

One time Dad went hunting with a bunch of guys from work. They were supposed to focus their energy on hunting deer, then set up a camp in the wilderness, then hunt deer some more, and then return home at the end of the weekend with a deer each to put in the freezer.

Instead, they headed out in the back country and proceeded to get too drunk to hunt. Their designated driver was a guy who limited his drinking to two or three beer while he drove. The headlights were not engaged, as that, they all agreed, would be cheating. The driver stopped the car when he could no longer see in the dark, and they all bumbled about in the night trying to set up tents and make fire and things like that. Basically, as Dad told the tale, they were simply incapable of much more than curling up in sleeping bags under a moonless sky and passing out. A couple of fellows camped in the car.

The next morning when they all woke up, it was to discover the car had stopped the night before about three giant steps away from a sheer rock cliff that would have seen them plunge two hundred feet to their inevitable deaths. Since the men had gone hunting without any clear idea as to *where* they were going, a search party would have been useless, and their petrified and/or skeletal remains would have been discovered in due course by berry pickers or day hikers years after all the children were grown and their wives had remarried.

So they abandoned the deer hunt and went home to recover. Dad was certainly clear that he bore precious little responsibility for the inexcusable lunacy of the Guy's Getaway, and I'm sure his position was shared by all other participants.

Flash forward several years, and Dad's gone hunting again. This time, having not much luck hunting the apparently Nearly Extinct Moose from the comfort of his Chrysler New Yorker, Dad decided that perhaps duck hunting might be more rewarding.

And so it was that Dad, my little brother, David, and I found ourselves hunkered down in the wilderness on a chill autumn morning beside a small, still pond bedecked with scores of ducks.

The ducks were sound asleep, and I envied them that.

David and I were frequently reminded to remain stock-still. Also, we were forbidden to speak. What fun we had with that—not! Dad was allowed to smoke because we were downwind from the sleeping ducks, although he smoked in slow motion so as not to frighten the canny fowl. This may have been a hunting tip he picked up on the tame shores of the mid-city duck pond of his youth. His shotgun lay across his lap.

Being an Ultimate Sportsman, my Dad could not be tempted to shoot a sitting duck. I know this because as David and I grew weary of remaining silent and motionless for seven million hours in the cold predawn, we began to advocate a massacre, albeit very quietly.

At bloody last, the ducks flushed! They had been dead asleep one second, and the very next they flapped up in a skirmish and lifted from the water's surface.

Dad leapt to his feet, swung his shotgun to his shoulder, sighted down the barrel, and at the precise moment he pulled the trigger, we saw a flash from the shore exactly opposite us as another hunter opened fire.

"JESUS H. CHRIST!" Dad exclaimed before yelling, "HOLD YOUR FIRE!" to the probable lunatic hidden in the woods.

Well, finally! Some excitement! We had actually been *shot at* and Dad had *nearly killed* a deranged armed man in camouflage across the pond! And now our Dad was going to take action by stomping over to confront the madman in the wilderness and give him a piece of his mind. David and I trailed behind, hoping that if there was to be bloodshed on this terrible morning, it would not be Dad's, although a glancing wound would be okay because it would make a sweet story for Show and Tell the next day.

As Dad and the probable killer strode toward one another, we realized there was a second, smaller accomplice also hanging back a ways from the obviously enraged head psychopath. David recognized him first.

"Daryl—is that *you*?" David squeaked.

It was our cousin, Daryl. Uncle Bubby was the Weapon Wielding Assassin. Uncle Bubby, who once shot a wild rabbit which turned out to be a neighbour's prize pig.

Dad and Uncle Bubby laughed and shook hands as the ducks vanished overhead. We sat together and shared an amicable early lunch before heading back down the logging roads, onto the highway, and home for an afternoon nap.

I was relieved that we didn't shoot any ducks. It turned out that the reason my brothers and I were included on such excursions had little to do with family bonding time and everything to do with the fact that *if we were present* when a duck was shot, our contribution to the whole affair would be to pluck and clean the duck once we got home.

My brothers would terrorize me and each other with disarticulated body parts. I would make the little webbed feet tap dance on the cutting board or maybe slap someone on the cheek with a wing. One particularly memorable duck post mortem involved my big brother Ken, who made the grisly discovery that he could make a headless duck quack.

No one liked to eat duck. No one.

The duck hunting thing was pretty short lived.

So, Dad took up pig farming as a hobby. Gerry style.

A SNOWBALL'S CHANCE

Fiction

Jeanine Manji

It was the early 1970s, just after my twentieth birthday, when my fiancé Gary talked me into leaving my home in the city, to be modern pioneers in northern British Columbia.

"It'll be our chance, Jess," he urged. "Only a few years of sacrifice and we'll be able to save enough for a down payment on a house here. It's a good company. I can really get a start there."

I remember looking at his earnest face and thinking I could survive anything for that man. So I agreed to go for the three years of his contract with the mining company, and he agreed not to make me stay a moment longer unless I liked it.

We married and spent our honeymoon driving the six hundred miles north. When we arrived in late May, after travelling the last one hundred miles beyond Prince George on gravel road, I wanted to run right back home. The town where the mine was being developed hadn't been built. Our first real home together was a single-wide trailer identical to all the others the company had carted up that same long drive we had just taken.

The first few weeks there, I became obsessed with keeping the mud that coated the town out of the trailer. I swept the floor every few hours, but the dirt just settled back in. Yet despite what would become an annual losing battle, I would learn to look forward to that spring mud as a welcome respite from the winter.

Winter was an unrelenting black night that clung to the earth for months. The dark was a constant companion—there upon awakening and there long before we rested our heads. The snow was its stark counterpoint, padded mountains separating us from the bleak dark nothing. In those early days, before the company installed street lamps and sidewalks, the snowbanks even separated us from our neighbours. Gary was a hard worker and, at twenty-seven, had more experience than a lot of the younger men. He was appointed foreman on his crew that first year and to maintain morale and help some of those newer to town to find their footing, he took it upon himself to get to know the crew socially. This meant that he often brought them to our place after work, for dinner and a drink.

That's how I met John Grey. He was a young happy-go-lucky kind of guy, and new to Gary's crew, having had a tussle over a woman with one of the foremen on another shift.

That night, I felt his eyes follow me as I moved around the table serving the pasta I had cooked. Later, when I was doing the dishes, he came into the kitchen on his way through to the bathroom at the back of the trailer. He brushed up against me, and dread crept up my spine.

"You've got pretty hair," he said in a low voice as he reached up to take one of my blond curls in his fingers.

"Thank you," I stammered, and then ducked under his arm to move away from him and toward the living room where Gary was sitting with the rest of the men. Gary's eyes caught mine, and concern crossed his face. He patted the seat beside him.

"Come join us," he said, and I did, feeling better that I had him close by. That night Gary apologized for the way John had acted. "He won't do it again," he promised.

The next time the crew came for dinner, Gary made sure that those who had wives brought them along. With the buffer of other women around I was comfortable again, and though I felt John's eyes watching me, he never made another advance. Instead he got interested in Sheila Morgan. Sheila was a buxom brunette with a voice that sounded like stone on stone. She had come to town a good six months before we had, when her husband got on with one of the first crews.

One night, when I went to the back of the trailer to get a sweater from our bedroom, I was shocked to find them up against the wall. Sheila's arms were wrapped around John's neck, his hands roaming over her body as they kissed. She saw me before I could turn around and leave.

A few minutes later, she cornered me in the kitchen where I had retreated. I knew my face was still beet red and my hands were shaking in the dishwater as I rinsed the dishes.

"If you tell anyone—I mean anyone—what you saw, I'll turn every woman in town against you," she warned me. Then she walked into the living room and perched next to her husband Charlie, laughing at the joke he'd just cracked.

I kept silent, afraid of what Sheila could do.

Just before winter set in that first year, John went south, called away on a family emergency. When he returned several weeks later, we were all surprised to find he had married and brought his new wife home. Madison Grey was movie-star beautiful and moved with a grace that I hardly believed possible.

John lounged at the table with Madison so closely tucked next to him they didn't need two chairs. She had a quick wit and a laugh that tinkled when the men at the table joked with each other. They all looked at Madison with longing, the same way men from my father's generation had looked at Marilyn Monroe.

Sheila was at dinner that night, and I watched as her face soured. Her husband Charlie was smitten as much as the rest of them, but Sheila's eyes were on John, her sneer of contempt reserved for Madison.

"So are you ready for the winter?" she asked Madison.

"Oh yes," Madison gushed. "Johnny's letting me decorate our trailer any way I like, aren't you, Johnny?"

"Anything to keep my girl happy," John answered, a lazy grin on his face as he watched his animated wife. "Maddy's great with a sewing machine. Can sew pretty much anything."

"And then, once we start to have children, well, that'll keep me busy. I was just at my sister's lying-in a few months ago. After the baby came, she was so busy she didn't have time to do anything else."

Sheila was now staring hard at John. "Yes, children do tend to be quite a bit of work," she answered. "Those who are lucky have them early. There's nothing like a baby to keep a girl busy during the long winters here."

The other three women there nodded in agreement, and Sheila added, "And those who are not so lucky have to wait for what can seem like forever."

I cringed inwardly. Sheila was already a mother of two and so a reigning queen of sorts to those of us who had not yet achieved motherhood. In my case, I hadn't been one of those lucky enough to get pregnant.

Charlie spoke then. "Well, if you ask me, there are lots of things to do besides changing brats' diapers and warming bottles on the stove for a two a.m. feeding."

"Yep," John agreed.

"Yeah, but most of those activities end in those two a.m. feedings," Graham, one of the men in the room, quipped in return.

His wife, Charmaine, batted at his arm. "You're embarrassing me," she said, blushing while looking pleased because, as everyone knew, she was now expecting their first child.

After that day, Maddy and I, and a few of the other women, began a sewing circle. John had not sung false praises—Maddy really was a wiz at sewing. She was also a generous and patient teacher who quickly taught us more than the basics we had all picked up in our high school home economics classes. She even shared some of her fabrics with us before we received the material we ordered through the Sears catalogue.

One of our regular group projects was to produce a baby quilt for each of our friends as their bellies began to grow. One by one, babies were born and our friends were drawn away from us to join the ranks of motherhood, forming bonds with others who had achieved that status.

"I learned to sew from my mother," Maddy said one day, not long after our sewing circle had dwindled to just the two of us. "She was the seamstress in the town where Johnny and I grew up, and she was always busy. I helped her until Johnny and I left town five years ago."

I nodded and listened, not sure if I should ask for details that didn't seem to fit with the story I knew of their relationship.

"You see," she said without stopping, "I've only seen my mom once since I left town." Her voice cracked. "Daddy refused to forgive me for what we did, and he told me the Lord would never forgive me either."

My mind was racing now. What was she talking about? "I'm sure that whatever you did can be forgiven," I said.

She looked up at me, her face stark. "Can I trust you to keep a secret?"

"Of course," I said, a little tentatively.

She lowered her voice to nearly a whisper, but in the quiet house I heard every word as clear as could be. She began to talk, and once she started, the words tumbled out one after another.

"Johnny and I, we got pregnant the first time we did it. I was seventeen. He was eighteen. Daddy wouldn't let us get married. Said Johnny was no good and would never amount to anything. Said he'd kill Johnny if he ever came near me again. Johnny had sworn he loved me and that nothing would keep us apart, but he didn't count on what Daddy could do. So he finally left."

I stopped sewing the hem on the slacks I was making and looked up, listening intently.

"Daddy made me pack up my stuff, and in the middle of the night he drove me to my aunt's house five hours away. I stayed there for six months, until the baby was born."

"What happened to the baby?"

"The doctor came to the house to deliver the baby. They didn't let me see her," she said, her voice dead of all emotion. "I heard them talking as I drifted off from the exhaustion of the birth. The couple they had found to adopt would be pleased it was a girl. They had only boys, and a girl would be cherished. I have held onto that hope ever since." She looked up at me, smiling through tears. "That my mistake could bring joy to someone else and that the baby wouldn't suffer for my sins."

I sat with her in silence and watched her face express a myriad of emotions as she searched for the thread of the story and finally began again.

"When I woke up she was gone. My aunt gave me two days to recover and then packed my bags and gave me a bus ticket to a town where Daddy and Mama had arranged for me to work as a seamstress with a woman Mama knew. I was sent on my way as though the whole thing had never happened."

"What did you do then?" I asked.

"When I got there, I was put to work sewing for a wedding. The woman I worked for was demanding, but fair. She even let me keep the scraps of leftover fabric so I could make things to sell. She gave me a place to live and fed me. It was almost like living at home again."

She paused again and took a deep breath as though gaining the strength to continue to climb to the top of a steep hill. I waited, casting my eyes down to my lap and finding myself surprised to see the pants I was hemming sitting there.

"I never saw Daddy again," she said. "A few weeks after I started working for the seamstress, my sister sent a letter saying that Daddy had died from a heart attack."

"Oh, Maddy, I'm so sorry." I squeezed her hand, trying to hold back a sob that was rising in my chest. My own father was larger than life, and I couldn't imagine him gone.

"I travelled home to pay my respects to Mama, but she didn't want to see me. She said it was my shame that had killed him, and she told me to leave and never come around again. "

"But how did you find John again?" I asked, not wanting to leave that detail uncovered.

She smiled at the memory. "My little sister Julia. She and I still keep in touch, and she married one of Johnny's friends. So, when Julia moved away with her husband and Mama couldn't afford to make the trip to go to her lying in, I went to her to help, and she told Johnny I would be there. So, it was my sister who helped me to find Johnny again. You have no idea how happy I was to see him."

"So, that part worked out at least," I said in a lame hollow voice.

"Yes, I thought so too, but now—" Her voice began to crack. She took a deep breath and whispered, "Now I think God is punishing me for going against my Daddy's wishes."

"What do you mean?" I asked.

"I can't get pregnant," she said. "I've tried and tried for months, and I can't get pregnant."

"I've been married for nearly a year," I said, "and I'm not pregnant yet."

"Thanks for saying that," she said, squeezing my hand. "But I got pregnant so easily last time I'm sure I'm being punished. Johnny is being so brave. He says all he needs is the two of us anyway, that kids would only get in the way. But I know he doesn't mean it. What man wouldn't want to have a son or a daughter of his own?"

"Well, I'm glad that you and I aren't pregnant yet," I said, trying to lighten the mood. "I still need to learn how to do a French seam without tearing it out three times."

"You're such a good friend," she said. "Thank you for listening. Promise me you won't tell anyone?"

"I promise." Feeling as though I needed to take some sort of action, I pulled my sewing from my knee and stood up. "Let me make us a cup of tea."

Maddy had returned to her sunny self that afternoon, and for the next few weeks she looked as though she had put down a large burden and left it in the path behind her. Then three months later, when I visited the clinic in September, the blood tests confirmed what I had begun to suspect. I was finally expecting a baby.

Gary was over the moon with excitement, so much so that it was him, not me, who broke the news to Maddy and John when they were over for dinner a few days after he heard the news.

Maddy smiled at me and asked how I felt. I told her that I was fine, just a little bit of morning sickness but nothing to worry about.

"Why didn't you tell me?" she asked when the men went to the living room after dinner for a beer.

I looked away, afraid to meet her eyes. "I didn't want things to change between us."

"Why would they?" she asked, but we both knew the answer to that.

"I guess you're right," I said, "I still have a lot to learn about sewing."

"Yes, you do," she said with a straight face that melted into a grin.

Maddy and I began to drift apart after that night. At first she would visit and leave after a half an hour or so, but soon, as my belly grew to become a wedge between us, she found excuses not to come and stopped extending invitations.

I tried to console myself with the books my mother would regularly send to me, and with the familiar voices that came to me through the CBC radio station, but I was lonely. When Charmaine began to invite me to socialize with her and a few of the other women who were in their first months of motherhood, I jumped at the opportunity. It was good to spend time with them, learning more about what to expect, and how to care for the baby once it arrived.

It was during one of those visits that Sally, a woman who was closest to Sheila, let slip a secret I wish I'd never kept. Sheila was not there; she and I had avoided each other since the John incident.

"I'm so glad you stopped spending time with that loony woman," Sally said.

"Yes," Charmaine said, "I was beginning to worry you'd become a recluse like she has. It's not healthy."

"She doesn't feel like she fits in." I said. "If she had a baby, perhaps it would be different."

"Maybe, but all the same, I'm glad you're part of our group now." Charmaine stood up. "I'll be right back, I have something to show you."

When she was gone, Sally leaned in toward me and spoke in a low voice, though the only other occupants of the room were Charmaine's infant, fast asleep in a playpen nearby, and Sally's little boy who was too engrossed in playing with blocks to hear. "But that's what's so odd," she said. "It's like she thinks she can get pregnant on her own."

"What do you mean?" I asked.

"Well, I can tell you, since you already know about Sheila and John's little affair last year." I blushed at the memory and she continued. "Sheila told me that John had a vasectomy."

"What do you mean?" I said in a low whisper, hoping she would tell me what a vasectomy was.

"He told Sheila she didn't have to worry about any little Johnnys ruining her marriage. That he got himself fixed after he knocked up some girl in high school."

"You mean he can't have children?" I was stunned and almost forgot to keep my voice low.

"That's why it's so odd that she keeps going to the clinic to get pregnancy tests," Sally said. "I think she's going a bit loony."

"I wonder if she knows," I said.

It was Sally's turn to be shocked. "You mean he didn't tell his own wife?"

"I don't know."

"Don't know what?" Charmaine asked as she rejoined us in the kitchen.

"I don't know if I'll be ready for the baby," I answered, improvising quickly.

"Oh, you'll be a great mom," Charmaine patted my hand. "Now look at the block I made for your quilt. I hope you like it."

The last time I saw Maddy, it was a Tuesday in the dead of winter. I took care dressing that morning to go to the clinic for my biweekly checkup. I wore a pair of black stretchy pants I had sewn the week before from material that had finally arrived three months after I placed the order, and applied some pale pink lipstick and a bit of blush.

The sun still hadn't risen when I started out at 8:30 that morning, and I was pleased the car started on the first try. The block heater hadn't failed us yet.

I drove slowly to the clinic. I had promised Gary that morning that I would drive carefully. His face had been drawn with worry, so I smiled brightly, brushing away his concern with my hand. "Driving is easy now," I told him. "You taught me well. The trouble will come when the snow melts. What will I do then? I don't know if I remember how to drive in the summer."

"I'll teach you," he said, smiling that slow grin of his, and I smiled back, happy that I had eased his concern.

I waddled through the front door of the double-wide trailer that served as our medical clinic and crossed the puddle-strewn linoleum to check in with the nurse.

I then walked to the crowded waiting area and was surprised to see Maddy seated alone in a corner. It had been several months since we had seen each other and I was alarmed at the change in her appearance. Her usual coiffed hair hung dull and limp, and she wore no makeup on her pale drawn face.

As I started toward her I passed Sheila, her brown hair in a new style, her lips sporting a slash of scarlet lipstick. She appeared to be reading one of the tattered magazines from the table in the middle of the room, but I saw her sneer as I lowered myself to the seat beside Maddy.

"Slumming, Jess?" she asked, and a few of the other women in the room tittered. I raised my hand to shield my baby from the negative atmosphere and turned toward Maddy.

"Hello, Maddy," I said.

"Hi," she said, not looking at me. She was too busy knitting a pair of pink booties.

I waited, not sure what to do. Sheila and the other women were sharing smirks.

"You're lucky you don't have long to wait," Maddy said. She was staring at my stomach now with an intensity I was finding uncomfortable.

"Yes, only eight weeks left," I whispered. "How have you been?"

A shadow flitted across Maddy's face. "I feel different this month, you know? I'm sure I'm expecting. I can feel it."

"Maddy…" I wanted to tell her but noticed Sheila's eyes boring into me

"I hope it's this month. I have the room ready, you know. Oh, and look." Maddy showed me the little bootie. "I have oodles of clothes for her. Been sewing and knitting for months now."

"Mrs. Grey," the nurse called from the doorway.

"Oh, that's me." Maddy jumped. "Watch my coat for me?"

I squeezed Maddy's hand and whispered, "Sure, I'll be here when you come back."

"Thank you," she said. "If it doesn't happen soon, I think I'll go mad."

Sheila curled her lip as she listened to the exchange. "Don't get your hopes up, honey," she shot vehemently as Maddy scurried toward the nurse. "You've got a snowball's chance in hell of not being disappointed."

"Mrs. Morgan," the nurse called next.

"It's about time," Sheila muttered as she rose and followed after the nurse.

Sheila wasn't there when Maddy returned. "Not this time," she smiled through teary eyes as she retrieved her coat. "But that's okay," she reassured me, trying to smile brightly. "I have a feeling it will be a boy now. I think I'll go home and order blue paint, just in case."

"Take care of yourself," I said to her. "Maybe we can get together soon?"

"Maybe. Yes. Soon. I have to go." She paused as she buttoned up her coat and looked at me. "Thanks for being there for me, Jess."

"That's what friends are for," I answered, guilt growing in my chest as I watched her leave.

"What a crazy loon," one of the women in the room said to me. "I don't know why you bother with her."

I ignored the barb, picked up a magazine to flip through, and fought a war with myself while I waited. By the time my name was called I was resolved. Tomorrow I would go to Maddy and tell her what I knew about John.

The next morning I was awakened by a loud banging on our front door. "Maddy! Are you in there?" I tied my robe around me as I rushed down the hall to open the door.

"Is she here, Jess? Is Maddy here?" John asked as he stepped inside.

I shook my head, looking up into his feral eyes and stammered out, "N-no."

"When did you last see her?"

"Yesterday, at the clinic."

"The clinic? Is she sick?"

"She was there about a pregnancy test," I told him. "We used to go together every couple of months before I…" I looked down at my belly.

"Oh God. This is all my fault," he said.

"What's up, John?" Gary came down the hall, sleep still pulling at his eyelids.

"Maddy's gone. I gotta go after her."

Gary frowned. "Of course," he said. "Anything we can do?"

"No, I need to find her. She told me a few days ago she needed to get her dad's forgiveness. I didn't listen."

"But she told me her dad—"

"Yeah, I know Jess." He looked at me in anguish, then turned to Gary, "I gotta go. I gotta find her before it's too late."

"But—"

"Let him go." Gary put his hand on my shoulder, and John turned, opened the door, and plunged back into the cold.

"But, Gary," I said, turning to him and looking into his eyes, "her dad is dead, so I don't understand how she can go and talk to him."

"Damn," he said running his hand over his face. "Jess, stay here in case John comes back. I need to go get help."

That day dragged on more than most, and Gary didn't come home for hours. When he finally returned, I had drifted to sleep on the couch waiting for him.

"Jess," he said, shaking me a little. "Jess, wake up. Let's go to bed."

"Did you find her?"

He looked at me hard in the faint light coming from the kitchen. "Yeah. We found her."

"Where is she?"

"Jess, Maddy's gone."

"Where did she go?"

"Jess, honey." He sat down on the couch beside me and took both my hands in his. "Maddy wasn't in her right mind these last few months. She packed a suitcase of clothes, baby clothes, and walked to the outskirts of town. We found her there this afternoon, frozen in a snowbank."

His face was drawn, making him look much older than his twenty-eight years.

"She wasn't going south like John first thought, Jess. She left letters addressed to her sister, her mother, John, and you."

"Me?"

He reached into his coat and pulled out a pink envelope and handed it to me. "I wasn't sure I should give this to you but … well, Jess, I realize I can't protect you from everything."

I looked up at him and then down at the envelope that bore my name in Maddy's perfect cursive. My hand shook as I carefully opened it.

> *Jess,*
>
> *Thank you for standing by me and for being my friend. I have never had a real friend like you before. I wish you joy until we meet again.*
>
> *Love, Maddy*

TANGLE WITH AN ANGRY MOOSE

Fiction

Danell Clay

Ray shifted gears in his 1963 International pickup. The truck was eleven years old, but he babied it, and the paint still looked good. In three months, when the snow started to slick up the roads, he'd have to add weight or the backend would fishtail, but the truck's motor had never given him any real worries. Not like the cargo he was currently hauling. That was a headache, no mistake about that. He glanced in the rearview mirror to see his stepdaughter, Trudi, and her friend in the truck bed, laughing and waving their hands over the side, the August sun making their faces glisten. Couldn't they just stop squirming and sit still?

Ray was only driving to a backroad in the woods near Prince George, so he didn't see the attraction, but the girls had been bored and asked to come along, provided they could ride in the back. His wife, Denise, had made it clear that he'd better try getting along with Trudi—she and her daughter came as a package deal.

"Trudi is going on thirteen, it's a difficult time," Denise had said. "I wasn't all joy and light myself at that age. There are a lot of changes happening in our lives, and you need to give her time to adjust." But Trudi just plain didn't like Ray, and the feeling was mutual. He'd never have gotten away with talking to his old man the way that girl smart-mouthed him.

Ray turned off the main road and the tires started crunching gravel while the dust rose behind them. Trudi made a big production of holding a hand over her mouth and coughing. It was the middle of summer, so what did she expect? Roads were going to be dry. It hadn't been his bright idea to ride in the back. Still, he slowed down, and the bumps from the ruts in the road kept the girls more worried about keeping their seats than complaining. That was Trudi for you. She could go from acting like a silly six-year-old to a screaming harridan with a faster acceleration than the old International had ever clocked.

Ray turned his attention back to the road. Prince George called itself "The Spruce Capital of the World," and the way the pine seemed endless every which way you looked, Ray thought the moniker was about right. You could feel swallowed by the forest out here. The truck pulled around another corner, and there was a clearing and what remained of a dismantled saw and planer mill. There wasn't much left of the mill now, just the beehive metal burner and a pile of sawdust.

It had been a family-owned business, and Ray had liked working here. He missed the six-man crew and how they stopped all the machinery at noon so the men could pull up their stump-chairs into a circle and open their metal lunchboxes. If it was a nice day, they'd start a campfire or if there was rain, they'd huddle under the shed. They would rib the young guy whose job it was to keep feeding the waste to the conveyor belt, or Jon would tell a long story in his heavily-accented Czech that would end in a joke. The two brothers, sons of the owner and supposedly their supervisors, were always bickering. They were okay to deal with when you got them alone but together they were oil and water. It was all very predictable, until one day, it wasn't. The family shut down the operation. Just like that.

Ray pulled up the truck by the burner.

"Stay out of the woods and off of the sawdust pile," he said to the girls. Trudi rolled her eyes.

He grabbed a coil of wire that he had "helped himself to." It had been left inside the fence of an electrical power substation. He wasn't usually a light-fingered man, but money was an issue. In a way, this was Trudi's fault, too.

"I can't wear those jeans to grade eight," she'd screamed, her face twisted, tears running down her cheeks. "Everyone will think I'm a dork. My first year in high school, and I will be the dork-girl." She wanted jeans with flared legs like all the other kids. But Ray had a Sears card and no room on the other credit card for fancy jeans.

Ray stood in the middle of the burner and started a small fire using the sawdust as tinder and dead branches he'd gathered. The fire would melt the black cable and he would be able to sell any copper wire he salvaged. He'd heard that the pulp mill was hiring and had put in a resume. He figured he had as good as chance as anyone at getting hired but for right now, money was tight.

Bang! Bang! Bang!

The metal inside of the burner reverberated with the sound of rocks being pitched against its side. Ray clenched his teeth as the sound clanged in his ears.

"Ray, we're bored," Trudi said, her face appearing at the entrance. "There's nothing to do out here."

Ray didn't answer, and the girls disappeared. He concentrated on stripping away the melted covering from the wires. After a while, when the job was nearly done, Ray realized he could no longer hear the girls talking to each other and hadn't heard them for a while. He wondered if they had climbed to the top of the sawdust pile despite his warning. Sawdust could be dangerous. It had killed more than one person by collapsing, pulling them into its centre and filling their lungs. Ray imagined his problems disappearing into a hill of sawdust. Now you see her, now you don't. He picked up the copper and searched the clearing. There were footprints around the base of the sawdust.

"Trudi," he yelled. "Let's go." No sign of the girls. He turned in a slow circle, searching for movement. Fireweed was always the first plant to reclaim a clearing and along with the red paintbrushes they had made a good start on turning the mill site wild again. The forest wanted back what had it had given up.

Would it have killed Trudi to listen to him just once?

"Trudi, time to get going." Ray wiped a palm across his face. The girls wouldn't really have climbed the sawdust pile, would they? Oh Lord, Denise would never forgive him.

A twig cracked, and Ray saw the white of Trudi's shirt through the trees.

"Geez, Ray, we heard you the first time," she was saying, but Ray was watching the forest behind them. The tops of the trees were shaking and something was traveling fast through the brush.

"Get to the truck, now!" said Ray.

"You can't yell at—"

"Go!" Ray grabbed her arm and pushed her along. She finally picked up his urgency and the girls started to run.

He glanced back. A moose burst out of the forest. Splintered remnants of branches were clinging to its antlers. Its ears were laid back, and the fur running down its neck and between its humped shoulders was standing straight up. It lowered its huge antlers and charged. The girls weren't going to make it.

Ray ran at the moose. "Back off, back off!" he yelled, arms above his head, waving the copper wire. The moose veered off, its hooves throwing dirt, then swivelled around and faced Ray. The truck doors slammed. Ray did a ninety-degree turn and ran towards the truck, but the animal, 1300 pounds of rage, was right on his heels.

He wasn't going to make it. Then the truck horn sounded, and the truck drove towards the moose. As the vehicle pulled forward, Ray threw himself down and rolled under the truck without even slowing down. His elbow hit the frame with a jolt that had him gritting his teeth. The truck stopped. Ray could see hooves and legs in a cloud of dust as the truck rocked and jerked backwards. The moose hit the pickup hard. Metal scraped as antlers raked up the fender. Another impact sent the truck rocking back. Ray rolled away from the tires, hearing antlers raking up the truck's frame again.

Ray could see hooves pacing. He peered around the tire well. The moose shook his antlers from side to side then stood still. It twitched his ears forward and looked off into the forest as if hearing a call that eluded Ray. It lumbered back into the forest.

Silence.

Ray stood up and opened the truck door. The girls were huddled on the floorboard of the pickup. "You girls okay?" he asked.

They nodded, eyes wide. Ray stretched, feeling his bruises and his hurt elbow. He threw his hard-won copper wiring in the truck bed and swung into the driver's seat.

"That was something, wasn't it?" he said after they were safely back on the highway.

"You slapped that moose on the nose with wire," Trudi's friend said.

Had he? He didn't remember that. He just remembered waving the wire in the air. "Nah, I don't think so."

"Oh yeah, you did. You should have seen the look on that moose's face." She giggled, but it sounded more like relief was bubbling out of her.

"He was probably amazed by my monumental stupidity. Anyway, it was good thinking of you girls to start beeping the horn and let the truck roll forward," he said. "It probably saved me a good stomping."

"That was Trudi's idea," said her friend. Ray supposed he really should learn the girl's name.

"It was good thinking, Trudi," he said.

"But Ray, the moose really ripped up the front of your truck," Trudi said, speaking for the first time. Even from the inside, Ray could see the dents, ragged tears in the paint and even a few punctures through the metal. The moose had really packed some force into his charge. But what a thing for her to worry about.

"Better the truck than any of us," he said. "I can pound out dents, but I'm not so great at fixing broken bones."

Ray was thinking that maybe he would take some of the copper and make the girls a couple of bracelets. Kind of like a memento of this day. The day they'd all faced down a mad moose and escaped. Later, when they were alone, he'd ask Denise to tell him the other girl's name.

Drawing by Chase Greenaway

CLOSE CALL ON AN ICY NORTHERN LAKE

Memoir, 1970, Prince George – Vanderhoof area

Wendy Squire

In the late sixties, my family built a cabin on the edge of Bednesti Lake, and all of us looked forward to spending every possible weekend there all year round. It was at the end of a long gravel road that wasn't serviced in the wintertime, so this meant we'd have to commute via snowmobile for the last part of the trip. We could ride the snowmobiles along the gravel road, but once the lake froze over, the shortest, fastest, and easiest route was from the truck stop and store at the northwest end of the lake. During one of our first winters at the cabin, we had a close call.

On a typical Friday night early in the 1970 winter season, my parents parked our yellow station wagon at the store to commute to the cabin by snowmobile. It was a good twenty below, but the cold didn't stop my brother and me from playing on the snow banks while Mom and Dad unloaded the snowmobiles from the trailer. I was seven and my brother was five and a half, and we loved making footprint patterns in the newly fallen snow.

We had a skimmer Dad had made using an old fiberglass army stretcher to haul our supplies and us kids. It reminded me of a big banana peel. Dad hooked it to the back of his machine. The cabin was well stocked before the road was snowed in but we needed to bring food that didn't like to be frozen, as well as drinks and clothing. Once my brother and I were packed in the skimmer with all the supplies, we headed out with Dad in the lead and Mom following on her snowmobile.

Not wanting to disturb anyone, we rode as quietly as possible past the little motel buildings, and I watched the snowflakes dance in the light from the big yard lamp. They quickly added to the already thick layers of snow on the swing set. The bright light tickled the snowflakes into twinkling, making the whole swing set sparkle.

We continued down the steep hill, launched straight off the end of the dock, and rode out over the frozen lake. The foot of freshly fallen snow provided a soft ride. That night, the only wind was caused by the snowmobiles. Above the perfect flatness of the lake, the stars were brilliant wherever they peeked around the clouds. The skimmer shushed over the snow between the friendly growling Ski-Doos. Rounding the small island in the centre of the bay, we crossed towards our cabin.

Running along about a hundred feet from shore, we were halfway to the cabin when Dad started slowing down. The snowmobile engine was screaming louder and louder, but we were going slower and slower. Dad waved Mom to go around him but it was too late. Dad's Olympique was bogged down in the soft ice of the lake, and Mom's little ten-horse didn't have the power needed to swing out and break a new trail. She was stuck too. Because of the insulating properties created by the latest dump of snow, the ice was soft and our machines were trapped.

Mom and Dad shut off their Ski-Doos, enveloping us in a snowbound silence. They looked at each other for a long moment before breaking that silence. I could see they were worried but didn't know why.

Dad looked at me and my brother. "Do not get out of the skimmer." We both obeyed without a word.

Mom stayed on her machine behind us and Dad cautiously stepped off into the deep soft snow. He began tramping down the snow on one side of his sled.

"Can I help?" I offered.

"Stay in the skimmer, both of you." He was using his no-nonsense voice. Unhooking the skimmer with us on board, he pushed it a few feet back along the fresh snowmobile trail.

Taking a firm grip on the rear bumper of his snowmobile, Dad heaved upward to swing it on to the newly trampled pad of snow. The Ski-Doo didn't lift up, but Dad went down! When the ice broke, his arms shot straight out from his sides like airplane wings and he sank to his armpits. He didn't say a word but smoothly turned his entire body to face his family and he looked very, very serious.

"Dad! Can you touch bottom?" I knew if he could touch the bottom of the lake, he wouldn't drown and we'd all be okay. I didn't notice the cold biting, or snow falling, or anything but Dad. Dad looking at me with his amazing ice blue eyes alert but calm. He gave no sign of the danger we were all in, especially him.

"Just," he assured me. He looked like he was doing the tippy-toe dance, bobbing off the bottom of the lake so I felt better. Years later I learned the lake was at least ten feet deep there and everything was not okay. His training as a firefighter kept him calm and in control. Dad carefully and deliberately hauled himself out of the water using the Ski-Doo's bumper for assistance and keeping his body flat against the surface of the ice. Like a big yellow fish, he slithered onto the packed snow. He stood slowly, testing his weight on the ice. His snowmobile suit glistened in the moonlight as water droplets started to freeze on its surface. He brushed the chunks of snow off his suit, always moving but never rushing.

"We'll have to go back." He didn't complain and he didn't waste any time. Mom and Dad quickly unloaded our supplies off the skimmer, hurriedly deciding what stayed and what got piled onto the patch of packed-down snow. Usually my brother and I were told to help but this time, despite our offers, we had to stay in the skimmer. And sit still. Everything but the liquor and us kids stayed behind.

Carefully tramping a trail around the ten-horse and turning the skimmer around, Mom and Dad dragged it back onto the trail we'd just made to get there. Very little had been said during all the activity. Everything was done efficiently, as if we'd rehearsed it back in town. Mom and Dad took turns pulling us and the liquor back towards the store, one of them always walking behind the skimmer. Their feet sank six or eight inches with every step, and each footprint filled with water. The wet snow quickly froze to the bottom of the skimmer, making it cumbersome and heavy. It lurched through the snow instead of skimming over it.

They could make maybe fifteen feet before needing to rest and catch their breath, which billowed around their heads as if they were steam locomotives. Like the old trains, we made slow steady progress. It was too cold to rush or to stop for long, and the lake was too unpredictable to not respect.

Once we got back around the island the ice was more solid, so Mom and Dad asked if we would mind walking to give them a bit of a rest. My brother and I were happy to finally be helpful in some way. We climbed out and they banged the frozen snow and ice off the bottom of the skimmer. Walking behind it, my brother and I were careful to follow strict instructions about where to put our feet. We did not stray off the snowmobile trail.

This was serious business and I knew it, though I didn't understand it. Even though he shivered, Dad never once complained about being cold or wet. No one else complained either—there was nothing to complain about, really. We each had a part, and we performed it as a privilege. We were a single unit with a single purpose. We were a family.

The cold, the difficulty walking, and my uncertainty about what just happened did not distract me from noticing how beautiful and quiet the night was. The kind of peaceful silence that can only be found in a snow-filled winter night. The soft plod of our boots in the deep snow, the muffled rush of our breath through scarves, and the rhythmic shushing of the skimmer were the only interruptions. Starlight twinkled on the tiny flakes of snow floating silently through the darkness to add another layer of fresh snow. I felt quite safe.

The store was closed by the time we made it back to our station wagon. We piled our wet clothes on the back seat and cuddled together in the front with the engine running and heat blasting. Mom and Dad broke open a bottle of rye from the salvaged liquor to help the warming process. My brother and I were each given a sip. It burned my throat, and a welcome fire spread out from my belly and tingled my cold toes. I was asleep before we pulled out onto the highway back to town.

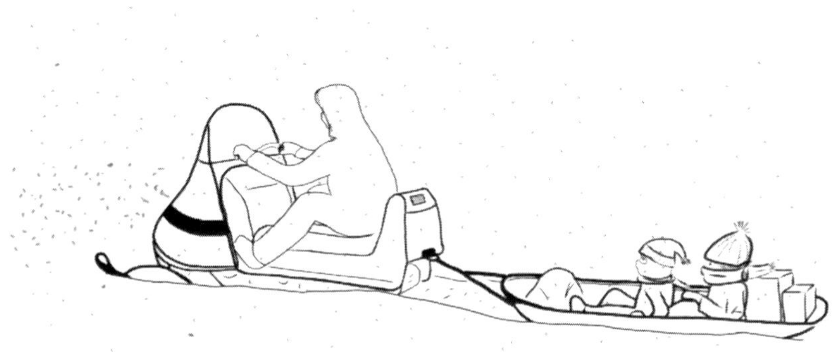

Drawing by Wendy Squire

THE GRIZZLY'S CLAWS

Creative Nonfiction

Tony Stark

After spending my life as an engineer, working on major projects around the world, I decided to retire with my family in the immense wilds of British Columbia. I had always been a dedicated fly fisherman and had learned to fly a float plane, so now I was determined to fish as many lakes and streams as I could in the Northwest of BC.

My wife was an intrepid soul and endured my frequent floatplane trips to the terra incognita with gentle good grace. However, on what was my final excursion into the wilds north of Highway 16, Lucia took me aside and looked me intently in the eye.

"Do not take Hector into the west, Vincent," she whispered to me, her Italian accent thicker through sentiment.

"Sweetheart," I replied kindly, "I was just out that way last week. The weather is gorgeous. I promise you, nothing is going to happen to me." I kissed her on the forehead, trying not to merely dismiss her good advice.

I turned to see our family friend, Hector, bustling fishing gear into the de Havilland Beaver I had operated for nearly twenty years. Hector's ruddy face was flushed with effort. His girth hardly fit into the door of the plane, leading him to carefully push the cargo for the flight as far back into the cabin as he could, puffing his round cheeks out with each lunge.

My gaze moved from my plump friend back to Lucia. "You think he's gonna have a heart attack?"

Lucia made a sour face. "No, not until the winter," she said sagely. "I just know some misfortune will befall him out there. He is a *cattiva influenza* upon you in the air."

I twitched at the Italian for "bad influence." It was one of Lucia's phrases of power. Every wife has a few that hit so very close to all the rough spots on her husband's shining armour that the sound of them gives him pause, even as they might raise indignance. Despite years of trust in my wife's hunches, I had to bite back the urge to remind her that we had just been out west to Oona Lake the day before, and that Hector couldn't get very far into trouble without me spotting him.

Instead, I sighed. "Let's leave it up to Hector, shall we?"

Lucia clucked her tongue and threw her hands up in the air, but said nothing. I motioned the civil servant over to us.

Hector arrived, mopping his brow with a red bandana. He was grinning with excitement.

"Lucia doesn't think we should go today," I said simply.

There was no need to explain further. Hector knew about Lucia's unerring hunches as well as any family friend. "Do you want to stay, and we can smoke our catch?" he asked.

"I've only got two days left in this gorgeous country, kind hostess," he said, and shrugged. "God knows, at the rate I'm expanding, I'll never fit in Vincent's plane ever again. I think I want to see those highland lakes—even if it kills me."

Lucia, a devout Catholic, crossed herself twice and glared at Hector as though he were refusing to wear his mittens on a winter's day. "Let it be on your own head," she said. "I'll keep the two-way radio on and wait to hear from you."

Hector and I had designs on Peta Lake, a beautiful lake nestled at about 800 m in the highlands north of Highway 16. There were several little round lakes, untouched, pristine ones, perfect for the short landings of the Beaver. As Hector noted, he was determined to experience as much of this wild country as he could before his holiday ended and he was sent back to Ottawa. The day was fine and clear, the green just starting to come into the cottonwoods. The ice had disappeared off of all but the highest of the lakes, leaving the water cool, fresh, and renewed.

Landing on the western shore of Peta Lake, I brought the plane into a tiny indent that served as a cove. We climbed out and sat on a log by the shore, letting the water and its invisible fish settle after the plane's disturbance.

We did not speak of the possibility of misfortune. Sometimes, only sometimes, Lucia was wrong. If she was, it was because her warning gave reasons to be extra alert to danger. If we friends were quieter than usual, it was because we were listening with all our ears, watching with all our eyes, for trouble.

We fished Peta Lake for three or four hours, caught a goodly amount of kokanee and one lake char that was as large as Hector's not insubstantial bicep. We fried up some of the fresh catch for lunch and passed my flask back and forth a few times. The abjurations of Lucia faded proportionately to the fullness of our coolers with catch and our bellies with my brandy.

Part of the draw for the aging bureaucrat to this particular vacation was his love of thrill flying. Hector's girth had always prevented him from obtaining his pilot's license, but he had loved spending time in the air with me, asking with childlike innocence if I was able to accomplish this feat, land the plane here or there.

In short, Hector was indeed a bad avian influence on Vincent Stark.

Hector finished frying a third fish for himself. He tossed a nip of my brandy on the pan, and he and I grinned boyishly as the excess raised bright magenta and blue flames that licked our nostrils.

"I wonder…" Hector would always begin this way when he fell into his *cattiva influenza* state. If Lucia had been there, she would have cried to the heavens and crossed herself at the speaking of those two words.

I also knew what those words meant.

But I had a belly full of fish I had caught myself that was warmed by brandy I had made myself from my own saskatoon wine. I felt like I was eight again, with the whole of the Great White North open to me and my pal—and this eight-year-old had one of the most versatile float planes ever made.

"What do you wonder?" I asked, eyebrow cocked.

"I wonder," Hector continued musingly. "That tiny, Lilliputian, miniscule lake just over there." He pointed back to the east shore of Peta Lake. "Could you land your plane there?"

"The round one," I asked, "or the—"

"That amazingly artificial-looking rectangular one," Hector replied. "The one that looked from the sky like it was carved out by a machine. So narrow it looked like you could reach out and touch the trees on either side."

I grinned. "You bet I can."

We two boys cleverly disguised as aging men piled our kits into the float plane, Hector puffing and reaching and pushing things into the tail with his angling rod. I hopped into the pilot's seat and lit myself a cigarette. I turned and watched idly as Hector began his boarding process.

This was a delicate affair for the large man. It involved a shimmying of his large carcass through the cargo door of the Beaver in slow degrees. First he would turn himself sideways, favouring his left side so he would be facing forward when he was done. Turning himself around in the Beaver was an emission of momentum that rocked the floatplane hard enough to produce whitecap ripples. It was best avoided when both men were full of fish and vinegar, as it were.

Hector eased his left arm and leg into the plane; he was already perched rather delicately on the reinforced steel boarding plate I had riveted onto the float to ensure he no longer dented it with his footsteps. Once his two limbs were inside, Hector gripped the handle on the ceiling tightly and slowly lifted and shoved his substantial gut into the plane with his right hand, pushing off with his right foot as he did so to add force where maneuvering failed. The entire process took at least two minutes.

When he had finally boarded the plane, he once again wiped the sweat from his brow with his classic bandana and retucked his lumberjack shirt into his jeans. I held onto the overhead handholds as the Beaver slowly came to a rest on the water. Hector settled himself in the passenger seat and, as was customary, I hopped in the back and threw a bit of ballast behind his seat to keep things level.

"Ready for some action?" I asked, grinning around my cigarette.

"Indubitably!" Hector clapped his hands together.

The de Havilland Beaver was one of the most remarkable aircraft ever made. With its clever design and powerful engine, the float plane could safely take off and land over a space of as little as fifty feet—if the pilot was good and the winds were obliging. This they both were.

We circled our campsite once more, taking in the vista on such a golden spring day, then we hopped over the little ridge and took a look at the target lake in question.

"That one!" Hector cried, pointing at the strange confluence of nature that had produced a lake, nearly 900 metres in the highlands, that looked like a small, perfect rectangle.

The lake was one of those odd pits that collect water in the Bulkley Nechako region. As I looked down upon it, the shadow of the plane gliding over the terrain, I knew it could be one of those rare sinkholes that went down as much as several hundred feet. The water was black, absorbing most of the light that fell on it, bespeaking much inky, still water beneath its surface. The trees on the west bank were growing right out of the water, leaning in the prevailing wind over the lake's surface and narrowing the wing room for the landing.

The east bank had a bit of rocky shore, however, and the trees were a few feet back from the water. The lake itself was long enough to land upon, especially if my passenger didn't mind steep inclines—which Hector didn't.

"Yeah," I nodded. "I can do it."

Hector clapped and laughed like a boy on Christmas morning as I brought the plane around. We came in so close to the tree tops that some intrepid spruce brushed their spiky new growth on the floats.

"Here we go!" I drew deep on my cigarette and dropped the nose down like I was drawing a line over the terrain with my propeller. The plane coasted down, and its floats touched the water with the gentle caress of a pre-Raphaelite in a medieval swoon. Barely six feet from the shoreline, my plane had plenty of room to coast to a stop.

The problem would be turning the craft around.

Once we stopped, we leaned forward and looked at the trees in the west leaning over the bank at this northern end of the lake.

"That's a little farther over than it looked from the air," I said, starting to doubt my ability to do this.

"It wasn't so severe where we came in," Hector said.

"Well," I shrugged, "we'll have to get out and push."

A singular look of incredulity blanched Hector's face. "How do you mean?"

I winked at him and coasted the plane to the northeast shore.

I hopped out onto the sharp basalt rock chunklets that made up the northern beach. They skittered a bit away from my hiking boots, but being a sure-footed little man, I positioned myself by the wing with ease.

"Like this." I motioned with my cigarette-holding hand in a large circle. "We spin the Beaver, then reverse our steps."

Hector's wide face filled the small cockpit window. "How do we keep the craft, once in motion, from spinning its way into those western tree trunks? It is, after all, on the water."

"It's not going to build up that much steam," I said, laughing. "Not with your fat ass inside. It'll just…" I grunted, "glide...gently *around!*"

As I spoke, I was attempting to move the Beaver by shoving on its wing. It barely rocked in the water. My short arms were trembling from the effort.

"It's not hung up on something, is it?" Hector's eyes were huge.

I shoved the plane with all the might I could muster a few more, futile times, then glared at my friend. "Only on you, Hector. We're going to have to reverse roles."

"I'm not set up for this sort of manual labour," Hector said. A large, well-manicured hand gripped at his chest. "Especially not on such irregular terrain."

"There's only two ways out of this box," I said, hopping back into the pilot's seat. "And only one way brings my plane and saves your arches."

Hector sighed dramatically and began his laborious exit process.

"Now, this baby'll spin right around with you pushing and me in it," I advised, lighting another cigarette. "So I'm going to fire up the prop and use it as rudder. Just give it a little shove and we can get reoriented."

"Don't leave without me!" Hector said, puffing. The sudden confinement in nature's majestic grip was taking its toll on the Ottawa man. I couldn't help but smile to myself. At least Hector would have a couple of neat stories to share back on the Hill.

"I won't," I promised.

The plane rocked once more as Hector stumbled out onto the rocky shore.

"And how, exactly, am I to get to the door once I have rotated the craft?" he asked me petulantly.

"You'll have to walk around the end of the lake," I called. "You can do that now, or after we get turned around, but where you are now has better footing for the pushing."

Hector looked down at the rocks and poked them with the toe of his boot. He squinted under the plane at more sheer boulders on the other side. "You'll have to bring the plane in close, Vincent!"

I nodded out the window, firing up the engine. "Yeah, I know. Now, let's get this thing done!"

Hector's face screwed up in disgust and he plugged his nose. He turned around and scanned the trees just behind him. As he told me later, about five feet from him lay a deer carcass, rotted from the melt. Its guts had been spread over the rest of its body, and the first flies had yet to settle on it. Hector held back the urge to retch.

He called out urgently to me, but at the time I was unable to hear him over the revving engine. Instead, I made a rotational movement with my hand and nodded at Hector's animated motions.

Hector cast a last glance at the carcass, then put his back into the wing of the plane. Without his heavy weight in it, the Beaver started to rotate gracefully in a small arc. Aided by the propeller, the plane was turning slowly in its miniscule runway.

Hector raised his hands to clap in satisfaction when he heard a snapping of a limb. At first he thought he had broken the wing of the craft and his heart caught in his throat. He realized it was the sound of wood snapping. He looked above him, certain he had pushed too roughly and the wing had clipped one of the low-hanging trees.

Then he heard the growl.

He turned, slowly, and saw the biggest grizzly bear in Creation. Mangy from its hibernation and hollowed out by hunger, the bear was drooling slightly over its fortuitous carcass. Rightly disturbed by the arrival of the airplane, the grizzly had hidden back in the trees as the dreadful machine with its whining propeller came right for him. Hunger and territoriality hadn't kept the grizzly at bay for long, however. Perhaps perceiving the starting of the engine as the creature coming for his cache, or perhaps just angry at the large presence on the shore by the machine, the grizzly had waited long enough.

Hector's eyes were huge. He stood stock still.

The grizzly's oddly pointed nose flared and flared again. His upper lip rippled in an undulating snarl. His immense paw and its three-inch claws scraped the rocks, tossing ones as large as Hector's head up into the air and over as though they were mere pebbles.

And, audible over the whine of the engine, was the growl...

"Vincent!" Hector cried weakly.

The grizzly had exited the forest to the east of the plane, effectively blocking Hector's only path to the door of the Beaver. Hector edged slowly to the east, wading slightly into the water to give the grizzly his distance.

The grizzly, unimpressed by the circling of both the strange machine creature and the plaid-coated bear in front of him who challenged him by rearing constantly on his hind legs, took a threatening step toward Hector

In the aircraft, I had turned the plane effortlessly and checked its rotation with ease. I looked out the passenger window in the cockpit, expecting to see Hector coming around to start his boarding procedure. There was no mass of MacGregor plaid coming into view.

Frowning, I peered out the window. Nothing.

"Don't tell me you turned an ankle," I rolled my eyes and moved to the cargo door. I stuck my head out, looking down the fuselage.

"Holy..." I murmured. My cigarette dropped out of my mouth and into the water with a hiss.

I was just in time to see Hector take his last, successful step toward the east. The grizzly charged him, drool and snarl and teeth and claw and what must have been, despite the winter, nearly half a ton of power behind him.

I knew better than to distract Hector with a yell. Instead, I watched, powerless, as the grizzly swiped at Hector with his immense claw. I felt the impact and winced. Hector doubled over as much as his girth would let him.

To my amazement, Hector, still bent nearly double, turned and stumbled toward the east and the open area of the shore.

I jumped into the cockpit, strewing curses, and sidled the plane over as far as I could make it. Even over the engine's noise, I could hear the roar of the bear.

Turning to leave my seat and help my friend, I was shocked to see Hector's girth flying gracefully in the air toward the open cargo door. His plaid shirt hung in tatters about his shoulders, and drops of scarlet blood dripped from the three gaping gashes in his huge belly. In the split second I had to look before I turned and took to the controls, I could see that

Hector's giant belly had saved his life. There was golden fat hanging out of the wounds and plenty of blood, but as the big man stretched himself out in flight there was no sign of even the muscle underneath, just fat at the base of the wounds.

As Hector made contact, the Beaver rocked dangerously toward the west, groaning on its float supports.

"Go! Go-go-go!" Hector screamed in a high register, hearkening back to his youth as a choir singer.

At the moment the Beaver rocked, and I hadn't heard a splash, I gunned the engine. The Beaver listed dangerously to starboard and rocked back and forth as Hector struggled to board the plane.

"We only got the one shot at this!" I advised, watching the end of the lake fast approach.

"I don't care!" Hector screamed. "I'm lodged! Go! Take off!"

I cast a quick look back at my friend. His jeans were bloody, but his left arm and left leg were securely in the plane. His belly was pushed up by his chin, sealing the gashes shut for the moment with the pressure of the door and his body.

"Hang on!" I advised and lifted the plane off the lake.

We crested the trees and circled around and landed back at Peta Lake, leaving Hector's right side to experience the miracle of flight without a cockpit for protection. I cut the engine and clambered out of the pilot's seat to check on Hector from the outside.

"How are you doing, Hector?" I asked. Hector turned his head to face me. I touched his arm. His visage was ashen, but his skin was not too cold or clammy.

"Remarkably, the pressure of the door seems to be easing the pain somewhat."

His eyes grew huge as he asked, "I didn't lose any of my ... insides, back there, did I?"

I laughed. "No, Hector, I didn't see you trailing any guts."

Hector gasped, then winced at the vivid image. I palpated the edges of the wounds. They were free from debris but were hardly bleeding from the pressure of Hector's girth against the metal frame.

I looked up at Hector appraisingly.

"Infection will be a risk, of course...grizzlies don't clean under their claws like they should," I advised. "But are you comfortable here?"

Hector was pinking up for being assured his internal organs were still just that. He nodded and smiled bravely.

"Remarkably, yes. I'm not too tired on my feet, and it really doesn't hurt too much for the pressure being applied."

"We can try to move you into the cargo hold," I told him as I balanced on the float of the plane. "But jiggling your gut around is going to open up the wounds—and hurt like hell. I don't know how much blood you lost on your way to the plane, but you could start bleeding afresh, and I'm not sure if you've got enough left in you."

Hector nodded. He looked me square in the eyes for a long moment.

"How serious is it?" he asked.

I shrugged. "Not as bad as you'd think, for being mauled by an irate grizzly bear. Your fat took most of it. I couldn't see that his claws even got close to your musculature, which is handy, otherwise you would be holding your guts in your hands."

"That's horrible!"

"Well, this isn't," I advised him. "Though several inches deep, you've pretty much just got three nasty flesh wounds."

Hector paused and considered. "Lucia is going to have a field day with this, isn't she?"

I nodded emphatically. "Oh my, yes."

Hector closed his eyes in mortification. I noticed the man wasn't too hypovolemic to blush fiercely.

"You're going to have some 'show' to go along with your 'tell' when you get back to the Hill," I remarked.

"Let's just get me home." Hector sighed as best as he could in his compacted position. "I can't imagine struggling into, then out of, this tin can."

I clapped him on the back and jumped in the passenger door. "Can do, old friend."

The engine fired up once more. Instead of hitting the throttle immediately, though, I grabbed one of the cargo straps and tied it to the hook welded to the side of the plane opposite the door. Then I cinched it firmly around Hector's hips. I tied another around his left arm, and a third around his left leg.

"What in heaven are you doing?" Hector asked me.

"If you pass out, you might relax your stomach muscles and fall right out of the plane. I'm not fishing your fat ass out of a pine tree between here and home on top of everything today!"

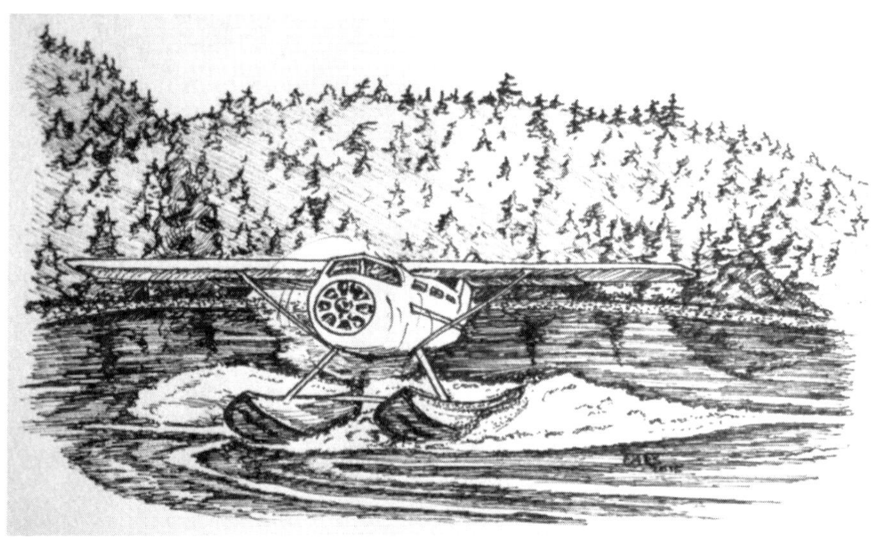

Drawing by Tony Stark, 2015

MCBRIDE LAKE

July 31

Vic Parsons

Cotton-prowed clouds drift
By a milk-faced moon
Over hills where mineral treasure lies.
Mist lifts from the Morice; beyond
Snow-capped peaks stand in gray solitude
In dominion over the lake.
Southward, across the lapping McBride waters,
Sits the watchful Tableland,
Shadowed clefts where the samplers go.
Five months ago this wintry shore
Was domain of wailing wolves
Now the bears hold sway.
The chill morning is mostly quiet,
Save for the generator's hum
And the low mumble of breakfast voices,
On the site where moose and grizzly tracks
Now stand fossiled side by side.
The bug-red wood interrupts the forest green
A sign that all passes in time
And briefer still this interlude.

WOLVERINE

Creative Nonfiction

Virginia Carraway Stark

It was a beautiful day for gardening. At least, it was a beautiful day in theory.

In practice, what can appear to be the perfect day by Dry Williams Lake just outside of Fraser Lake, British Columbia, can in reality be an almost impossible day for gardening. It starts with the hordes of black flies that emerge from the moist soil in late April or early May. This progresses to mosquitoes that dot the air like fleets of black helicopters and finally climaxes in wasps and hornets that build their nests quickly and wildly everywhere in a mad dash to finish before the first frost. After that, it's winter again and there is nothing to beset you until the snow-fleas freckle the leaving snow starting as early as February.

When I say it was a beautiful day for gardening, what I actually mean was that it was a day when there was a bit of a wind so the black flies weren't eating me too badly, and it was too early for mosquitoes and wasps to be in attack mode yet. Also, when I say "gardening," I actually mean hacking at overgrown brush to clear it enough for it to one day become a garden.

I had my hair tied back and tucked up into a baseball cap. My pants were tucked into my socks to keep the creepy crawlies out, and the long sleeves of my shirt were tucked into my gloves. Somehow, those areas would still be invaded by the end of the day by bits of bracken and black flies, but it was better than what would happen if I didn't take those measures!

I had a set of long snips with a mouth on them like a parrot's, and I was using it to snip the little willows and poplars that spring up and grow quicker than you can cut them before the hardness of the frost even leaves the ground. Those long snips were the first thing I thought of to use as a weapon when I met Checkers.

There were going to be complications to arming myself that, as I was working on taking down the brush and imagining the beautiful garden that would one day grow there, had in no way crossed my mind at that point. The complications started with ten little goslings, who all believed me to be their Mama Goose.

Anyone who knows goslings knows they bond fiercely with the first person they see, and in the case of these ten little babies, I was their mother. It must be a reciprocal connection, because I was crazy about those little goslings. They would come out and garden with me and eat the bugs out of the air and the weeds out of the garden bed. Geese are nature's best weeders, if you teach them when they are babies to eat the weeds you want to eliminate. They naturally develop a palate for whatever you feed them most and will avoid weeds or plants with which they are unfamiliar.

Ten little goslings fluttered around me on the ground, and my puppy played guard dog to them, romping and playing around them. I sang little bits of nonsense to them and myself to amuse us as we worked, "*Goose-girl, goose-girl, the boundaries between us have become decidedly loose.*" Silly little things that you say to animals and plants who will never judge you for being silly.

After working for a few hours, I set the clippers down and sat on the ground. I was instantly swarmed by the goslings, who ran under the edges of my over shirt like it was a skirt of Mama Goose feathers, and nuzzled into me. With goslings around me and my puppy on my lap it was almost easy to ignore the insects that swarmed to me nearly as quickly as the goslings had when I stopped moving and became an easy target.

It was in this pleasant moment when the forest was quiet except for the peepings of the baby birds that I noticed that it was altogether too quiet.

Then I heard it: A heart-stopping sound when you are in the wild—something BIG moving through the brush.

It sounded huge. Whatever it was, it was moving without any thought of being careful or quiet. It was completely unafraid, and it was headed right for me and my little family.

My first thought was that it was a bear or a moose. It was just so loud! I tucked my puppy under one arm, and the goslings, roused from their nap, headed off in all directions looking for more tasty weeds.

My heart was pounding in my ears, and my adrenaline was surging. How could I round up all ten of them before whatever was running at us made an appearance?

Rule one when being in the bush: Don't ever be too quiet.

Chances are that wild animals will try to avoid you. If you accidentally surprise them, as I was about to surprise the beast I would come to call "Checkers," they will act like a wild animal and do whatever they think is necessary to protect themselves.

"Hey," I called out. "Whatever you are, I'm not sure you noticed, but there's a bunch of us over here. You might want to take another path!"

I was saying whatever came to mind, just talking so that the beast would hear us and hopefully run away. The "bunch of us" was a bunch of baby goslings and a puppy. I looked around for my shears, a big metal tool I could use as a weapon in a pinch. What on earth sort of animal was I dealing with? I tried to remember the various rules for if it was a moose or a bear. Should I play dead? Run? Not run? What were the rules, and how could I get my awkward slow-moving goslings to safety? We weren't very far from the barn, the house, and safety, but even a short distance was much too far for us. The beast in the bushes paused. I could hear him listening.

I piled a couple of goslings on top of my puppy, who was squirming. All the baby animals were completely unaware of the possible danger. The animal was upwind from me, and I got a whiff of something nasty. It was a carnivore, that was for sure, and it had musky stink to it that made me tremble from the adrenaline pumping through my veins.

"Hey, Drew," I called one of the goslings who was fighting with one of his sisters. "Do you hear that racket? Maybe we should go inside?"

I couldn't even see the snips. The loud noise of a big animal approaching came closer. It was more cautious than it had been, so that was good. It knew we were here now, so however this was about to go down, we had at least removed the aspect of surprise from the equation. I finally spotted the aluminum snips about twenty feet away in the opposite direction from our safe retreat and the barn. They were too far away so I abandoned the idea of grabbing them and instead shooed the goslings towards the house. I kept up a dialogue, the goslings chatting back to me happily in their language of peeps and squeaks that would one day become formidable honks—assuming I could keep them all alive long enough to get their pin feathers! I was worried at that moment that we were all about to become some predator's lunch.

From the musky odor, I was pretty sure it would be a bear or perhaps a cougar that emerged from the bush. Imagine my surprise when an animal with a smooth, black head emerged from the undergrowth. My first thought was that he was one of the black otters that lived in the lake that had for some reason come all the way up the hill away from the water to explore.

"Oh, hello," I said in surprise.

The goslings had become suddenly aware of the danger and ran behind me with alarmed cries. I looked down at the animal, both of us frozen in place, inspecting the other and equally unsure of what our next move would be. He didn't seem nearly large enough to have made such a racket coming up the hill. I looked down at his paws and realized that whatever he was, he wasn't an otter. He had large, formidable claws that were easily four inches long. They were stuck like razors coming out of his hands, like that superhero, like ... the wolverine. I realized that must be what this animal was. I looked back up and met his gaze, and his mouth opened in a snarl. His teeth looked like they were too big for him to ever close his mouth around them. Thick strands of saliva clung to his open mouth and then dripped to his chest.

"We were just going," I said, incoherently. I spotted a branched stick and picked it up. Acting entirely on instinct I held it over my head like antlers and took a sliding step to the side and away from the wolverine. It quit snarling and cocked its head.

"Yeah," I said, trying to think of words to say and continuing my shuffling sidestepping.

Rule number two: Don't run away. Don't act like prey.

I don't know what I was acting like. I don't remember what else I told that wolverine, but I kept up a steady, talkative stream while he watched me. With every shuffle step, my little flock of geese ran behind me. I must have looked like the strangest and possibly craziest animal in the forest with my faux antler on my head and my puppy and two geese in my arms and eight more scurrying behind me. Whatever I was acting like, the wolverine must have decided that I was pretty funny. It sat down on its haunches and scratched the side of its face with one of its terrifying paws. Its head cocked and its mouth closed, almost like a funny-looking dog watching us.

It was no dog though. It was a wild animal, and I could see the calculating intelligence in its gaze as it watched my bizarre pantomime. After a moment of this, I truly swear that it smiled at me like a nearly human smile. It stood up and faster than I could imagine, turned and galloped away from me and my little family.

I watched the wolverine run off and dropped the stick, took off my shirt, gathered up the goslings, and ran them back to the barn and barricaded them in. I was in a panic at first. What if the animal came back for us? How could I garden or ever feel safe again?

It was that night that it hit me: Why should I feel threatened? Sure, he had come, but he had also been respectful, and he hadn't hurt so much a piece of down on one of the gosling's heads.

The next day, I walked around my property, looking for telltale signs of wolverines. They like to make perches on bowers and bent-over trees, where they watch for prey. They will fall on someone like death from above before you even know what is happening. They spend their time sharpening their teeth and claws, so their perches are easy to see if you look for the white exposed flesh that their claws leave on their lofty lookout points.

I found a lot of them, some of them older and some of them quite recent. The reality is that when you live in a place like British Columbia, you are living in wild beauty, and part of that beauty is the danger of the wild. That wolverine had been there for a long time, and he had chosen to do me and mine no harm. Wolverines travel through a wide area, hunting, patrolling, and marking.

It was a while before I saw the wolverine again, and by that time I had dubbed him "Checkers" as an ironic and perhaps panic-induced nod to Nixon's spaniel.

I saw him just as he was leaving. He had left something on the grass on the farthest edge of my land. He took off away from my land and I walked down the hill to the little brown bundle he had left on the side of the road. It was half of a tawny brown rabbit.

I looked at it and then turned towards the tree line where Checkers had vanished. "Thank you!" I called after him.

I picked up the rabbit half with a bit of Kleenex in my pocket. I had no idea how I was going to dispose of it, but the last thing I needed was for a watching wolverine to see me spurn his gift.

The perches where Checkers had watched for prey became weathered with age over the seasons—he did not return to mark them again. I never found another wolverine perch on my property again. Every two or three months, however, I would find part of a rabbit or maybe a dead bird or something unidentifiable left in the same spot at the border where my land met the road. It was in an exact line from where our confrontation had occurred.

That's the difference between people from British Columbia and people in the rest of the world: They have cats bring them "presents," and in BC, we have wolverines do the same thing.

Wolverine drawing by Tony Stark, 2015

BEAR LAKE LOGGING CAMP

Memoir

Beverly Fox

Fly in your mind, north of Prince George, BC, to the Bear Lake sign post, then turn east and trace winding logging roads 85 kilometres farther into the forest. Zoom in. You may spot half a dozen campers and heavy equipment—evidence of a logging camp, the seasonal home to some of our province's intrepid loggers. But beware—the journey is far more arduous in northern BC's winters than it is during the summer months. I was destined to discover that firsthand one winter.

This story began on December 1, 2013, when my husband, Dave, and son, Ed, headed off to camp for the winter logging season. Originally the company had intended the remote, least accessible wood east of Bear Lake to be a summer project. But the Ministry of Forests shut the operation down after a couple of weeks, citing earth compaction as an environmental threat, thereby leaving the company with the unexciting prospect of finishing the job after freeze-up.

Compounding the problem was the fact that, to keep the men working, the company had immediately flipped the crew over to the timber they'd originally intended for winter logging, located closer to home in Quesnel. So when it came time for the summer's problem to get dealt with, tough decisions had to be made: Machinery was shuffled, elderly machines were pressed into service, and the crew was split between the two locations.

With Bear Lake's sole, condemned motel having permanently closed that year, the unenviable task of setting up an impromptu winter camp obviously fell to the camper owners in the crew. What with temperatures diving to below –35 Celsius, the lack of facilities, and the prospect of contending with frequent breakdowns from older machinery, it was some grouchy loggers that got started on December first. And that was *before* the big snow.

Nostalgic summer memories still filling my head, the dubious wisdom of following my husband into the BC winter—in a camper designed for summer use—was easily rationalized. After all, prior to forestry descending on us in helicopters after only two weeks' logging that summer, hadn't I had a glorious time out there? I'd enjoyed picking blueberries, lazing by the creek reading a childhood favourite, *Wind in the Willows*, watching the dogs chase martins into hiding in the river bank, and dreaming

I might catch a glimpse of Mr. Toad or Ratty punting past if I was quiet enough.

Was I really naïve enough to believe that what had been an adventurous trek in summer would not be transformed into a complete nightmare by December? That washed-out roads, teetering precariously alongside remote lakes, would not become ominous toboggan slopes later in the year? I hadn't realized that a winding three-kilometre canyon, where visibility of oncoming logging trucks was virtually nil in the summer, would be far worse in a blizzard. Or that the single-lane arched bridge with puny one-foot side rails, straddling the Parsnip River, would turn into a terrifying skate when covered in ice.

The first weekend after setting up winter camp, both men had arrived home cranky.

"Dave's trying to freeze me out, Mom. He's so stingy with the camper heat, I'm a block of ice in the morning. Speaking of which, how's a guy supposed to sleep when he's up so early? I don't know why he has to bang and crash about so much!"

Not to be outdone, Dave was just as vocal: "Kids! They've got no stamina, dear. That boy barely puts in twelve hours a day. And filthy! You should see the pigsty he's made the camper. Drops into bed in his clothes half the time. And I bet he hasn't used the washbasin once this week."

Whether you call it naivety, ego, or being tricked into it, my response of "You only have yourselves to blame, living like cavemen. This situation needs a woman's touch, before you kill each other," was received with enthusiasm. Accordingly, I rearranged my schedule for a couple of days and followed Dave back to camp Sunday afternoon to fix things.

The "intrepid logger's wife," supporting her husband. Qualified? Heck, I'd spent several days with Dave out at camp when the children had to visit their father for Christmas years ago. Back then, he'd only owned a tatty twelve-foot camper outfitted with a woodstove. Now we had a twenty-five-foot luxury model. No sweat.

After a "Toad's Wild Ride" sort of trip in, I noted the camp had been relocated away from the creek, and it was less than idyllic. Five campers were lined up like train boxcars, chained together by heavy electrical cords linking them to a large generator for power—the same generator that had conked out for a day the first week, plunging everyone into a minus-35-degree nightmare, alleviated only by the rabid usage of everyone's backup propane heat.

I started getting nervous, taking mental inventory of how many propane tanks we'd brought, wondering if Dave's old camper with the woodstove might have been a wiser choice. Back then, we'd been located closer to town and in milder conditions, so we could run back to Quesnel whenever obtaining fresh supplies became more important than guarding the company's fuel supplies from marauders. But this Bear Lake lark was in the backside of nowhere.

Early Monday's light illuminated the austere camp scene that had been partially hidden the evening before. Concentrating on rendering the camper shipshape, then taking inventory of food supplies, I wasn't too alarmed by the harsh environment outside. After all, I only had to tolerate it for a couple of days.

Unwilling to tear himself away from his new girlfriend until the last minute, Ed arrived in camp mid-morning and left me dinner ingredients and a request for his new favourite dish. I was happy to comply, as the "plenty of food" Dave had insisted the camper still held consisted mostly of forty precooked meals I'd sent them in with the week before, perma-frozen in a Tupperware tote behind the camper. This was going to be a long couple of days, if the only raw ingredients I had to entertain myself with consisted of utilizing the few suspicious remnants the fridge offered.

Matters didn't improve at two am Tuesday, when I struggled to see Dave off to work. Camp was roaring to life, as the crew hustled to take advantage of the darkness, before sun glinting off the snow made logging less comfortable with eye strain. Bright headlights lit the camper interior, daring anyone to sleep in, as machinery began thundering past. Suddenly, summertime's spacious camper had shrunk. Manoeuvring around and stumbling over discarded boots, damp coats, and a six-foot catatonic son sprawled on the pull-out couch was challenging. Skirting a ninety-five-pound dog to reach bread and get it into the precariously perched toaster was not fun. Wrestling a five-gallon water jug onto the nonexistent counter space to fill a pot with water for coffee proved next to impossible.

I didn't attempt to repeat the process three hours later, when Ed began his work day.

As I struggled unsuccessfully to go back to sleep, it seemed three adults and two dogs had exhausted the oxygen in this cramped little hole. With electric heaters going full bore and the backup propane making up any deficit, it was dry as the Sahara. A sore throat and raging headache finally subsided mid-morning, and I managed to wash up and shampoo my greasy hair in a tiny washbasin (our water lines having necessarily been winterized with anti-freeze prior to arrival).

Soldiering through the rest of Tuesday, I came up with a passable meal of corned beef hash. Two sad apples and instant maple - brown sugar oatmeal became an apple crisp that both men declared better than I usually made at home, a backhanded compliment I decided to accept graciously. After all, I was going home the next morning, so I could afford to be nice.

But cabin fever was becoming a reality. I gave up my two-day Sudoku stint, as the only pen I had malfunctioned, and the puzzle book reached the stage that required surreptitious flipping to the back to peek at the solutions. With nothing fresh to cook, what else was there? Special touches like dinner table candles and real plates seemed wasted on men who were working like maniacs seventeen hours a day so they could get out of there as soon as possible. They'd return late, wolf down their food, and drop into bed. Gone were the evenings of wine and crib games. Anyway, I had important stuff waiting to get done at home to get prepared for Christmas.

Speaking of which … enough people must have been "dreaming of a white one," because on Tuesday night the snow started.

Upon my arrival, the existing few feet had appeared manageable. The skidder had done a neat job of clearing the parking area. Looking out the camper at the surrounding white-cloaked evergreens was a serene panorama I had enjoyed—until I woke up Wednesday to find everyone scrambling to contend with three freshly fallen feet of it.

Despite spending an hour digging my vehicle out of its snowy grave so the skidder wouldn't accidentally run over it, my optimism that I could make it out of there evaporated by lunchtime. The verdict was official: Dave declared I wasn't leaving that day. A loaded logging truck had failed to make it out that morning and flipped. The machine that went to help the truck had gotten stuck. Eighty-five kilometres of road was impossible to clear fast enough for anyone to make it in or out before fresh snow rendered it impassable again. The trick would be to make a run for it as soon as the snow stopped long enough for one clear track to be made.

The next three days alternated between mind-numbingly boring, exhausting, and expectant. The snow was interminable. I shovelled snow away from the camper, so the skidder could plough without smacking our living quarters, then shovelled more to unearth our buried food supplies.

That evening, truck headlights directed onto the camper roof, Ed shovelled the snow load off.

"Change sides, Ed!" Dave yelled at him after a few minutes. "The machines can't get behind the campers to clear the snow where you're flinging it. Besides which, it's completely burying the main power supply cords back there."

I looked nervously out one of the windows. "Holy cow, love. There's a seven-foot snow mountain back there, threatening to avalanche into the camper broadside!"

"Never mind that," my husband tersely replied. "Come and help me finish chipping this little glacier off the doorframe, before we freeze to death in here. We've got to get this front door closing better."

By Thursday, every man in camp had utilized their machinery to climb onto their camper roofs, following our lead to save their accommodations from caving in. In turn, those who'd forgotten to bring shovels borrowed ours. Some light relief was afforded when the company's owner made the mistake of jumping off his roof on the snow mountain side, briefly disappearing completely. But really, no one was laughing at that point.

After I spent Friday morning unburying my truck yet again and loading garbage, dirty laundry, empty water containers, and propane tanks in anticipation of escaping my snowbound hell, Dave returned by early afternoon, announcing that everyone except himself, Ed, and the skidder operator had already quit work. Gone. Vamoosed on the freshly cleared road. His great plan was that I drive out immediately, following Ed's lead, before it started to snow again. But he intended to stay and work through the weekend.

We'd already had talks about this. With the other faller/buncher operator working close to town, Dave had been struggling to stay ahead of this crew's machines. And with record snowfall slowing him further, he felt the pressure to keep going. After all, no one could finish before he was done cutting. And Lord knew no one wanted to stay out there a second longer than necessary.

The more information I got, the less I liked it. The skidder operator was leaving as soon as he'd opened up the next stretch of road so Dave could move to a new block of timber. With Ed hightailing it to Quesnel for the weekend with his girlfriend, no one would have Dave's back. He had a repeater channel…which might be monitored sufficiently for a distress radio call. He had a satellite phone … assuming he could reach it in an emergency. The company's mechanic was scheduled to arrive the following day … provided the snow didn't restart before then.

I tried to talk Dave out of staying, but reasoning, blackmail, and bullying all proved ineffective. Meanwhile, Ed had abdicated from the "discussion" in disgust and headed home. Finally, we compromised: I would stay with Dave and monitor him hourly on my truck radio. The trade-off was that we would follow Ed out as far as the Bear Lake gas station to stock up on supplies. After all, the dogs had been existing on leftovers and crumbled saltine cracker rations for the past forty-eight hours, and we were down to our last two gallons of water. Dave's truck needed gas (the company's diesel tank storage being the only one that still had any supply left), and he'd promised me a gas station hot dog for dinner. How could a girl refuse? Besides, I would use any excuse to escape my frozen prison for a few hours. It wouldn't take long—eighty-five k there and eighty-five k back. We'd leave the dogs and be right back.

Right.

Thirty kilometres out, Dave began cursing the grader operator who'd supposedly cleared the road. I honestly think I might have done a better job. It was exceptionally bad on a four-kilometre downhill stretch with several switchbacks, where more snow had been smooshed, tracked, and rutted across the road than had been removed from it. We struggled to remain out of the snowbanks as we skated down, wondering how everyone else had made it out successfully. In truth, the road told a story: several guys had spun badly, and it appeared that Ed had narrowly escaped skidding off the edge of a poorly cleared cliff turn.

Despite this we continued on. After all, we'd heard a plough truck operator on the radio on his way to assist the green grader. It would be cleared up for sure when we returned.

Then the snow restarted in earnest. Monster sized flakes.

By the time we reached Bear Lake, we had to grab our supplies and run. But not before the gas station owner relished describing how the only other grading machine in Bear Lake was sitting burnt out beside the highway, having broken in half attempting to plough snow.

I tried not to choke on my hot dog on the return trip, as we listened with growing disgust to the plough truck and grader operators' radio dialogue about the Christmas party they were anxious to attend. Refusing to pull out at a convenient place, they forced Dave to back his truck two kilometres through the winding canyon pass—nebulously responding to his enquiry of the road conditions ahead of us. It didn't need a rocket scientist to decipher they'd jointly disfigured even further the four kilometres of switchback ahead of us. They raced off towards Bear Lake, anxious to vacate the scene of their joint crime before we arrived.

We sat in the truck, in front of the Parsnip River bridge, debating our next move.

"I don't believe it! I said. "How could they actually make the road worse than before! Now what do we do?"

"Well, we're over half way to camp. We could head back to Bear Lake. From there we'd only be an hour from the nearest motel in Prince George."

"And what about the dogs? The camper will be uninhabitable if we leave them alone in it for two days. We can't do that to them!"

"Then we have to continue."

"But we'll never make it up that hill."

"Then we'll have to walk."

"Thirty five kilometres? Wouldn't that take seven hours … in the dark … in grizzly country?"

"When you've done stating the obvious, Beverly, you'd better make up your mind. What's it to be, forwards or back?"

We struggled into our snowpants and fitted studded tire chains to all four wheels of our old work truck. There was no time to regret the decision we'd made based on the erroneous assumption that the grader operator would be competent. Hindsight, though a scab begging to be picked, was an unaffordable luxury. Our pets needed us to try.

Chains finally installed, we pointed the truck toward the four-kilometre uphill switchback looming between us and camp. I audibly prayed to God to aid His two latest nitwits. Dave gunned the engine, yelling, "COME ON, BABY!" We fishtailed up, ignoring the gouges in the snowbanks announcing the grader and plough truck defeats. I had a distinct impression of what God would be seeing as He looked down on us: an awkward, black metallic salmon bucking and fighting its way uphill against all odds on the current of an enraged, white river.

He shook His head … and helped us through, anyway.

That night, we thanked Him, hugged the dogs, celebrated with a glass of wine, and slept soundly.

And that weekend Dave cut enough timber to keep the returning crew supplied with several days' worth of work.

Near Tumbler Ridge, BC. Photo by Murphy Shewchuk

FORT ST. JOHN, DAWSON CREEK, ALASKA HIGHWAY AREA

ONE SMART MOOSE

Creative Nonfiction

Virginia Carraway Stark

From Telegraph Creek to Vancouver, to Cranbrook and Dawson Creek, British Columbia has been my home. I have travelled to many places across the world but never, ever, is there a place that sings to me like British Columbia.

When I was a child, my father was a hunter. He would hunt deer, moose, bear, elk, you name it—if it was wild with four legs in BC, chances are he hunted it. To be honest, he wasn't just a hunter, he was also a degenerate poacher. When my father was a young man, there was no animal that was safe in a radius near him. If he saw it and had a way to kill it, he would find a way to put it in the freezer regardless of such "petty" matters as hunting permits, tags, or seasonal restrictions.

Some of my earliest memories are of helping my father with a kill. When I was just a tiny girl, even before my fourth birthday, my job was to operate the meat grinder. I would turn the metal handle for hours, using my weight to pull it down and then pushing it back up with all my strength. The grinder was nearly bigger than I was, and in between turning the handle, I would put chunks of meat into it and watch them get eaten by the big silver twirling blades and come out in what I thought of a the time as "meat spaghetti."

Dad was a notorious hunter and was actively pursued by law enforcement officials and game wardens. He was never caught red-handed, not by any human, but this is the true story about how even the hunted have a knack for finding revenge.

It was early spring in the Peace River Region. We lived out at Arras, about a thirty-minute drive southwest of Dawson Creek, British Columbia. The freezer was full and the day was beautiful and bright.

"I was thinking of going for a walk," my dad said. At the time, this was generally code for "I'm going to see if there is something for me to kill."

My mom sighed. "The freezer is full."

I didn't blame her for sighing. I wanted to go outside and play. I didn't want to spend several days processing whatever Dad brought home. That's one thing people don't realize: killing anything equals a ton of bloody work.

Dad smiled and grabbed his Cannon camera from where it was hung on the wall by the neck strap. He kissed my mom and teased taking a picture of her. She fussed about her hair and he laughed. "I'm not taking my gun, just a camera today."

"Just your camera? What are you hoping to hunt with that?"

"Nothing…well, nothing for me. I promised Dale I would take a picture of a moose for him. He's never seen one, and since we have so many around here, I thought I would take the camera and grab him a picture."

"Oh, he gets a picture of a living moose and everything?" I said.

"Yep, it's not going to even have its head cut off for the picture. I'm going to walk until I find a moose and shoot it with the camera, no gun required."

He kissed the top of my head and headed out.

It was a beautiful day. As he told us in great detail later, he started off towards the big clearing at the far end of our land. There were almost always moose grazing out there. He was hoping to find a whole family of moose, or at least a cow and her kids. It would be a peaceful slice of British Columbia that he could send off to his friends. He walked for miles. He saw a doe and her fawns, some pheasants, and a fox, but no moose. He didn't mind at all though. It was nice to walk and stretch his legs, and the camera was much lighter than carrying a gun. He wouldn't have to worry about hauling a kill back to the house afterward either, and he felt light and happy. More than that—he felt like he was doing the entire world a good service by choosing on this one day in early spring not to kill.

He continued past the clearing—not a moose in sight. There, the underbrush was thicker and there were few trails. He pushed past the sentry trees and scrubby willows that guarded the border to the real wild lands and walked deeper into the woods.

He walked for miles, and it was coming onto dusk when he decided to have a look in the next clearing and rest for a few minutes before heading back. This far into the woods there were still drifts of snow. He examined some deer tracks briefly and rested his back against a birch tree. He was shaking his head in surprise at their elusive behaviour as he murmured under his breath, "I should have brought my gun. This camera is unlucky."

He closed his eyes to feel the breeze on his cheeks that were sweaty from his efforts. It was then that he heard a snuffling snort and opened his eyes.

It had come to him at last: The bull moose of his dreams. Its rack was something any man would be proud to hang up in his rec room. There was enough meat on that animal to feed a family throughout the entire winter. The moose stood only fifteen feet away, so it was the perfect picture. All he had to do was take off the lens cover, raise the camera, and click a photo that would stun and amaze beyond all expectations.

His hands trembled as though he was loading his gun instead of just unscrewing the lens on his camera. The camera made a faint whirring noise and the bull moose cocked his head. His eyes were bright and fierce. His smell was angry and in rut. Frank narrowed his eyes and the moose narrowed his back and ripped up a clump of sod the size of a poodle. That was all the warning Frank got. The moose's muscles rippled as he braced himself for a sprint that would pin Frank between the impressive rack and the pine tree at his back.

His heart thumping madly, Frank turned and raced up the tree, his feet miraculously finding footholds and his hands sticky with sap, not noticing the pokes and prods of needles and branches into his fingers. Just below his feet he felt the moose impact the tree, ramming it hard with his shoulder to protect his massive antlers. The antlers weren't good for ramming trees, not unless there was a nice squishy man between the moose and all that hard wood.

The impact made Frank drop down a couple of branches, to within antler reach of the moose. He scrabbled back up before the moose had a chance to regather himself for another run in with the pine tree.

Thud! Whump!

The moose connected with the tree again. This time Frank had a better handhold, and he managed to stay on the same branch. The swaying impact shook a sprinkle of pine cones and needles onto his head. A squirrel screamed at him angrily and leaped into another tree where there weren't any strange men to accost him. Nearby, a small murder of caws called out to him and laughed raucously. They had not been immune to his bullets and traps and tricks either. They settled nearby, occasionally calling out to him mockingly.

Sweating with fear, Frank climbed as high as he could in the tree and propped himself among some branches, then looked down. The moose was rooting around in the snow at the bottom. Feeling temporarily safe, Frank calmed down a bit and laughed ruefully. He had been thoroughly treed by a moose. Well, the least he could do was to get a picture of the sucker who had done this to him.

He reached for the camera strap and couldn't find it. Down below he heard the sounds of crunching glass and metal. Bits of black camera were being explored by the moose on the ground. This seemed to mostly be accomplished by him smashing it apart with a hoof the size of a dinner plate. After he was done strewing the remains of the camera around the base of the pine tree, he took a couple more rams at the tree. Frank was braced for these impacts though, and except for some crow laughter and the squirrel becoming freshly outraged, there was little effect on the man clinging to the tree.

Frank shook his head. The moose would probably leave shortly, and he could limp home, minus one camera, but at least he could have a hot bath and nurse his wounded pride.

The moose looked around, gauged the man in the tree and the black shards on the ground, and took a few steps to leave. It was as though he had second thoughts about it and gazed over his shoulder with a look that Frank could only think to describe as mischievous. The moose turned around and rubbed the bark off the pine tree as ardent as a lover. Bits of sap stuck to him, and Frank's cheeks were coated in resin and pine needles from hugging the trunk of the tree. After satisfying himself that all of his itches had been scratched, the moose turned around in a circle three times and settled down in the snow at the base of the tree, like a dog beside his master's bed.

After about twenty minutes, Frank heard a rumbling noise: the moose was snoring. He crept down a branch, and the crows started to call out. The moose raised his head and looked at Frank, who thought he saw the moose shake his head as though he were disappointed in him. Then he settled his head back down into the snow.

Frank sighed. With any luck, the animal would get bored or have business to attend to. Maybe he would get hungry and go look for something more to his taste than broken camera. He straddled a branch as best as he could and hugged the tree. He was high enough up that he could interlace his fingers around it.

Darkness fell and the moose snored on, but one branch breaking under Frank's feet would see the large animal immediately alert, and the first place his gaze would go was up that tree.

The moon rose and Frank, exhausted and chilled, managed to catch little snippets of sleep now and again. How he wished he had brought a gun. How he wished he had stayed home in bed. His socks were wet and his face and hands were so sticky they could barely unstick from the branches he clung to. It was a long night, with many sudden starts and then falling into restless, nervous fits of sleep. Every dream brought the nightmare of a fall, and he woke from them to clutch the tree trunk harder.

Peering down in the moonlight, he could still see the bulky shape of the moose, and sometimes those dark eyes looked up at him.

He woke up in the false light of predawn and saw that at last his tormentor had left him. Or had he? Frank looked around nervously. The moose could be trying to lure him down, make him think it was safe, and then pin him at the base of a tree.

The crows had left, and only the squirrel remained. It seemed to be used to him now and ran around him with only a brief scold now and then to remind Frank that he was out of his usual place and really wasn't welcome up here.

As true dawn lit the sky, Frank took a chance and squirmed down the tree. He dropped to the ground and looked around. No moose. His arms and legs had fallen asleep, and he could hardly walk. The camera had been decimated. He picked up the pieces, waiting to see if the moose would run back as soon as his feet were on solid ground. When he had finished picking up all the pieces, he crept home, limping and exhausted. He got there just as his family was starting their chores for the day. His wife's eyes were huge when she saw his hands, cut bloody by the tough pine bark, and his face, covered in resin, dirt and needles.

I ran my dad the bath that he had been waiting for all night as he told us the story of the moose. His voice was full of wonder that the animals knew he was harmless for the first time and convinced they had plotted to make him have the worst night of his life in vengeance for his acts of violence against them.

He swore that he would always take a gun and never a camera after that, but the truth was, he forgot his gun more and more often. Eventually, he stopped hunting altogether. He said he just didn't have the appetite for it anymore, but I always wondered if he wasn't trained out of it by one smart moose.

THE FIRE'S PATH

Seanah Roper

We only heard rumours
Of the forest fire that nearly swept our town away.
As the Alaska Highway carried us north, homeward,
On both sides, the burnt aftermath of battle
Unfolded before us
Charred brush against a blue muted sky
And to our surprise, it was beautiful.
We were struck by the stark obscenity
Of these black, tousled remains of trees
Leaning over each other in defeat.

How the animals must have fled
Did they all get out?
I thought of Pompeii and the ashen statues of people huddled in corners, taking cover.

What will grow to replace the trees, and will it carry a part of them?
Perhaps the soft veins of new growth will whisper something of this.

This is what we do,
Endure,
Face things bare, raw,
There is dignity here,
In the purple lupins that smile
Beside the dark, obsidian corpse of forest,
Life blooms again.
The mushroom pickers will have work next year.

CONTRIBUTORS

in alphabetical order by last name

JOHN ARENDT lives in Summerland and is the editor of the Summerland Review. His experiences covering the news and his bicycle trips in the area and beyond, often to unusual and out-of-the-way places, serve as the inspiration for his fiction.

HOWARD BAKER was born in Victoria, BC, and lived in the Fraser Valley for forty years. He published in many genres during his teaching career, including poetry, tall tale fiction, and craft writing. In retirement he edited two popular memoirs by Pat Ferguson, *Gone Huntin'* and *Cowboys, Good Times and Wrecks*, and has written a novel, *Unfinished Business,* set in northern BC and the Shuswap. Mr. Baker lives in Merritt with his wife, Stephanie.

MICHELLE BARKER lives in Penticton, BC. A recent graduate of UBC's MFA program in creative writing, Michelle has published poetry, short fiction and non-fiction in various journals. Her YA fantasy, *The Beggar King,* was published by Thistledown Press (2013). A chapbook, *Old Growth, Clear-Cut: Poems of Haida Gwaii*, came out with Leaf Press (2012). Her picture book, *A Year of Borrowed Men*, will be released in November (Pajama Press). Michelle works an editor and mentor, and teaches writing workshops. Please visit her at www.michellebarker.ca.

DELLA BARRETT has had four short stories, numerous poems, and a mini-memoir published in the past few years. One of Della's short stories won second place in a 2014 anthology by Red Tuque Books. Della grew up in the Bridge River Valley and later, in Keremeos, B.C. After living in the Yukon, the NWT, and Alberta, Della has returned to Keremeos, where she continues to enjoy writing short stories, memoirs and poems. Della also has a novelette in progress.

MIKE BIDEN is a man who likes living on the edge! He has had the privilege of parachuting, riding in hot-air balloons, tanks, jet fighters, World War II vintage airplanes, aircraft carriers, and even submarines. He has served more than 30 years as a ground Search and Rescue technician, rescue driver, and Search and Rescue pilot, and is also an experienced survival instructor.

CLAYTON CAMPBELL was born in Northern Quebec, spent his early childhood in Eastern Canada, then moved to Bralorne/Pioneer, then Lake

Cowichan, where he finished high school. Clayton worked in mining/rock construction, then for the Tunnel and Rock Workers Union, then WorkSafe BC. He studied law while teaching blasting courses. In 1979, Clayton was elected as a Councillor for the City of Surrey and commenced a law practice, specializing in personal injury, which he continues to date. Clayton presently lives in Vancouver, where he explores writing.

FERN G. Z. CARR is a Director of Project Literacy Kelowna Society, lawyer, teacher and past President of the Society for the Prevention of Cruelty to Animals. A Full Member of and former Poet-in-Residence for the League of Canadian Poets, this 2013 Pushcart Prize nominee composes poetry in six languages. Carr has been published extensively from Finland to Mauritius and has had her work recognized by the Parliamentary Poet Laureate. One of her poems is currently orbiting the planet Mars aboard NASA'S MAVEN spacecraft. www.ferngzcarr.com

VIRGINIA CARRAWAY STARK has a diverse portfolio and has been writing professionally for nearly a decade. Over the years, she has created a wide range of written products, including screenplays, novels, articles, blogging, and travel journalism. She works with other writers, artists, and poets to hone her talents and to offer encouragement and insight. Virginia received an honorable mention at Cannes Film Festival for her screenplay, "Blind Eye," and was nominated for an Aurora Award. She currently lives in Fraser Lake, BC.

DANELL CLAY is a long-time resident of Prince George, BC, where she works as a library technician in a small medical library. Books are one of her favorite vices. She attends a writing group and has been dared to write 50,000 words in the month of November, as part of the National Novel Writing Month (NaNoWriMo).

LINDA CROSFIELD'S poems have appeared in *Room Magazine, The Minnesota Review, Labor*, *Ascent Aspirations*, and *The Antigonish Review*. She's been a featured poet in *The New Orphic Review.* In 2014 one of her poems was short-listed for Room Magazine's annual contest and in 2015 she participated in Rocking the Page, a program that involved presenting poetry online and in classrooms in the West Kootenays. She lives in Ootischenia, near Castlegar, on the Columbia River.

DEBRA CROW, a Syilx Grandma, has read books all her life. That was her entertainment as a child, due to no electricity. She started out with a love of horse books—anything to do with horses. She also spends her time hunting, gathering, catering, sewing, casket-making, counselling, facilitating at a Youth Empowerment Camp, swimming, canning, card reading, and being a grandma, a mom, and an aunty. Now that she is older, she is inspired to put her stories down on paper to share with others.

SHIRLEY BIGELOW DEKELVER worked for over forty years as a paralegal in Calgary, then she and her husband Don retired to the Shuswap in 2007. Her two young adult novels, *The Trouble with Mandy* (2012) and *Lilacs & Bifocals* (2015), were published by Solstice Publishing. She also has three short stories and a poem in *Kaleidoscope V*, an anthology published by the Shuswap Writers Group. Her short story, *Ziggy's Revenge,* was second place in Askew's Foods' Word on the Lake Writing Contest (2014). Shirley is an avid photographer and artist. www.shirleydekelver.com

KEITH DIXON is a retired social worker. He has had poetry, short fiction and a history book published, and has done freelance journalism. While a member of the Alberta Canadian Authors Association, Keith published their newsletter and managed their website. He lives in the Okanagan and releases his creative energy through photography. Keith is a member of the Summerland Scribes writing group and is currently writing a novel.

ELAINE DURST is a journalist and published author of short stories. BC is near and dear to her heart, having been born and raised here. Many of her stories are about treks she and her husband have taken through Canada and the US. Eventually she would like to publish this collection in a book form. They retired to Kelowna in 1986 and reside in Sunrise Village. Contact her at redurst@shaw.ca.

BERNIE FANDRICH, a pioneer of Canada's whitewater rafting industry, has a passionate relationship with the Thompson River that began in 1973. Originally from Vernon, he graduated from UBC and was a university and college instructor for eight years. Bernie and his family continue to share the river's rapids and stories with enthusiasts of all ages at his Kumsheen Rafting Resort (www.kumsheen.com) near Lytton, BC. He shares his whitewater expertise and love of the region's history in his second book, British Columbia's Majestic Thompson River (www.kumsheen.com/majestic).

BEVERLY FOX was born in Ontario and educated in England. After eight years on Vancouver Island, she moved to northern BC's interior where she now resides in the Cariboo with her husband, three children, and a menagerie of dogs, horses and farm critters. She is currently working on the third novel in her Piper Trilogy (Essence Publishing), was the Bronze medalist in the 2015 Illumination Awards for the second novel, and has been published in *Chicken Soup for the Soul: The Power of Forgiveness*.

RM GREENAWAY has worked in nightclubs, darkrooms, and courthouses. She writes the B.C. BLUES crime series, featuring RCMP detectives Leith and Dion. Her first novel COLD GIRL, winner of the 2014 Arthur Ellis Unhanged award, will be released 26 March 2016. Interested to know more? Check out RMGREENAWAY.COM

STERLING HAYNES is an octogenarian writer of creative nonfiction and zany poetry. His stories and poetry have been published in the *Harvard Medical Alumni Review, Okanagan Life, North of 50, The University of Alberta Alumni Review, The Medical Post, BC History, The Canadian Journal of Rural Medicine,* and *The Rocky Mountain Goat.* His story "No Strings Attached" won the Joyce Dunn Award for creative non-fiction in BC in 2008. His three books, *Bloody Practice*, *Wake Up Call*, and *Where Does it Hurt Now?* are all selling well.

DIANNE HILDEBRAND is an editor, writer and former teacher who lives in the old George Ryga House in Summerland, BC. She writes biographies and family and community histories, along with some poetry for fun. She loves to work, swim, draw, dance, and spend time with her children and grandchildren, as well as with friends.

NORMA J HILL is a professional tutor, editor and writer. Based in Penticton BC, Norma engages in an eclectic assortment of writing activities, including poetry, short stories, memoir, blogging, magazine articles, curriculum, newsletter writing and more. She is a member of Penticton Writers and Publishers (PWAP) and the BC Home Learners Association (BCHLA). Norma can be contacted through http://penandpapermama.com/ or email nlhills@shaw.ca.

EILEEN HOPKINS retired from her post-secondary administrative career in Calgary and moved to Osoyoos, BC, to launch this new phase of her life in 2014. Eileen blogs about her own retirement experiences – from planning it to embracing it – with a growing audience of boomers from around the world. She has authored several short stories and was recently published in the anthology, *An Okanagan Tapestry*. You can read more at http://boomerspotofgold.blogspot.ca/ or on her Facebook page at Boomer Pot of Gold.

YASMIN JOHN-THORPE is a co-founding member of the Penticton Writers and Publishers group. She is a children's author, mentor, and publishing consultant. Yasmin also enjoys writing romantic fiction.

CHRIS KEMPLING is a retired counsellor/teacher living in Kamloops. Primarily a columnist, he got his inspiration from the great "Dr. Foth" (Allan Fotheringham of *Maclean's* magazine), and penned a satire column for the *Quesnel Cariboo Observer* under the pen name of "Johnny Quesnel" for over 10 years. He currently writes a religion column for *Kamloops This Week*, but dabbles in stories, songs and poems as well.

DENISE KING grew up in Penticton, but has lived in Osoyoos, Vancouver, Chilliwack, Hope, Kelowna, Prince George and Revelstoke. She is currently settled in Kamloops. She has her undergraduate degree in Communications from Simon Fraser University and a Certificate in Creative Writing from the Humber School of Creative Writing. Through support from the Kamloops Art Council, Denise has been working on her first novel with editor/mentor Michelle Barker. She works full time, is married with two girls, and hopes to one day be a career novelist.

LINDA KIRBYSON lives in Okanagan Falls. Her roots in the Okanagan go back to the early 1900s when her great-grandfather retired in Summerland. In third grade, she was bitten by the writing bug when her story about a postage stamp was read at the awards assembly. When not writing, she likes to travel and is always searching for the next story. She has published several short stories and is a member of the Penticton Writers and Publishers. To learn more, visit her at www.penwriters.com.

VIRGINIA LAVEAU, currently living in Barriere, BC, was born in Penticton, BC. From an early age she had an interest in writing poetry and prose, and during the last ten years she has pursued a writing career. Her interests vary, including fiction, nonfiction and poetry for children and adults. In 2000 and 2002, she took children's literature courses, improving her craft. She has short stories, an article, and one novella published.

LOREENA M. LEE, AFCA, was born in Edmonton, Alberta, and moved to BC when she was two years old. Her family moved around the province during her growing-up years and finally settled in the lower mainland. A professional artist, writer and art teacher, her paintings hang in corporations and private collections in Canada, the United States and Europe. View her paintings, published novels, and illustrated children's books at www.dragonlee.ca, and connect with her Facebook page: Loreena Lee. Loreena lives in Abbotsford, BC.

DENISE LITTLE was born in Newfoundland and grew up in Prince George, BC – The White Pine Capital of Canada (please hold applause). Her work experience informs her writing and includes Burger Flipper, Denture Cleaner, Parenting Four Kids, Graphic Artist, and Bicycle Mechanic. Denise now owns a Nail Bar and Spa in Osoyoos, BC, where her *real* work is as a nondispensing Spa-sician and Spa-chiatrist. She and her husband live in Oliver, BC – The Wine Capital of Canada.

ALAN LONGWORTH moved from the lower mainland to the Okanagan in 1997. He has produced six novels, a book of short stories, two children's books, and a book of humour, all self-published. Two of his novels are available as e-books. He has an unpublished collection of poetry, including cowboy poetry, and his latest novel, *Fortunes*, is as yet unpublished.

KEN LUDWIG spent the spring of 1969, at age 25, in Anahim Lake, BC. In 1972 he bought a farm in Tatamagouche, NS. After that disaster, he retreated to Ann Arbor, Michigan. He wrote *Hard Country* in 1995. He also wrote 1000 poems in that period while mending from a divorce and rebuilding his life. Ludwig also wrote technical publications and scholarly articles while teaching Sociology at Eastern Michigan University and Entrepreneurship at the University of Michigan. Contact him at kludwig@umich.edu.

JEANINE MANJI actively returned to writing in 2014 after taking a ten-year hiatus to pursue an alternate career. While her children were young, Jeanine wrote children's stories, which have appeared in several magazines. Jeanine is now working on a collection of short stories for adults and has completed the first draft of a novel. Jeanine has lived in various regions of British Columbia, including the Interior, North Coast, and Vancouver Island. She now resides in the lower mainland with her husband.

KATIE MARTI is an award-winning writer of fiction and creative non-fiction. She makes her home in the mountains of Revelstoke, BC, but still keeps one foot in the Maritimes where she grew up. She is currently working on a novel for young adults set in the Kootenays and has her sights set on completing an MFA in Creative Writing one of these years...

KATE MCDONOUGH: Although born and raised in the USA, Kate and her husband immigrated to the Cariboo-Chilcotin region of British Columbia in 1968. Starting in Anahim Lake working on a ranch, they gradually moved into the Kleena Kleene Valley, where they lived with their two children for eighteen years. Kate has been writing since childhood, and her work has been published in several magazines in years gone by: *Interior Woman, North of Fifty,* and *Mother Earth News,* as well as in local newspapers.

HERB MOORE was born in Penticton eighty-five years ago. He lived in various small towns of the Fraser Valley and elsewhere, including Vernon and 108 Mile Ranch for sixteen years, where he wrote cowboy poetry, which was published in *Western Horsemen*. Magazines such as *Our Canada* and local newspapers frequently featured his short stories. His story, "Angelina's Christmas," won a first prize in a writing contest. Herb has written three novels of Western romance, which he hopes to publish someday. He now enjoys living in Oliver, BC.

JANICE NOTLAND's first book of poetry, *Dreams Laid Down*, released in 2012, was inspired by her time living in a rural area outside of Nelson, BC. A former community mental health care worker, she is currently writing about dementia and Alzheimer's disease. She also loves humorous short stories and is exploring writing in that genre. Notland moved to Kelowna in 2010. For more information, go to http://bcwriters.ca/notland

SYLVIA OLSON is a writer and a former board member for the Federation of BC Writers. She is the coordinator of the Kamloops Writers Festival since 2010. Sylvia has been published in anthologies and magazines and has also written a newspaper column for *Kamloops This Week*. When she is not writing you may find her kayaking on one of our many beautiful BC lakes.

JAMES OSBORNE is a novelist and author of more than 100 short stories. Based in Vernon, he is a former investigative journalist, teacher, corporate executive, business owner, and army officer. Osborne has published two books this year, the bestselling thriller about terrorism, *The Ultimate Threat,* and a collection of his short stories, *Encounters With Life – Tales of Living, Loving and Laughter*. Samples of his work can be found on his blog, www.JamesOsborneNovels.com.

VIC PARSONS was a national journalist for 30 years. He is author of *Bad Blood: The Tragedy of the Canadian Tainted Blood Scandal*; *Ken Thomson: Canada's Enigmatic Billionaire*; and his first novel, *Lesser Expectations: Charles Dickens's Son in North America*. He has written award-winning short stories and some poetry, and intends more as the spirit moves. He lives in Victoria, has lived in Vancouver, and spends part of his summers in Smithers. His email is lvparsons@shaw.ca.

L.M. PATRICK lives in Penticton, British Columbia and writes supernatural and spiritual fiction. You can find his website at http://lmpatrick.com/ and his blog "Alive at 50 – A Survival Guide to God" at http://lmpatrick.com/blog/. L.M. Patrick can be reached at lmpatrickwrites@gmail.com.

WILLIAM S. PECKHAM is a novelist, columnist, and short story writer. For 30 years, he hosted a home improvement call-in radio show, and in 1990, he became host/writer of a national home improvement television series. Peckham is an inspirational speaker. He began writing fiction at 72, after moving to Kelowna from Niagara Falls in 2002. He has published a non-fiction book and two short-story collections. He released his first mystery novel in 2013, followed by the sequel in 2014. www.williamspeckham.com

ANITA (A.D.) PERRY has called the Okanagan her home since 1997. A Registered Music Teacher for over 30 years, Perry is also a composer and has written works for orchestra, concert band, piano, voice and choir, as well as seven children's musicals and five ballets. In 2012, she was honoured with the Summerland Arts Appreciation Award. Perry teaches piano, composition and theory rudiments in Summerland. She has a dog named She-Ra and a cat named Jasmine, and is currently building a cabin entirely made of recycled materials.

SETH RAYMOND has resided in the Fraser Lake and Prince George region of BC for over 30 years. He has worked primarily as a teacher, a counsellor, and a behaviour specialist. He is retired now. As regards his writing, Seth is principally interested in plays, nonfiction, and children's literature. He has started a blog site at constructivemeanings.com to promote his views regarding meanings and the role they play in our lives.

JODIE RENNER, a former teacher and librarian with a master's degree, is a sought-after fiction editor and award-winning author of three craft of writing guides, *Fire up Your Fiction*, *Captivate Your Readers*, and *Writing a Killer Thriller*. She has also published two *Quick Clicks* e-resources for word usage and spelling, and is organizing and editing several anthologies. Originally from BC, Jodie has travelled a lot and moved a lot, and now makes her home in Penticton.
www.JodieRenner.com, www.JodieRennerEditing.com;

SEANAH ROPER is a BC-based writer of fiction and poetry. She has been published in *Undercurrents Anthology, OnSpec Magazine, Writing Without*

Direction Anthology, and *Filling Station Magazine*. Her work explores the darker facets of human experience, often playing with history, allegory and narrative. She lives in northern British Columbia, where she works for a non-profit literacy society. She holds a Bachelor's Degree in English Literature from Thompson Rivers University and is a current graduate student working toward a Master's Degree in Adult Education through Athabasca University.

RON B. SAUNDERS undertook fiction writing as a late-in-life pursuit after a thirty-year professional career and then another ten years operating a woodworking and cabinetmaking business in Naramata, in the South Okanagan. Numerous short stories launched his new passion; however the compulsion to draft a larger work soon became irresistible. He is currently writing *The Aurykon Chronicles*, a dark novel about secret global geopolitical and macroeconomic trends that threaten our comfortable way of life.

PAUL SEESEQUASIS is a writer, editor, cultural activist and journalist. He was a founding editor of the award-winning *Aboriginal Voices* magazine, and the recipient of a MacLean-Hunter journalist award. He was a program officer for a number of years at The Canada Council for the Arts. His short stories and feature writings have been published in Canada and abroad. His novel, *Tobacco Wars*, was published by Quattro Books, and his latest book, a collaboration with Mayan artist, Jesu Mora, *pop wuj: An Illustrated Narrative of the Mayan Sacred Book*, will be launched in Mexico City in 2015. He is currently editor-in-chief at Theytus Books and resides in the Okanagan.

MURPHY SHEWCHUK has been writing and illustrating newspaper and magazine articles and books since the mid-1960s. More than 400 of his magazine articles and 1500 of his photographs have appeared in a variety of publications. He has also written and illustrated over a dozen books. In addition to his life-long interest in photography and exploring the mountains of western Canada, Murphy is also an active member of Trails BC, the organization involved with the Trans Canada Trail in British Columbia.

WENDY SQUIRE was born and raised in the heart of British Columbia. She left Prince George to pursue a career as a Registered Nurse in northern Alberta, but it wasn't long before she returned to BC where she settled in the Okanagan. Nearly a quarter century later, Wendy moved back to her roots. Wendy enjoys writing scripts for stage and screen as well as fiction and nonfiction short stories. Her interests include a love for the outdoors, wood and stone carving, drawing, and photography. She almost always has a cat or two and a secret stash of dark chocolate.

KRISTINA STANLEY is the author of the Stone Mountain Mystery Series. Her books have garnered the attention of prestigious crime writing organizations in Canada and England. Crime Writers of Canada nominated DESCENT for the 2014 Unhanged Arthur award. The Crime Writers' Association nominated BLAZE for the 2014 Debut Dagger. She is published in the Ellery Queen Mystery Magazine. www.KristinaStanley.com

TONY STARK comes from a long line of readers, storytellers and explorers. He is a paramedic and an adventurer who has thoroughly explored the province by air, foot and wheel. He currently lives in the shadow of Fraser Mountain. A trained engineer, Tony applies this knowledge to his science fiction, where he writes for the GAF Universe. He has written numerous short stories and scientific papers, as well as two novels. In addition, he is the CEO of StarkLight Press, where he cultivates a welcoming environment for first-time authors from all over the world with his notable Speculative Fiction Anthologies.

CHERYL KAYE TARDIF is an award-winning, international bestselling Canadian suspense author. She is best known for *Children of the Fog* (over 100,000 copies sold worldwide), *Submerged, Divine Intervention, Divine Justice, Divine Sanctuary, The River, Lancelot's Lady* and *Whale Song*. In 2014, she penned her first "Qwickie" (novella) for Imajin Books™ new imprint, Imajin Qwickies™. *E.Y.E. of the Scorpion* is the first in her E.Y.E. Spy Mystery series. Booklist raves, "Tardif, already a big hit in Canada … a name to reckon with south of the border." Twitter: @cherylktardif; Facebook: CherylKayeTardif

MAHADA THOMAS was born in Ontario and moved to beautiful British Columbia in 1993. She has lived in Vancouver and Tofino and presently resides in Penticton. She is a Reiki Master and a Shamanic practitioner, and she writes with an inspired pen. Her extensive genre of writing includes spiritual/contemplative prose and poetry, nonfiction, fiction, and children's literature. Email: madathomas@yahoo.ca.

ROSS URQUHART is a retired eccentric and grump who spends his time writing when the rest of his chores are done and the weather is too abominable to do anything outside. His latest book, *Being Reasonable, Plain Talk About Living in the Future*, is now out in a print edition. He may be contacted through his blog, "Middle of the Road Radical," or simply at ofbandg.com. He and his wife are longtime residents of Lytton.

PHOTO CREDITS

Murphy Shewchuk – cover photo and many interior photos
Mike Biden – four Okanagan photos
Chris Czajkowski, wildernessdweller.ca - Chilcotin Cowboys
Keith Dixon – photo of KVR train trestle bridge
Kim Lawton – photo of Lillooet
Jodie Renner – two photos of Similkameen Valley
Gary Doi – photo of Kimberley, BC
Donna Beckley Galanti – photo of deer
Kumsheen Rafting Resort – photo of Bernie Fandrich, whitewater rafting

INDEX

CONTRIBUTORS & CONTRIBUTIONS:

CONTRIBUTIONS BY GENRE
FICTION, CREATIVE NONFICTION, POETRY:

FICTION:

NONFICTION & CREATIVE NONFICTION
(memoirs; true stories; based on true stories):

Creative Nonfiction:

Nonfiction:

POETRY:

STORIES ACCORDING TO THE ERA IN WHICH THEY TAKE PLACE:

Contemporary – 1980 to present:

World War II to 1979:

ABOUT THE EDITOR

Jodie Renner, a former teacher and librarian with a master's degree, is a fiction editor, well-known blogger, and award-winning author of three editor's guides to writing compelling fiction, *Fire up Your Fiction*, *Captivate Your Readers*, and *Writing a Killer Thriller*. She has also published two time-saving clickable e-resources, *Quick Clicks: Word Usage* and *Quick Clicks: Spelling List*, and is busy organizing and editing several anthologies. Her next anthology, to be released in 2016, entitled *Childhood Regained – Stories of Hope for Asian Child Workers*, is also for charity. She hopes to compile and edit more BC anthologies in the future.

Jodie grew up in the interior of BC, attended UBC and SFU, and taught in Vancouver and on Vancouver Island. She has travelled a lot and moved a lot. After living in Ontario for 30 years, she is thrilled to be back in BC and around her family. She now makes her home in Penticton, where, when she's not editing novels and short stories, writing, judging stories for contests, or presenting writing workshops, she enjoys dancing, music, photography, travel, and spending time with family and friends.

Websites: www.JodieRenner.com, www.JodieRennerEditing.com
Blog: http://jodierennerediting.blogspot.ca/
Previous group blogs: The Kill Zone, Crime Fiction Collective